Imaging the
WORD

Imaging the
WORD

An Arts and Lectionary Resource

Kenneth T. Lawrence, Editor

Jann Cather Weaver

Roger Wedell

Volume 1

United Church Press

Cleveland, Ohio

Thomas E. Dipko	Executive Vice President, UCBHM
Ansley Coe Throckmorton	General Secretary, Division of Education and Publication
Lynne M. Deming	Publisher
Sidney D. Fowler	Editor for Curriculum Resources
Monitta Lowe	Editorial Assistant
Marjorie Pon	Managing Editor
Kelley Baker	Editorial Assistant
Lynn Keller	Business Manager
David M. Perkins	Marketing Director
Cynthia Welch	Production Manager
Martha A. Clark	Art Director
Angela M. Fasciana	Sales and Distribution Manager

United Church Press, Cleveland, Ohio 44115
© 1994 by United Church Press
Imaging the Word has been designed to be used with the New Revised Standard Version of the Bible.
All scripture quotations, unless otherwise noted, are from the New Revised Standard Version of the
Bible, © 1989 by the Division of Christian Education of the National Council of Churches of Christ
in the U.S.A. Adaptations have been made for clarity and inclusiveness. Used by permission.

Printed in Hong Kong on acid-free paper
First printing, 1994

Design: Kapp & Associates, Inc., Cleveland, Ohio
Cover art: Duccio, *Dispute with the Doctors,* detail, 1308-1311, Siena Museo dell'Opera
Metropolitana (Scala/Art Resource, N.Y.). Used by permission.
Jonathan Green, *The Congregation,* detail, 1991, Jonathan Green Studios, Inc., Naples, Fla.
Used by permission.

Library of Congress Cataloging–in–Publication Data

Lawrence, Kenneth Todd, 1935–
Imaging the Word : an arts and lectionary resource / compiled by Kenneth Todd Lawrence,
Jann Cather Weaver, and Roger W. Wedell.
p. cm.
May be used in conjunction with "Word among us" Sunday School curriculum published by
United Church Press.
Includes bibliographical references (p. 260–267) and index.

ISBN 0–8298–0970–8 (cloth : v. 1). — ISBN 0–8298–0971–6 (pbk. : v. 1)

1. Church year. 2. Revised common lectionary. 3. Bible—Illustrations. 4. Bible—In literature.
5. United Church of Christ—Education. 6. United churches—United States—Education.
7. Reformed Church—United States Education. 8. Christian education—Textbooks for adults—
United Church of Christ. I. Weaver, Jann Cather, 1955– . II. Wedell, Roger William. III. Title.

BV30.L39 1994   94–823
263'.9–dc20   CIP

Contents

Acknowledgments

A volume so complex in design and construction as *Imaging the Word* has many contributors. To list all those who have done so much to make this book possible exceeds practicability. But certain individuals and institutions must be acknowledged for their indispensable contributions. In addition to the staff of United Church Press and Kapp & Associates, we would like to thank the following:

Derin Tanyal, art historian on the staff of Art Resource in New York City, contributed untold hours of patient and enthusiastic assistance in locating photographs of desired artworks and in obtaining permissions.

Sister Mary Madelen, lecturer at the Catacomb of Priscilla in Rome, provided generous assistance of central importance in the interpretation of early Christian frescoes.

Ronald Flowers, chair of the Department of Religion at Texas Christian University, contributed not only personal support but indispensable budgetary support for staff assistance in the process of preparing the final manuscript.

Clayton Holmes, student assistant at Texas Christian University with enthusiasm for the learning process, ably assisted with the detailed process of finding locations for permission requests, typing forms, and assembling photos and manuscript.

Faculty colleagues and friends of the three co-authors and editor were sources of support and encouragement.

Robin Hutchins and Ben Taylor spent many hours assisting in widely varied ways during the final days of manuscript preparation. Ms. Hutchins contributed refined insights through her contribution to "Imagine That: An Introduction for the Young."

Carol Jane Lawrence was careful critic, patient source of unceasing encouragement, provider of assistance at odd hours, and is due much praise for her part in the completion of *Imaging the Word*.

Kenneth T. Lawrence, Editor
Jann Cather Weaver
Roger Wedell

Foreword

The Bible and the arts are inherently and historically linked. The lectionary, selected portions of Scripture to be read in worship, itself is a form of art. Since the fourth century in the Christian era, congregations have been guided by the lectionary's imaginative and disciplined journey through the Bible. This systematic reading of Scripture has its roots in the reading of the Torah (first five books of the Hebrew Scriptures) and the Prophets in the Jewish synagogue. Although some lectionaries used by the early church included readings from the Hebrew Scriptures, the church often reserved its ordered readings for portions of the Gospels and the Epistles. Today the lectionary includes readings both from the Gospels and other Christian Scripture as well as from the Hebrew Scriptures, including the Psalms. *Imaging the Word: An Arts and Lectionary Resource* brings together those readings with poetic and visual arts.

In recent years, an increasing number of Protestant congregations as well as Roman Catholic parishes have begun to use the lectionary for worship and preaching. Church leaders have discovered the wealth of potential for building the life of a congregation centered around common readings of scripture. Congregations that have used the lectionary have been enlivened and enriched. Because of those possibilities, the United Church Board for Homeland Ministries of the United Church of Christ developed *Word Among Us: A Worship-centered, Lectionary-based Curriculum for Congregations* to assist and enhance congregations' ministry with the lectionary. *Imaging the Word: An Arts and Lectionary Resource* is a central component of that comprehensive curriculum.

In the development of *Word Among Us*, congregation members were asked questions that recognized the intimate relationship between the lectionary and worship. They were asked how they came to know God and understand the Bible through worship rather than through the more traditional approaches of Sunday school. Answers included through experience and prayer, but especially through the arts. Respondents affirmed that poetry, liturgy, music, movement, drama, and visual arts stirred their hearts and engaged their intellects in a deeper knowledge of God and the Bible.

Through the use of the lectionary in worship, the Bible and the arts can be brought together in a significant way. The liturgy, music, colors, movements, and celebrations of the church year from Advent through Pentecost and ordinary time are undergirded by the traditional readings of the lectionary. At the same time, the interpretation of scripture and the imaginations of worshipers are enhanced by the arts.

Imaging the Word was created to provide a well of images and words for individual worshipers and congregations to draw from in their experience with the Bible readings. For each Sunday and several festivals of the church year, *Imaging the Word* provides art, liturgy, photography, prose, poetry, prayers, or commentary, based on a selected reading from *The Revised Common Lectionary*.

Far from what has been characterized as "bathrobe art" or the style of illustrations in the traditional Sunday school curriculum resource, the works in *Imaging the Word* comprise ancient, contemporary, European, and cross-cultural images and words. Children, youth, and adults may draw inspiration from these works as they imagine, engage, and pray the scriptures.

Imaging the Word: An Arts and Lectionary Resource may be used in several ways.

1. It is designed for individuals to use in a personal way for reflection, garnering of new insights, or devotion in connection with the lectionary readings. Some may use it as a guide for personal weekly meditation or as a spiritual journal.

2. It can be enjoyed in a family setting in which members of all ages use it together for discussion and family worship or devotions.

3. *Imaging the Word* may be used in a congregation as a resource throughout the church year for worship, fellowship, group study, meditations and devotions, and in activities across generations.

4. The book may be used in connection with the age-level resources for *Word Among Us: A Worship-centered, Lectionary-based Curriculum for Congregations*. These resources have been developed to coordinate with the resources of *Imaging the Word*.

The two introductions are intended to assist you in fully using this resource. In "Arts: Imaging the Faith," the nature of art as a means of expressing faith and theology is briefly interpreted. Also, approaches to the interpretation of art are proposed through an example of two paintings. "Imagine That: An Introduction for the Young" is designed especially for children and younger youth, though older youth and adults may find the section engaging as well.

See, read, take in, argue with, and pray with the images of *Imaging the Word*. Talk with others. Create your own imaginative expressions of the lectionary readings. May you recognize the Word in the world around you.

Sidney D. Fowler
Editor for Curriculum Resources
United Church Press

Arts: Imaging the Faith

Children, youth, and adults all can encounter an expression of art and experience it in ways that are meaningful based on their own experience and faith. A small child enters into important experiences through a work of art that might not be adequately explained in words. An eight-year-old child grasps something "of God as a strong, nurturing presence" through the picture by Käthe Kollwitz in the unit for Lent 2, page 154. A teenager is overwhelmed by grace while reflecting upon the painting *The Return of the Prodigal Son* by Rembrandt in the unit for Lent 4, page 162. Or an adult experiences a film or music in a deep way and some aspect of life and faith is clarified, such as in *Babette's Feast* in the unit for Easter 3, page 192. At such moments, one can say, "I really *know* what that means."

This book employs many forms of the arts; through them you may have a rich experience of and gain insight into the focus of the scripture readings from the lectionary. The book is divided into units, one for each Sunday and major church festival in the church year. Each unit first presents a selected scripture reading. Then, poetry, music, visual art, film script excerpts, stories, photography, drama, liturgies, or interpretive commentary is presented as a means of opening up the reading. Some of these selections refer directly to the scripture reading; others are focused on some insight or experience suggested by the scripture. Possibly one or many of these selections will have an impact on you, based on your experience, your questions, your insight, or your own faith. No two people will gain the same insight from the selections and commentary. They are included as means to stimulate individual reflection or group discussion at home or places of worship and study.

Käthe Kollwitz, *Seed Corn Must Not Be Ground*

Writers, artists, and composers all have insights into and experiences of meaning or significance in life. They feel compelled to express that meaning, that moment of insight, in some way. Sometimes they may want simply to celebrate the discovery. The expression may be emotion filled or it may be one of intellectual enlightenment. It may celebrate joyously or uncover pain or bewilderment. When this happens, artists not only express themselves, they provide opportunity for others to reflect on their own lives through the artist's work.

The artist finds ways to give form to the insight or experience—for example, through words, paint, movement, or stone. Without form, insight has no avenue through which it can reach its audience. All the forms of human expression serve some effort to communicate. (The communication may not always be consciously intended, but nevertheless it is there.)

The arts have an especially great power to represent not only the ordinary in our experience and faith, but the very deepest aspects of it. Sometimes these representations become so powerful that they not only represent, that is, point to something beyond themselves, they also become joined with that for which they stand. When this happens, they may take on such power in a person's experience or point of view that they are called symbols. Thus, they not only point beyond themselves to something else, they *contain* some essential element of what is represented within themselves. The representor (the form that is doing the representing) *fuses* with what is being represented. For example, in the painting *Last Supper* by Tintoretto (see the unit for Maundy Thursday, page 174), Jesus' meal is the basis for Holy Communion or Eucharist, in which the bread and wine become potent symbols for the body and blood of Jesus. The table is transformed into the altar of sacrifice or the banquet table of the Resurrection feast. The divine is present in the symbol.

The many forms of expression used in this book were selected because they have potential to illuminate the scripture readings in some way. Some may strike you powerfully. Others may puzzle; some may be unappealing. Whatever your response, the arts may enter your own world of experience and enrich or clarify it. Whenever it has seemed useful, we have composed concise commentaries to assist you in experiencing the context in which an artwork was created or ways the form of the art may disclose meaning. Always, such commentaries are intended to open more possibilities and not to restrict your own interpretation.

For those who want to explore further . . .

Interpreting Objects of Art

On the next page and in the section in this book devoted to the festival of Good Friday, beginning on page 178, a painting by a French artist, Valentin de Boulogne, is presented as an imaginative way to enter into events of the day of Jesus' crucifixion. (It would be helpful to read the lectionary reading in John 18:1–12.) Briefly, what are some questions that you have about the painting? What do you feel as you look at the painting? What do you notice first in the picture? What seems to be happening? What are some methods that can be used to enter more deeply into the representational power and communication of the painting?

When you first encounter this image, you may be struck by the faces, the strong light and deep shadows that both define and envelop the figures, and all the contorted lines that suggest not only movement, but also struggle. Specifically, how do these elements of *form* in the art object affect your perceptions of what it is representing and the meanings it may suggest?

Light is an important factor in this image. The face most strongly lit is in the upper portion and to the right of the center of the picture. What is the source of the light? How is it used? In looking to the source, the eye is moved to the left. At left, deep in shadow, a man holds a torch to give light to the scene. (Because of the lectionary reading, you know that the event takes place just before dawn.) His facial expression exhibits his struggle to throw light on the man they seek. Opposite, in a straight line across from the torchbearer's face, in the extreme upper

Valentin de Boulogne,
The Taking of Christ

right of the picture, a young man, startled by the event unfolding before him, shields his eyes from the glare of the torch. Who might he be? Is he one of Jesus' disciples?

Another face is brightly lit from another light source. In the lower right segment and foreground, Peter reacts in defense of Jesus by pushing down one of the men sent to make the capture and raises his knife to cut off the man's ear. As the man falls, the door of his lantern flies open and the bright light illumines Peter's face and arm. Already, it becomes clear that the artist is interested in shaping the viewer's perception of the moment as one filled with much simultaneous movement, even violence.

Near the center of this active, violent scene, two soldiers with armor struggle to take hold of Jesus, who clearly is the man in the upper right whose face is brilliantly lit by the torchlight. The soldier farthest left grabs at the neckline of Jesus' garment. (His armor is painted to reflect brightly the torchlight.) The other soldier, presented with his back to the viewer, reaches out with his right hand in front of Jesus to grasp Jesus' left shoulder or arm. The brilliant red of the soldier's sleeve accentuates the gesture. (Valentin, the painter, uses a deep red for the sleeve color that heightens the aggressiveness of the capture.) Added to the actions of the soldiers, Judas' left hand is placed on the center of Jesus' chest while his right hand rests on his right

Paying attention to aspects of the form of this painting helps us to gain more from it. The artist's use of many oblique and curving *lines* that intersect make it very active. The strong contrasts of *light and shadow* shape how we perceive the figures and contribute drama. Clearly, the use of *color* makes it possible to "model" the faces and bodies to make them seem natural and to direct our attention to important aspects of the message. The overall *composition* or organization of the picture is important. As suggested earlier, the fact that the main figure is not in the middle, that the composition is not symmetrical, suggests more of a swirling action into which the artist wants us to enter. The dark *space* accentuates those occupied by visible action. Finally, all the elements of form are used to suggest the *content* or meaning.

shoulder, thus indicating that Judas has his arm around Jesus' neck. Judas is in the position to identify Jesus by kissing him as a close friend would do when greeting in that time and culture.

Now, with attention given to the intentions of the figures through their gestures and hands, the artist presents Jesus' hands in an extraordinary pose for this scene. Jesus' hands are calmly clasped in front of him, in sharp contrast to the others in that moment. He is the calm in the storm created by all the moving lines of those who would identify and capture him. His head is turned away from the blazing bright light of the torch; he faces Judas, who is very close, and gazes directly into his face. Valentin presents Judas' face as turning away from the close encounter with Jesus' eyes. Judas appears unnerved.

Thus, in this moment Jesus has accepted the betrayal of his supposed friend, understanding the motivations that drive the man and the confusion of his other followers. Calmly, if sadly, he stands facing Judas and the confusion of reaction around him. He accepts the burden he must bear to express an unqualified love, a love that he offers despite the weakness of those around him. Such moments exalt for this interpreter the presence of God's love in Jesus. Jesus endures the giving of himself completely for others that they might begin to incarnate that same love in their lives. What meanings and interpretations do *you* bring to this dramatic painting?

Whenever it is possible, learn about the historical or social situation in which an artistic statement was produced. This will shed light on its meaning. For example, we know that Valentin de Boulogne was active in France, a nation that remained Catholic after the Protestant Reformation began in Germany and spread elsewhere in northern Europe. Further, we know that artists in Roman Catholic regions frequently exhibited the Catholic Reformation in what we call the baroque era. Like some other great painters working for the church in his time, Valentin reflected the strong emphasis on individual emotional experience that became typical after the reformations. Especially important, he developed the capacity to capture and "freeze" a moment of action as a part of a sequence of actions. Finding out about the religious, political, and artistic circumstances surrounding a statement expressed by an artist, composer, or dramatist can clarify important aspects of the deeper meaning.

A strong contrast to the Frenchman Valentin de Boulogne's interpretation of a scriptural story is that of Wu Yuen-kwei, a contemporary Chinese artist who works in Nanjing. He sought to interpret the meanings he discovered in a story in chapter 7 of the Gospel of Luke. (This lectionary scripture is explored later in this book in Pentecost 2, beginning on page 218.)

Wu interprets a story of the encounter of a sinful woman who dares to enter the house of a proper Pharisee. Jesus has joined the host and others for dinner. There the woman expresses dramatically her grief at her status and seeks Jesus' forgiveness.

Wu Yuen-kwei,
Her Sins Are Forgiven

Wu employs watercolors and ink in this image in a traditional Chinese style. The woman's distress and the important interaction between Jesus and the other guests become the foci of the image. Wu places the woman in the lower foreground of the scene. She is dressed in a flowing red garment, and the curving lines of her gown seem to cascade forward toward us. In front of her, and nearer to us, sits the alabaster jar containing the valuable ointment she uses to anoint Jesus' feet. The red of her gown, the lines leading toward us, and the jar quickly engage us.

In composing the scene, Wu strongly connects the woman's experience to Jesus. She holds his foot gently in her arms and anoints it while her long, dark hair falls into the action. Her cheek seems to touch his shin as she weeps. At the same time, Jesus is presented as accepting her pleading action while interpreting it for his host and the other guests. By presenting Jesus at right center, in profile, Wu shows that Jesus' gesture is addressed to all the people around the table and not only his Pharisee host. The open, unfilled space in the center is given almost no detail and is defined as a table top only by the lightly brushed lines suggesting a tablecloth, and by the two simple suggestions of plates of fruit near the back of the surface. (Examination of many Chinese paintings reveals quickly the importance of empty spaces.) The person seated exactly opposite Jesus, to whom his hand gesture is directed, listens, but turns his gaze toward the viewer. Does he invite, perhaps dare our response? All around the table, the other diners respond in individual ways both to Jesus' words to them and to his response to the pleading woman. They lean forward and gaze at Jesus; one smiles in seeming bemusement, one gestures to attract another's attention, and some listen and muse quietly, looking at no one. Wu places two women in the far left background. One, dressed in red, carries a platter with large vegetables or fruit with which she is altogether occupied, quite uninvolved in the exchange before her. In contrast, the woman to her left, who carries a platter on her head, expresses interest in the surprising event through her curious, sidelong gaze.

The background provides little distraction to the central action. At the same time, the room is given definition by the use of simple, almost transparent lines that suggest draperies. An interpretive statement written in Chinese characters is superimposed over the lines representing drapes.

Wherever one directs attention in this composition, the eye continually is brought back to the subjects of the image—the woman and Jesus' response to her plea. It is a simple yet sophisticated and revelatory interpretation.

These Western and Asian art forms differ; yet each addresses in powerful ways the depth of meaning carried through the stories of the Christian faith. Perhaps the avenue to insight through artistic expression is to keep one's eye, like a camera lens, open long enough to assure a lasting impression.

It is hoped that the following pages, centered on the weekly lectionary scripture readings and festivals of the church year, will serve as a wellspring of disclosure, insight, and faith.

Kenneth Lawrence

Imagine That: An Introduction for the Young

Imagine that two-thousand-year-old stories from the Bible can still teach you very important things about God, about yourself, and about the world today. They can! This book is designed to help you see, feel, and think about the Bible through art. To get started, flip through the pages and look at the artwork, poems, and stories. You will find that every unit begins with a scripture reading quoted from the Bible. Then you will find art, music, and poetry that has been chosen to help you explore ideas from the Bible.

There are many ways to use this book. You may start anywhere. Choose something that you like: a poem, a painting, or a Bible verse. Look at it carefully. See if you can discover how it is related to the other items included in the unit. Talk about it, too. Show it to others. It can be fun (and sometimes surprising!) to find out what other people see and think.

For Those Who Want to Explore in Detail

There is a story in the Bible found in Luke 10:25–37 called "The Parable of the Good Samaritan." Read the story (below), and think about these questions as you read it.

- Who are your neighbors?
- Why does the Samaritan help the wounded traveler?
- Why don't the priest and Levite help the wounded man?
- What is Jesus trying to show the lawyer in the story?

Just then a lawyer stood up to test Jesus. "Teacher," he said, "what must I do to inherit eternal life?" He said to him, "What is written in the law? What do you read there?" He answered, "You shall love the Sovereign God with all your heart, and with all your soul, and with all your strength, and with all your mind; and your neighbor as yourself." And he said to him, "You have given the right answer; do this, and you will live."

But wanting to justify himself, he asked Jesus, "And who is my neighbor?" Jesus replied, "A man was going down from Jerusalem to Jericho, and fell into the hands of robbers, who stripped him, beat him, and went away, leaving him half dead. Now by chance a priest was going down that road; and when he saw him, he passed by on the other side. So likewise a Levite, when he came to the place and saw him, passed by on the other side. But a Samaritan while traveling came near him; and when he saw him, he was moved with pity. He went to him and bandaged his wounds, having poured

Jacopo Bassano, *The Good Samaritan*

oil and wine on them. Then he put him on his own animal, brought him to an inn, and took care of him. The next day he took out two denarii, gave them to the innkeeper, and said, 'Take care of him; and when I come back, I will repay you whatever more you spend.' Which of these three, do you think, was a neighbor to the man who fell into the hands of the robbers?" He said, "The one who showed him mercy." Jesus said to him, "Go and do likewise."

Luke 10:25–37

Now, after reading the story, what are your answers to the questions at the beginning? You can have a friend read the story, too, and then talk together about your answers and ideas.

Look at the painting called *The Good Samaritan* by the artist Jacopo Bassano (pronounced Yah-co-po Bah-sah-no) on the previous page. Think about words and ideas that you can use to talk about what you see. What do you think is happening in the painting? Can you identify the wounded traveler? The good Samaritan? The travelers who passed by without stopping to help? How do you know them?

Artists use colors and objects to help express their ideas. For example, dogs in a painting can often stand for friendship and loyalty, since many dogs are friendly and loyal. So the dogs in this painting may be a sign that the man in the red jacket is a friend or "neighbor," one who will help.

Why do you suppose Bassano decided to paint the moment in the story when the Samaritan is lifting the traveler? One reason may be that he wants us to think about the Samaritan and ask ourselves, "Why did the first two men keep walking?" Another reason may be that he wants us to ask ourselves if we would be the one to stop and help or would we pass by. That's a big question.

When Bassano painted *The Good Samaritan* he created a picture that would make the story seem real to people in Italy, where he lived four hundred years ago. He painted people who looked like Italians, wearing clothes like Italians wore then, and in a place that looks like the countryside in Italy.

Other artists have also made paintings depicting the good Samaritan, such as this one by Vincent Van Gogh. How is the painting different from Jacopo Bassano's?

How could you tell the story of the good Samaritan in a way that would make sense to your friends? Maybe you could create a picture of an injured person alone on the side of a street with someone in a car stopping to help. You could even make a home movie on videotape or write a play. Have you ever helped someone else who really needed it? Maybe you have your own good Samaritan story!

Painters can take a story or idea and make a picture (like Bassano did with the good Samaritan story). In the picture you can "see" the story. You can imagine the story and all the action. Now, think about something different. Like paintings, words can help a person to *imagine* new things. Words can help people to imagine and talk about God.

Trying to talk about God can be very hard because God is so big, so vast! God is really more than humans can imagine, but one can still talk about God and what God

Vincent Van Gogh, *The Good Samaritan*

might be like. Here are some ideas that Frederick Buechner (pronounced "Beek-ner") wrote about God.

Using the same old materials of earth, air, fire, and water, every twenty-four hours God creates something new out of them. If you think you're seeing the same show all over again seven times a week, you're crazy. Every morning you wake up to something that in all eternity never was before and never will be again. And the you that wakes up was never the same before and will never be the same either. —*Frederick Buechner, Wishful Thinking: A Theological ABC*

When looking at Bassano's painting, we found that it helped to think of words to use to talk about the story of the good Samaritan. *Words* also bring pictures and new ideas to mind. Do Buechner's words bring pictures to your mind?

The first sentence suggests that God is creating new things every day. People cannot see God but one can see what God makes. Can you think of ways that you can see God's creative work?

Every day trees grow a little. Grass grows a little. Ants all over the world move more grains of sand than anyone could count. Hot lava flowing out of a volcano builds layer upon layer as it cools. Over a long, long time it may build a mountain or even whole islands in the ocean. God is always creating. Every morning the world is new and will never be exactly the same again.

God is creating *you* all the time too. Can you think of ways God is doing this? Your hair grows a little every day and maybe your legs do, too. You see new things, think new thoughts, and feel new feelings—every day. You wake up every day a little bit different and you will never be *exactly* the same as you were yesterday.

By *looking* at Bassano's painting, and *reading* Buechner's words about God, you probably had ideas of your own. Maybe you would like to write your own ideas about God and paint your own picture of the good Samaritan. As you use this book, you will find more Bible readings and some of the arts that you understand and enjoy.

Think about what the examples of art, scripture, and other writing mean to *you*. You may find things you don't understand. When this happens you can learn a lot by asking other people what they think. You may agree. You may have other new ideas because you talked to them. This is a book you can look at, read, and enjoy over and over again and think new things each time.

Robin Hutchins and Kenneth Lawrence

Pentecost

Emil Nolde, *Christ Among the Children*

This is a time of

making connections—

a time for bridging

the words and

witness of Jesus

with our words,

our witness.

Green—the color is deeply imbued with notions of growth and life. Green is the color associated with those weeks after the festival of Pentecost. This "ordinary" time, not punctuated by great festivals of the church year, is a season when that which seems mundane is recreated in an extraordinary way. It is a time when growth in discipleship is gradual, multifaceted, and integrating. Roots are set deep. Ordinariness in relationships can be transformed by the discovery of the meaning and depth they possess.

Quiet growth can empower the hesitant person or community to risk. On All Saints' Day the church remembers the witnesses of the past, and their example gives new dimension to life. The scripture readings for this season challenge disciples to grow. The events of daily experience are explored for their significance and challenge to discipleship. That which divides is identified and confronted with the opportunity for integration.

This is a time of making connections. It is a time for bridging the words and witness of Jesus with our words, our witness. The scriptural reading for Pentecost 17, from the Gospel of Mark, and the painting by Emil Nolde, *Christ Among the Children,* suggest a bridge, a connection between Jesus, children, faith, the church, and you. By placing them in juxtaposition, we are challenged to look at our ordinary lives in new ways and to look to the child who is often forgotten as a bearer of God's presence.

The common acts of living and relating are made holy. Common bread and common juice are transformed into the presence of the living Christ. A child is lifted by Jesus, giving holy significance to the little ones.

ORDINARY TIME IS HOLY TIME

BE OPENED

*J*esus took aside in private, away from the crowd, a person who was deaf and had a speech impediment, and putting his fingers into the person's ears, Jesus spat and touched the person's tongue. Then looking up to heaven, Jesus sighed and said, "Ephphatha," that is, "Be opened." And immediately the person's ears were opened, the tongue was released, and the person spoke plainly.

Mark 7:33-35

Mark 7:24-37

Ephphatha!

BE OPENED!

German manuscript illumination, *Christ Healing the Deaf and Mute Man*

Jesus deals with a deaf-mute. He takes suffering to heart. Following his example, we want to be as caring for the deaf and residents with speech impediments in our community as he was in his day. Perhaps we will be able to make others experience what it means to be deaf and how awful it is not to be able to express oneself properly because of a speech defect. We call attention to the deaf and mute in our midst, and we want to show that one can also communicate with them, albeit in a different manner.

Gijs Okhuijsen and Cees van Opzeeland, In Heaven There Are No Thunderstorms: Celebrating the Liturgy with Developmentally Disabled People

Ephphatha

Now listen to this,
You hucksters of religion,
All you faith healers,
Gatherers of crowds,
Who come to smite the populace
With miracles, spectaculars;
When Jesus healed a deaf man,
He took the man aside, privately,
Away from gawkers.

Jesus did not yield to crowd promotion,
As do some who appear in his name (in vain?).
He took the man aside, apart, away
From the multitude. He put his fingers
Into the deaf-mute's ears. He spat
And touched his tongue. Does Jesus'
Spit offend you? He looked into heaven.
He sighed and said, "Ephphatha! Be opened!"

Do you think you know his secret now?
Do you think method is the key to power?
Repeat the procedure exactly.
Try the sequence in proper order.
Isolate the experimental subject.
Stick finger into ear. Spit on finger.
Place finger on tongue. Look heavenward.
Sigh. Say the magic word. Got it? Try it.

When his ears were opened
And his tongue released,
The [man] spoke plainly. Of course.

Now that we have rehearsed the event,
Do we understand it better?
Of course not.

Let's start with something easier.
Try listening to what others say.
Experience the loss of your own deafness.
Say how you feel, and watch your tongue come
    untied.
Get somebody you can trust to practice on.
Try it on your wife or husband,
Father, mother, brothers, sisters, children,
    friends.

You already know how to sigh.
Now learn to open up.
Ephphatha! Be opened!
See, that's all there is to it!

Wayne Saffen,

Duccio di Buoninsegna, *Jesus Opens Eyes of Man Born Blind*

The Gift I Need

Listen
only
listen.
Do not pursue me
as though you were God.
The gift I need
is your hearing
and your heart.

Thomas John Carlisle

The Italian painter Duccio, a visual interpreter of the Christian faith in the late medieval era, depicts Christ's healing encounter with a man born blind (as recounted in John 9). Duccio interprets the moment Christ speaks while touching the man's eyes. The drama continues in the right foreground of the painting where the man, now with eyes opened and healed, gestures broadly, opens his mouth to speak, and looks upward while he drops the no-longer-needed cane.

Duccio paints the healed man wearing clothing like the contemporary Italians of the painter's time, unlike the figures of Christ and the disciples. Christ's healing events, as interpreted by Duccio, transcend the barriers of time and enter contemporary reality.

To the immediate left of Jesus stands Peter, who gestures in astonishment as he moves closer. Other disciples and onlookers crowd closer. The follower immediately behind Peter turns his gaze toward the viewer and serves as an observer figure as he makes direct visual encounter with us, drawing us into the scene.

The brilliant blue and red of Jesus' clothing hold our attention as they are contrasted with the pale blue and pink of the surrounding urban buildings. The converging streets between the buildings and the overall scene heighten the dramatic moment of the healing.

Thousand Red Birds

We clutch our tiny bits of faith in tight fists
*   shoved firmly in our pockets.*
We clutch it suspiciously, so unwilling to let it go—
*   we don't want to lose it.*
We clutch it fearing that once it is spent,
*   we will be without hope,*
*   cast adrift, out of luck.*

Help us loosen our grip.
Help us to pull our hands out of our pockets.
Help us to uncurl fingers stiffened over time.

to grow,
to shimmer,
to pulse,
to explode into the air

like a thousand red birds.

Phil Porter

Donnelly/Colt Customstickers

This contemporary graphic is an effort to alert people to act and to speak out. It challenges persons to penetrate the consciousness of the world, promote education, and elicit responses to deal with the epidemic of acquired immune deficiency syndrome (AIDS). The pink triangle is a reminder of the badge worn by homosexual prisoners in Nazi prison camps. Many of them, like Jewish, gypsy, and other political and religious prisoners, were murdered because of a silence of indifference to the atrocity. The contemporary graphic demands speech and action in behalf of any group of persons who by violence or disease are forgotten.

TEACH AND BE TAUGHT

the Sovereign God has given me the tongue of a teacher, that I may know how to sustain the weary with a word. Morning by morning God wakens—wakens my ear to listen as those who are taught. The Sovereign God has opened my ear, and I was not rebellious.

Isaiah 50:4-5a

Isaiah 50:4-9a

Jesus Among the Teachers (Vie de Jesus Mafa)

Perceptive adults often are amazed by the penetrating, clear, pure insights children can offer.
In this painting, the artist interprets the experience of the old scholars of the community who are
fascinated and amazed by the wisdom of the child-teacher in their midst.

. . . and a little child shall lead them.
Isaiah 11:6

Education . . . becomes an act of depositing, in which the students are the depositories and the teacher is the depositor. Instead of communicating, the teacher issues communiqués and makes deposits which the students patiently receive, memorize, and repeat. This is the "banking" concept of education. . . .

Those truly committed to liberation must reject the banking concept . . . adopting instead a concept of humanity as conscious beings. . . . They must abandon the educational goal of deposit-making and replace it with the posing of the problems of humanity. . . .

In "problem-posing" education, people develop their power to perceive critically *the way they exist* in the world *with which* and *in which* they find themselves; they come to see the world not as a static reality, but as a reality in process, in transformation.

Paulo Freire, *Pedagogy of the Oppressed*

In an introduction to Faust, I remembered the writer/editor quoting Goethe as saying, "In the beginning was not the Word. In the beginning was the Act." I blurted aloud, "Ah! No! In the beginning was not the Word. In the beginning was the hearing."

Nelle Morton, *Journey is Home*

I can never teach your children everything they need to know. But I can teach them to be curious and discontent.

Marva Nettles Collins, quoted by Brian Lanker in *I Dream a World: Portraits of Black Women Who Changed America*

Morning by morning God wakens—wakens my ear to listen as those who are taught.

Isaiah 50:4b

MADRE DE LOS DESAPARECIDOS

Sting, a rock musician,

sings about women in Chile

who have danced with

pictures of their disappeared

husbands, sons, and fathers,

Los Desaparecidos,

as they protested

the Pinochet government.

In their dance,

a traditional Chilean

courting dance

called the "Gueca,"

these women taught

the world as suffering servants.

Robert Lentz, *Madre de Los Desaparecidos*

While trained in the classical traditions of Byzantine iconography and art style, Robert Lentz paints contemporary icons depicting men and women who communicate a vision of justice. Icons are intended symbolically to communicate the presence or action of the divine. Such images may be revered because of their power to "fuse" with that which they represent, that is, that which they represent is symbolically present in the art form.

They Dance Alone (*Gueca Solo*)

Why are these women here dancing on their own?
Why is there this sadness in their eyes?
Why are the soldiers here
Their faces fixed like stone?
I can't see what it is that they despise

They're dancing with the missing
They're dancing with the dead
They're dancing with the invisible ones
Their anguish is unsaid
They're dancing with their fathers
They're dancing with their sons
They're dancing with their husbands
They dance alone They dance alone
. . .
Ellas danzan con los desaparecidos
Ellas danzan con los muertos
Ellas danzan con amores invisibles
Ellas danzan con silenciosa angistia
Danzan con sus padres
Danzan con sus nijos
Danzan con sus esposos
Ellas danzan solas
Danzan solas
. . .
One day we'll dance on their graves
One day we'll sing our freedom
One day we'll laugh in our joy
And we'll dance

Sting

Jesus sat down, called the twelve, and said to them, "Whoever wants to be first must be last of all and servant of all." Then Jesus took a little child and put the child among them, "Whoever welcomes one such child in my name welcomes me, and whoever welcomes me welcomes not me but the one who sent me."

Mark 9:35-37

Mark 9:30-37

Emil Nolde, *Christ Among the Children*

In this rather abstract painting from the early part of the twentieth century, Emil Nolde presents
Jesus leaning toward eager, responsive children with his back to the viewer. The artist visually invites the
observer into this joyous encounter. Adults are presented in the left and darker segment of the picture.
It is they who have been preoccupied with an argument over who was greatest among them.

THE STORY OF THE CHILDREN'S FIRE

The whole community sits around a circle called a Medicine Wheel. Around that wheel are representatives of all the different aspects of the community. In the East, there's the fool. In the West, there's the witch. In the South, there's the hunter. In the North, there's the creator. Others positioned around the circle are the shaman, the politician, etc. And in the center of the circle is the children's fire. Next to the children's fire sit the grandfather and grandmother.

If you want to build a condominium in the community of Spirit Lake, you have to enter the Medicine Wheel in the East, at the position of the fool. The question you ask is, "May I build a condo on Spirit Lake?" The fool takes your question, turns it around backwards and asks, "What would Spirit Lake say about such a condo?" You then have to take the question the fool gives you to everyone around the Medicine Wheel. Each will respond to you according to their position in the community.

The last people you must ask the question to are the grandmother and grandfather who guard the children's fire. If these two decide that the request is not good for the children's fire, then the answer is "no." They are the only ones in the circle who have veto power.

The concept of the ultimate question is simple. Does it hurt or help the children's fire? If it can pass the test of the children's fire, then it can be done.

As heard from the elders of the Hopi Nation,
quoted in Kathleen A. Guy, *Welcome the Child*

Rohn Engh, *Young Girl Carrying Washtub*

Jesus and the Children

According to a rabbinic treatise, the resurrection of the people of Israel will happen when "God embraces them, presses them to his heart and kisses them, thus bringing them into the life of the world to come" (Seder Elijahu Rabba 17). Something like that has happened to the children. . . .

How did the children merit such a reception? Absolutely no condition is made. The children have not yet reached even "the age of the Law," and they therefore have no merit. Nothing is said about their innocence, their childlike confidence or any other such qualities. . . . God's will is to present the children with [God's realm], and against all human calculation this is done in a totally gratuitous way. . . .

This gratuitous love of God, assured to the children in Jesus' prophetic words and action, turns upside down... classifications. Children receive a place of preeminence, if human realities are considered from the point of view of God's [dominion].

Hans Rudi-Weber, *Jesus and Children: Biblical Resources for Study and Preaching*

Litany for the Children

Greenless Child

I watched her go uncelebrated into the second grade,

A greenless child,

Gray among the orange and yellow,

Attached too much to corners and to other people's sunshine.

She colors the rainbow brown

And leaves balloons unopened in their packages.

Oh who will touch this greenless child?

Who will plant alleluias in her heart

And send her dancing into all the colors of God?

Or will she be left like an unwrapped package on the kitchen table—

Too dull for anyone to take the trouble?

Does God think we're her keeper?

Anne Weems, from *Reaching for Rainbows: Resources for Creative Worship*

Defender of the oppressed and the orphan, we pray for all children in our nation and our world who suffer from poverty, injustice, and fear.
Hear the cries of your children, O God.

For children who are runaways, homeless, in institutions, or jails,
In your tender mercy, protect them, God.

For children who are disabled in mind or body,
In your tender mercy, encourage and strengthen them, O God.

For children who this day will not have enough to eat,
In your tender mercy, provide them food, O God.

For babies born at risk, for children who are sick, and for those who lack proper health care, especially pregnant teenagers,
In your tender mercy, help and sustain them, O God.

For children who are victims of race or class discrimination, poor education, drug or alcohol abuse, and hopelessness,
In your tender mercy, grant them lives of hope and a future, O God.

For children who daily experience the fear and pain of war and civil strife, especially the children of _____.
In your tender mercy, defend and protect them, O God.

Written for National Children's Day, June 1982, The Washington Cathedral, Washington, D.C.; adapted by Jann Cather Weaver

Little Children, Welcome

Words: Fred Pratt Green, 1973
Music: SAIPAN, by Roy Hopp, 1988

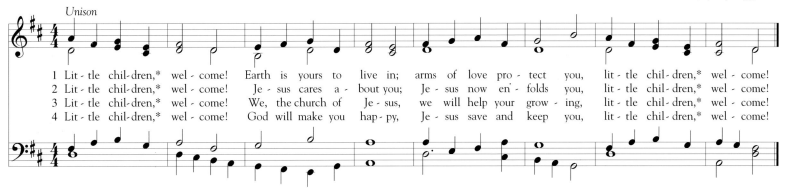

Unison

1 Lit-tle chil-dren,* wel-come! Earth is yours to live in; arms of love pro-tect you, lit-tle chil-dren,* wel-come!
2 Lit-tle chil-dren,* wel-come! Je-sus cares a-bout you; Je-sus now en-folds you, lit-tle chil-dren,* wel-come!
3 Lit-tle chil-dren,* wel-come! We, the church of Je-sus, we will help your grow-ing, lit-tle chil-dren,* wel-come!
4 Lit-tle chil-dren,* wel-come! God will make you hap-py, Je-sus save and keep you, lit-tle chil-dren,* wel-come!

* You may wish to substitute other words as appropriate; for example, "Sisters, brothers, welcome!" , "Little sister, welcome!", or "Little brother, welcome!"

DEEDS OF POWER

john said to Jesus, "Teacher, we saw someone casting out demons in your name, and we tried to stop it, because the one who did it was not following us." But Jesus said, "Do not stop such a person; for no one who does a deed of power in my name will be able soon afterward to speak evil of me. Whoever is not against us is for us. For truly I tell you, whoever gives you a cup of water to drink because you bear the name of Christ will by no means lose the reward."

Mark 9:38-41

Mark 9:38-50

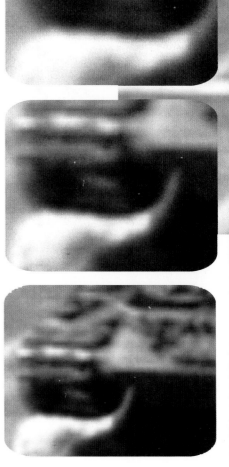

Man Stopping Tank, Beijing

In June 1989, this video image was broadcast around the world from the city of Beijing, China.
At the time, large numbers of students were protesting government policy. When troops moved into Tiananmen Square to end the students' protest, a lone man stepped in front of a long line of moving tanks. He held up his hand as he stood before the approaching tanks, ultimately halting the army's movement against the students for that day. While the identity of the young man and his fate are unknown to those in the West, his deed of power remains indelibly imprinted in the memories of millions of persons.

Brian Lanker, *Rosa Parks*

In 1955, Rosa Parks refused to give up her seat to a white man on a bus. Her simple deed of power gave birth to the historic 381-day bus boycott in Montgomery, Alabama, which for many marks the beginning of the civil rights movement in the United States.

We'll Carry It On

Sometimes I feel my dreams don't matter,
That I am just too small;
The game is theirs, the rules are set
And I don't want to play at all!
But then I think of one strong voice
Who dreamed nighttime into day—
Who broke the rules and changed the
game to one we all can play.
We gather there because that voice
makes love possible to do—
If you can have a dream, Martin,
Surely we can too.

Sometimes I feel like giving up,
The task is just too tall;
For every forward step we take
There's another backward fall!
But then I think of one simple act
That turned a tired movement 'round,
That said enough! we will not go,
We will stop and stand our ground.
We gather there because that voice
makes love possible to do—
If you can make it happen, Rosa,
Surely we can too.

We'll carry it on, we'll carry it on.
We'll carry it on, we'll carry it on. . . .

Susan Savell

When he saw that I was still remaining in the seat, the [bus] driver said, "If you don't stand up, I'm going to call the police and have you arrested." I said, "You may do that."

Two policemen came and wanted to know what was the trouble. One said, "Why don't you stand up?" I said, "I don't think I should have to." At that point I asked the policemen, "Why do you push us around?" He said, "I don't know, but the law is the law and you're under arrest."

Rosa Parks

Blessed Be These Hands

Blessed be the works of your hands,

O Holy One.

Blessed be these hands that have touched life.

Blessed be these hands that have nurtured creativity.

Blessed be these hands that have held pain.

Blessed be these hands that have embraced with passion.

Blessed be these hands that have tended gardens.

Blessed be these hands that have closed in anger.

Blessed be these hands that have planted new seeds.

Blessed be these hands that have harvested ripe fields.

Blessed be these hands that have cleaned, washed, mopped, scrubbed.

Blessed be these hands that have become knotty with age.

Blessed be these hands that are wrinkled and scarred from doing justice.

Blessed be these hands that have reached out and been received.

Blessed be these hands that hold the promise of the future.

Blessed be the works of your hands,

O Holy One.

Diann Neu

At an informal family Eucharist I celebrated last year during Lent, I asked the group to name persons whom they knew were suffering. A little girl sitting next to her father said, "My father's suffering but he will not tell anyone." While I was thinking of a response, she began to hug him. In embarrassment he said, "Oh, Beth, stop; you're going to hug me to death." "No Daddy," she exclaimed, "I'm hugging you to life."

John H. Westerhoff, III, from *A Pilgrim People: Learning Through the Church Year*

Jann Cather Weaver, *Homeless Hands*

THE WORK OF GOD'S FINGERS

When I look at your heavens, the work of your fingers, the moon and the stars that you have established; what are human beings that you are mindful of them, mortals that you care for them? Yet you have made them a little lower than God, and crowned them with glory and honor.

Psalm 8:3-5

Psalm 8

THE EIGHTH SONG

Yours are these stars
that spark and burn
and streak across the sky;
yours, this spectral moon
that mesmerizes field and
        meadow,
speaks with field-mice.

Who am I that
I am rooted here in wonder?
that something in me dares
to make reply?

I want to raise the window,
wake the world,
shout until the housetops
        answer—

God is alive, alive, alive!

Dorothy Hanson Brown

The Creation

Using the same old materials of earth, air, fire, and water, every twenty-four hours God creates something new out of them. If you think you're seeing the same show all over again seven times a week, you're crazy. Every morning you wake up to something that in all eternity never was before and never will be again. And the you that wakes up was never the same before and will never be the same either.

Frederick Buechner
Wishful Thinking: A Theological ABC

Jess, *No-Traveller's Borne*

In 1965, The artist Jess painted this vision of a vast universe based on an engraving by G. M. Hopkins that appeared in an 1869 issue of *Experimental Science*. Jess, who at one time worked as a radiochemist, integrates scientific and spiritual realities in this work.

Aaron Douglas, *The Creation*

Aaron Douglas based this painting on James Weldon Johnson's poem "The Creation." In the poem God steps out on space; spangles the night with moon and stars; claps hands so that thunder rolls; raises an arm so that birds split the air with their wings; scoops up clay from a river bed "like a mammy bending over her baby"; and breathes the breath of life into the clay—creating human beings.

Colorful Creator

Colorful Creator, God of mystery,

thank you for the artist teaching us to see

glimpses of the meaning of the commonplace,

visions of the holy in each human face.

Harmony of ages, God of listening ear,

thank you for composers tuning us to hear

echoes of the Gospel in the songs we sing,

sounds of love and longing from the deepest spring.

Author of our journey, God of near and far,

praise for tale and drama telling who we are,

stripping to the essence struggles of our day,

times of change and conflict when we choose our way.

God of truth and beauty, Poet of the Word,

may we be creators by the Spirit stirred,

open to your presence in our joy and strife,

vessels of the holy coursing through our life.

Ruth Duck

Dream Variation

To fling my arms wide
In some place of the sun,
To whirl and to dance
Till the white day is done.
Then rest at cool evening
Beneath a tall tree
While night comes on gently,
    Dark like me—
That is my dream!

To fling my arms wide
In the face of the sun,
Dance! Whirl! Whirl!
Till the quick day is done.
Rest at pale evening . . .
A tall, slim tree . . .
Night coming tenderly
    Black like me.

Langston Hughes

Michelangelo Buonarotti, *The Creation of Adam*, detail

Through the centuries, the creative and healing power of God has been represented through the gestures of the human hand and fingers. Beginning in the early Christian catacombs, frescoes showed God touching and healing through Jesus. During the Renaissance, Michelangelo dared to symbolize God's "human hand gesture" bringing humanity into being.

Great Creator, still creating,
show us what we yet may do.

. . .

Great Creator, give us guidance
till our goals and yours are one.

Catherine Cameron

GRACIOUS JUSTICE

Seek good and not evil, that you may live; and so the Sovereign, the God of hosts, will be with you, just as you have said. Hate evil and love good, and establish justice in the gate; it may be that the Sovereign, the God of hosts, will be gracious to the remnant of Joseph.

Amos 5:14-15

Amos 5:6-7, 10-15

The Prophets

The prophets had no theory
or "idea" of God. . . .
To the prophets,
God was overwhelmingly
real and shatteringly present. . . .
They lived as witnesses,
struck by the words of God,
rather than as explorers
engaged in an effort to ascertain
the nature of God;
their utterances were
the unloading of a burden
rather than glimpses
obtained in the fog of groping.

Abraham J. Heschel

Emil Nolde, *Prophet*

Pathos and Ethos

There is no dichotomy of pathos and ethos. . . . They do not exist side by side, opposing each other; they involve and presuppose each other. It is because God is the source of justice that [God's] pathos is ethical; and it is because God is absolutely personal—devoid of anything impersonal—that this ethos is full of pathos.

. . . God is concerned about the world, and shares in its fate. Indeed, this is the essence of God's moral nature: [God's] willingness to be intimately involved in the history of [humanity].

Abraham J. Heschel

THE AMISTAD ADVENTURE

On the morning of June 28, 1839, *La Amistad* (The Friendship) set sail from Havanna. . . . On board the little schooner were fifty-three Africans who had been abducted from West Africa and sold in violation of international law. Their intended fate was enslavement on plantations down coast from Havanna.

On the third day out, led by one Cinque, the Africans revolted and ordered that the ship be guided toward the rising sun, back to Africa, but each night the Cubans reversed direction.

Zigzagging for two months, the ship eventually was brought by northerly winds and currents to Long Island. The Africans were jailed and charged with piracy and murder.

In New York City, a group of Christian abolitionists . . . formed a defense committee. Attorneys, with help from former President John Quincy Adams, took the case to the United States Supreme Court, which ruled that the Africans were free. The Amistad Committee evolved into the American Missionary Association (A.M.A.), which since then has been in the forefront of the fight for freedom and justice.

The Amistad Research Center

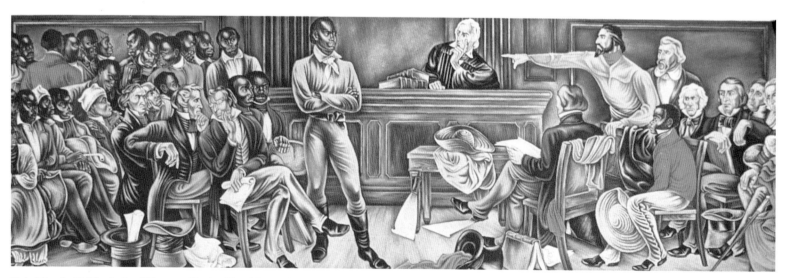

Hale Woodruff, *The Amistad Slaves on Trial at New Haven, Connecticut, 1840*

This painting is the second panel in a triptych by artist Hale Woodruff. The paintings served as a model for larger murals now on display at Talladega College in Talladega, Alabama. The murals were commissioned for the observance of the 100th anniversary of the Amistad Incident.

Faith and Gracious Justice

If a brother or sister

is naked and lacks daily food,

and one of you says to them,

"Go in peace; keep warm

and eat your fill," and yet

you do not supply their bodily needs,

what is the good of that?

So faith by itself, if it has

no works, is dead.

James 2:15-17

Claude Lorrain (Claude Gelée), *Landscape with Rest on the Flight to Egypt*, detail

The French Baroque painter Claude Lorrain placed the holy family, Mary, Joseph, and the infant Jesus, within a beautiful landscape. They rest as they flee the agents of Herod lest the child Jesus be killed (see Matthew 2:13-23). Throughout the Hebrew Bible recurs the theme that a *righteous remnant* shall remain to live the covenant with God and to be God's witnesses. The survival of Jesus from threat of death in childhood to be God's witness, God's very presence, in the world becomes a supreme example of this recurring theme.

The graciousness of God is suggested in this painting, not only in the supportive natural landscape, but in the symbolic presence of the protection of God by the placement of an angel with the family during their respite. Quite possibly the artist found subject suggestion in Christian apocryphal literature on the topic of the flight to Egypt; nevertheless the image is consonant with the passage from the prophet Amos: *Hate evil and love good, and establish justice in the gate; it may be that the Sovereign, the God of hosts, will be gracious to the remnant of Joseph* (Amos 5:15).

TRUE GREATNESS

So Jesus called the disciples and said to them, "You know that among the Gentiles those whom they recognize as their rulers lord it over them. But it is not so among you; but whoever wishes to become great among you must be your servant, and who-ever wishes to be first among you must be slave of all. For the Human One came not to be served but to serve, and to give up life as a ransom for many."

Mark 10:42-45

Mark 10:35-45

Fear not this goodness
as a thing impossible,
nor the pursuit of it as
something alien,
set a great way off;
it hangs on our own choice.

Fourth-century desert disciple

Giovanni Bellini, *St. Francis in Ecstasy*

During his latter decades as a painter, Giovanni Bellini emerged as one of the foremost Renaissance painters in Venice. In *St. Francis in Ecstasy*, painted c. 1485, Bellini's use of fine detail and exacting color catches the eye almost before one notices the figure of St. Francis.

With bare feet, reminiscent of Moses before the burning bush, St. Francis stands before God amid the larger context of the natural world and society. His eyes gaze up and outward, as though seeing an actual vision, while he opens his arms and hands to the glory of God.

In the distance looms the city, the location of most human activity. Bellini seems to indicate a relationship between St. Francis, his ministry of servanthood, and human society.

Behind St. Francis, the artist places a human skull on a prayer desk. Bellini seems to suggest that when standing before the presence of God, in service and in prayer, the ultimate transcendence of God provides the background of all humanity and all human deeds.

God, make us instruments of your peace.

Where there is hatred, let us sow love.

where there is injury pardon.

where there is doubt, faith.

where there is despair, hope.

where there is sadness, joy.

O Divine Maker,

Grant that we may not so much seek

    to be consoled as to console,

to be understood as to understand,

to be loved as to love.

For it is in giving that we receive,

it is in pardoning that we are pardoned,

it is in dying that we are born again

to eternal life.

St. Francis of Assisi, *Prayer for All*

Are we not all divine?

Are we not all made for a higher life?

Mother Teresa

When I Pray the Prayer of St. Francis

When I pray his prayer, or even remember it, my melancholy is dispelled, my self-pity comes to an end; my faith is restored because of this majestic conception of what the work of a disciple should be.

So majestic is this conception that one dare no longer be sorry for oneself. This world ceases to be one's enemy and becomes the place where one lives and works and serves. Life is no longer nasty, mean, brutish, and short, but becomes the time that one needs to make it less nasty and mean, not only for others, but indeed also for oneself.

We are brought back instantaneously to the reality of our faith, that we are not passive recipients but active instruments.

Alan Paton, *Instrument of Thy Peace*

To Touch This Strength

We touch this strength, our power, who we are in the world, when we are most fully in touch with one another and with the world.

There is no doubt in my mind that, in so doing, we are participants in ongoing incarnation, bringing god to life in the world.

For god is nothing other than the eternally creative source of our relational power, our common strength, a god whose movement is to empower, bringing us into our own together, a god whose name in history is love . . . which is just, mutually empowering, and co-creative.

Carter Heyward

Reconciliation is not feeling good; it is coming to grips with evil. In order to reconcile, Christ had to die. We must not deceive ourselves. Reconciliation does not mean holding hands and singing: "black and white together."

It means rather, death and suffering, giving up one's life for the sake of the other.

Allan Boesak

Are we helping the poor, the lonely, the oppressed? People want to see Christ in others. Therefore, we must love Christ with undivided love until it hurts. It must be a total surrender, a total conviction that nothing separates us from the love of Christ. We belong to Christ.

Mother Teresa

Eric Reisberg, *Mother Teresa*, © AP/Wide World Photos

Mother Teresa and her Missionaries of Charity were awarded the Nobel Prize for their work among the slums of the world.

Wherever there is need

among the poor and destitute

in India, Australia, the Middle East,

or anywhere else in the world,

I will set up a home and

send my nuns and brothers.

Mother Teresa

A GREAT COMPANY

See, I am going to bring them from the land of the north, and gather them from the farthest parts of the earth, among them those who are blind and lame, the women with child and in labor, together; a great company, they shall return here. With weeping they shall come, and with consolations I will lead them back.

Jeremiah 31:8-9a

Jeremiah 31:7-9

No matter

how bad the experience was,

the people survived,

not letting exile, or fear,

or helplessness defeat them.

They held on

to one another and

to their faith in God.

Hyemeyohsts Storm,
Untitled (Medicine Wheel)

In the tradition of the Plains Indians, this Medicine Wheel functions as an object for meditation and revelation. Its functions bear some similarities to the Eastern Orthodox Church icon. It is an object into which one gazes. It becomes a powerful focus for those who are a part of the religious community of which it is an expression.

Each one of (the elements) within the Medicine Wheel represents one of the many things of the Universe. One of them represents you, and another represents me. Others hold within them our mothers, fathers, sisters, brothers, and our friends. . . . There are also stones which represent religions, governments, philosophies, and even entire nations. All things are contained within the Medicine Wheel, and all things are equal within it.

Hyemeyohsts Storm, *Seven Arrows*

Beginning in the year 1833,

five American Indian nations,

the Choctaw, Cherokee,

Chickasaw, Creek, and Seminole,

were forced to march from

their homeland in the southeastern

United States to land far west

of the Mississippi River.

Almost every Indian tribe or nation has known some kind of exile and have lost a land that was once their home. Indian people, today, know what it means to feel forced out, helpless, and angry. Today, we understand the psalm's words "strangers in a strange land." (Psalm 137) They describe the experience of so many Indian people. The Trail of Tears is part of what it has meant to grow up Indian. We feel like strangers in our own land. . . .

. . . No matter how bad the experience was, the people survived (the Trail of Tears), not letting exile, or fear, or helplessness defeat them. They held on to one another and to their faith in God.

The faith and strength of . . . the Indian people (is) worth remembering, reminding us that if we believe in ourselves and in the God who watches over us, we will endure. The God of the psalms is the same God who walked the Trail of Tears with the people. . . . God does not abandon the people, even in exile. This is our hope. We are not strangers to this God who has been with us from the beginning and is with us now. We are God's people. And that's worth remembering.

In the Spirit of the Circle: A Christian Education Resource created by Native American Episcopalians

Michael Pavlovsky, *Movement to Overcome*, detail

This cast bronze sculpture, completed in 1990, is located at the National Civil Rights Museum in Memphis, Tennessee.

This grouping of figures suggests a movement or progression across time, boundaries and obstacles . . . the untold stories of thousands of people who lived—and are still living—the Civil Rights Movement and what it stands for and stands against.

Michael Pavlovsky

Out of Exile: An Affirmation

We are ministers of a new covenant:

We are coming out of exile!

We are afflicted, but not crushed:

We are coming out of exile!

We are puzzled, but we do not despair:

We are coming out of exile!

We are persecuted, but not overcome:

We are coming out of exile!

We are struck down, but not destroyed:

We are coming out of exile!

We bear in our bodies the death of Jesus,

that his life might show forth in us:

We are coming out of exile?

Miriam Therese Winter

Nikhil Halder, *The Kingdom Comes*

Nikhil Halder was born in Bangladesh and studied art . . . at Dacca University, Bangladesh. . . .
He painted *The Kingdom Comes*, which stresses the healing ministry of Jesus, for the inaugural
conference of the Asian Christian Art Association.

Masao Takenaka and Ron O'Grady

ALL YOUR HEART, ALL YOUR MIND, ALL YOUR SOUL

ne of the scribes came near and heard them disputing with one another, and seeing that Jesus answered them well, the scribe asked Jesus, "Which commandment is the first of all?" Jesus answered, "The first is, 'Hear, O Israel: God is one; you shall love your God with all your heart, and with all your soul, and with all your mind, and with all your strength.' The second is this, 'You shall love your neighbor as yourself.' There is no other commandment greater than these."

Mark 12:28-31

Mark 12:28-34

Blessed are those who keep God's testimonies,

who seek God with their whole heart

who also do no wrong,

but walk in God's ways!

Psalm 119

Preparation for the Shema

Let eyelids close, let disharmony disappear . . .

Shema (shem-ah'): Listen, hearken, let words' familiar sounds dapple the darkness . . .

Yisrael (yis-ra-el'): Israel is each of us, Jacob wrestling with God, our people wrestling with our doubts and our destiny . . .

Adonai (ad-o-ni'): Your Name, Your Innermost Name, the Name You love best, the compassionate Name we heard Moses call You face to face, the Name that means I am . . .

Eloheynu (el-o-hay'-nu): O God whose rule is just, God who promised Israel eternity like the stars, God with us . . .

Adonai (ad-o-ni'): Wherever we are You are, wherever the world is, You are . . .

Eched (e'-ked): You alone, You are life, Disharmony and harmony, shaded light and dappled [shadows], wicked acts, compassionate people, justice and cruelty, all find their hidden purpose in Your innermost Name. Let disharmony (soon, and in our own day) disappear.

Welcoming Shabbat: The Prayerbook of Chevrei Tikva (Friends of Hope)

Hear, O Israel

שְׁמַע יִשְׂרָאֵל

Dorothea Lange, *Migrant Mother,
Nipomo, California,* 1936

[*Migrant Mother*] centers on a manifestly
decent woman whose face is ravaged by
immediate worry; her right hand plucks at
her cheek, pulling down the right corner
of her mouth, which looks as though it
wants to be humorous. She is poor, and
we assume that her poverty and the uncertainty of her future cause her worry. But
the viewer is less concerned with her
poverty as such, and far, far less with feeling guilty about the social conditions that
imposed poverty upon her, than [the view-
er] is with understanding the profounder,
the humanly universal, results of that
poverty. For the picture is a sort of anti-
Madonna and Child. One sees on her lap
part of a sleeping, dirty baby; but the
mother, who, we feel without reservation,
wants to love and cherish her children,
is severed from them by her anxiety even
as they lean on her.

George E. Elliott, "Things of This World"

A Hassidic Tale

When the great Rabbi Israel Baal Shem-Tov saw misfortune threatening the Jews it was his custom to go into a certain part of the forest to meditate. There he would light a fire, say a special prayer and the miracle would be accomplished and the misfortune averted.

Later, when his disciple, the celebrated Magid of Mezeritch, had occasion, for the same reason, to intercede with heaven, he would go to the same place in the forest and say, "Master of the Universe, listen! I do not know how to light the fire, but I am still able to say the prayer," and again the miracle would be accomplished.

Still later, Rabbi Moseh-Leib of Sasov, in order to save his people once more, would go into the forest and say: "I do not know how to light the fire, I do not know the prayer, but I know the place and this must be sufficient." It was sufficient and the miracle was accomplished.

Then it fell to Rabbi Israel of Rizhyn to overcome misfortune. Sitting in his armchair, his head in his hands, he spoke to God: "I am unable to light the fire and I do not know the prayer; I cannot even find the place in the forest. All I can do is to tell the story, and this must be sufficient."

And it was sufficient.

Elie Wiesel

Christ Be with Me

I arise today

Through God's strength to pilot me;

God's might to uphold me,

God's wisdom to guide me,

God's eye to look before me,

God's ear to hear me,

God's word to speak for me,

God's hand to guard me,

God's way to lie before me,

God's shield to protect me.

Christ be with me, Christ before me,

Christ behind me, Christ in me,

Christ beneath me, Christ above me,

Christ on my right, Christ on my left,

Christ when I lie down, Christ when I sit down,

Christ when I arise,

Christ in the heart of every [one] who thinks of me,

Christ in the mouth of every one who speaks of me,

Christ in every eye that sees me,

Christ in every ear that hears me.

attributed to St. Patrick

AND THEY SHALL LIVE

Jesus cried with a loud voice, "Lazarus, come out!" Lazarus came out, his hands and feet bound with strips of cloth, and his face wrapped in a cloth. Jesus said to them, "Unbind him, and let him go."

John 11:43b-44

John 11:32-44

For All the Saints

For all the saints, who from their labors rest,
Who thee by faith before the world confessed,
Thy Name, O Jesus, be forever blest.
Alleluia, alleluia!

Thou wast their rock, their fortress, and their might:
Thou, Lord, their Captain in the well-fought fight;
Thou, in the darkness drear, the one true light.
Alleluia, alleluia!

From earth's wide bounds, from ocean's farthest coast,
Through gates of pearl streams in the countless host,
Singing to Father, Son, and Holy Ghost,
Alleluia, alleluia!
Amen.

William Walsham How

The Corporate Confession

LEADER: God, you send us saints . . .

PEOPLE: And we imprison them, or nail them on crosses.
Have mercy.

LEADER: God, you send us saints . . .

PEOPLE: And we persuade ourselves they are fools, or
meddlers or incompetents. Have mercy.

LEADER: God, you send us saints . . .

PEOPLE: And we hate them for reminding us that our
comfort requires the poverty of others. Have mercy.

LEADER: God, you send us saints . . .

PEOPLE: And we ignore them. Have mercy.
(*Some moments of reflective silence*)

Words of Assurance (Unison)

God's Word to us is a word of forgiveness, a word of assurance, a word of grace. We are loved and accepted because
we are we and God is God and nothing can finally separate
us from our Creator, our Parent, our sustainer. Amen.

Ruth C. Duck, ed., *Flames of the Spirit: Resources for Worship*

Sebastiano del Piombo, *The Raising of Lazarus*

In del Piombo's painting, the strong contrast between light and deep shadow heightens the drama of the event in progress in the foreground. Just left of center, with lips still open from uttering "Lazarus, come out!" Jesus has his right hand raised as if calling on power beyond himself. His intense gaze at Lazarus is directly in line with his extended arm in the commanding gesture used since the end of the second century to refer to God's power of healing extended through Christ. Lazarus is rising and extracts himself from the burial cloths which have bound his body.

In the lower left foreground, Peter falls to his knees in astonishment and reverence. Mary falls down opposite Peter and looks up into Jesus' face, while Martha reacts in fright, with hands raised. On either side of Jesus, people move wildly about in astonishment, while others in the background talk intensely about the meaning of the event.

Marcus Leatherdale, *Silent Scream*

Art thou any thing?
Art thou some god, some angel, or some devil,
That mak'st my blood cold and my hair to stare?
Speak to me what thou art.

William Shakespeare, *Julius Caesar*, 4.3

To us the ashes
of our ancestors are sacred
and their resting place
is hallowed ground.

Chief Seattle of the Dwamish
(Native American), *Words Upon
Surrendering His Land*

The DEAD LIVE

All see the glory of God!

All Saints Day

O Almighty God, who hast knit together thine elect in one communion and fellowship in the mystical body of thy Son Christ our Lord: Grant us grace so to follow thy blessed saints in all virtuous and godly living, that we may come to those ineffable joys which thou has prepared for those who unfeignedly love thee; through the same Jesus Christ our Lord, who with thee and the Holy Spirit liveth and reigneth, one God, in glory everlasting. Amen.

The Book of Common Prayer

FULLNESS OF THE GIFT

Jesus sat down opposite the treasury, and watched the crowd putting money into the treasury. Many rich people put in large sums. A poor widow came and put in two small copper coins, which are worth a penny. Then Jesus called the disciples and said to them, "Truly I tell you, this poor widow has put in more than all those who are contributing to the treasury. For all of them have contributed out of their abundance; but she out of her poverty has put in everything she had, all she had to live on."

Mark 12:41-44

Mark 12:38-44

Truly I tell you,

this poor widow has put in

more than all those

who are contributing

. . . out of their abundance.

Paula Modersohn-Becker, *Old Peasant Woman*

Penniless . . .

A while

Without food

I can live;

But it breaks my heart

To know

I cannot give.

Penniless . . .

I can share my rags,

But I—

I cannot bear to hear

Starved children cry.

Toyohiko Kagawa

His Widow Complex

. . . [Jesus] was sitting
that morning
in the temple
looking at the treasury-box
in which all kinds of people
were throwing their money
from rattling
and loud clanking bags.

And then
in that row of rich people
very politely and submissively
greeting by the temple—*askaris*,
. . . and all the others

     . . .

there is again
that widow
with her two five-cent pieces
carefully knotted
in her handkerchief.

She stepped in front of the box
unknotting her coins;
the others were getting impatient
already,
and she dropped her
two five-cent pieces,
and was pushed on
immediately.
Jesus stood up,
his disciples too,
and he said
to their astonishment:

" . . . She gave all she had,
everything;
she gave more than anyone else."

     . . .

. . . if our baptism in him
means anything to us,
then our lives too
should integrate
the example
of [the widow]
who gave all [she] had
in view of God. . . .

When he took his bread
that last evening
of his life,
when he took his cup
and said:
"This is my body,
this is my blood,"
he must have been thinking
of . . . that widow
. . . in the temple.

Joseph G. Donders

The Widow's Mite (Vie de Jesus Mafa)

This painting comes from an extensive series of scenes depicting the gospel through the eyes of the Mafa people in northern Cameroon, Africa.

To give and give, and give again,

What God hath given thee;

To spend thyself nor count the cost;

To serve right gloriously

The God who gave all worlds that are,

And all that are to be.

Geoffrey A. Studdert-Kennedy

GOD AMONG US

God is my chosen portion and my cup; you hold my lot. The boundary lines have fallen for me in pleasant places; I have a goodly heritage. I bless God who gives me counsel; in the night also my heart instructs me. I keep God always before me; because God is at my right hand, I shall not be moved.

Psalm 16:5-8
Psalm 16

Ground Me in Your Grace

Eternal One,
Silence from whom my words come;
Questioner from whom my questions arise;
Lover of whom all my loves are hints;
Disturber in whom alone I find my rest;
Mystery in whose depths I find healing and myself;
enfold me now in your presence;
restore to me your peace;
renew me through your power;
and ground me in your grace.

Ted Loder

A goodly heritage recalled by faith. A cup overflowing with charity.

Jack Beal, *Hope, Faith, Charity*

Although this post-modern painting is quite recent (1977-78), the painter has returned to several traditions used in the church in much earlier times to present a painting that can be "read" like a story.

Books, both on the stand atop the table and the one being held by Faith (the man) seem important in the image. Faith is rooted and nurtured in human history and in the reflections of those who have searched for God in the past as well as in our own time. He appears totally engrossed. Immediately to the left, Hope, the younger of the two women, leans close to Faith, suggesting the intimate relationship between faith and hope. She holds a red rose just opening in her right hand, for hope flowers in relationship with faith. Though Hope's face is toward that of Faith, her gaze does not appear to rest exclusively upon him. Her eyes seem partially to rest upon Charity, the more mature woman seated at right. Having found faith and hope, Charity gladly extends her gifts to one beyond the picture itself.

Carissa Etheridge, *Boy in Shelter*

This photograph was taken by a homeless fifteen-year-old person.

We Is Still Friends, Lord (Psalm 86)

Put your ear next to me, Lord,
I just want you to hear me and talk to me
'Cause I ain't got much.
Just remember I try to be like you
You are my man
So I ask for your help.
Make me happy when I'm mixed up inside.
We know you don't hold nothing against us
And you listen and hear us when we talk to you
And don't push us away.
So when we got troubles
We can call up you.

Help us remember you is only one
And everybody was made by you
And had sure better know it
And you are the only God.
Show me the right side of the street to walk on
So I can walk with you and even trust you
And not be afraid to say it
'Cause your love is just great.

When it seems like everybody is against me
And nothing goes right
And people is out to get me
Help me to know we is still friends
And that your love is here.
That's what helps me have heart.
So "give me some skin," Lord,
Then everybody will know where we stand.

Treat me Cool, Lord: Prayers of Kids from City Streets

Gertrude Myrrh Reagan, *Angel de mi Guarda*

Translation of text in the image: Guardian Angel, sweet companion, neither abandon me by night or by day. Four corners hath my bed, four angels to take care of me. Jesus Christ at my head. If I sleep, they care for me, if I die they watch over me with the eleven thousand candles with which the most holy sacrament of the altar is illuminated. Amen. Jesus, Mary, and Joseph. Guardian Angel, sweet companion, neither abandon me. . . .

As part of her series of engravings entitled, *No Puedo Decir lo Peor* (*I Can't Tell You the Very Worst*), artist Gertrude Myrrh Reagan graphically depicts people huddling during a bombing raid. Note the mother who protects the ears of her child. A Quaker, Reagan's work depicts especially peoples of Central America; and universally, she captures terrors all may experience in which God's presence is called for and found.

I keep God always before me;
because God is at my right hand,
I shall not be moved.

Psalm 16:8

I BRING THE TRUTH

Pilate asked Jesus, "So you are a king?"

Jesus answered, "You say that I am a king.

For this I was born, and for this I came into the

world, to testify to the truth. Everyone who

belongs to the truth listens to my voice."

Pilate asked Jesus, "What is truth?"

John 18:37-38

John 18:33-38

But what is the deepest expression of the truth that is in Jesus? Pilate asked Jesus, "What is truth?" Jesus gave no verbal response. However, not long after in the story, Jesus is crucified. The cross, God's self-giving love for the world, is the answer. "God so loved the world that God gave the Begotten One" (John 3:16). Jesus' reign is the reign of God's love. Truth finally is not words. It is the word made flesh in Jesus.

Paul Hammer

Pietro Lorenzetti, *Christ Before Pilate*

Now located in the Vatican Picture Gallery, this 1335 painting by the Italian artist Lorenzetti reveals both the central meaning of the scriptural passage from the Gospel of John quoted for this Sunday and new and powerful forms in Christian art at the end of the Medieval Era on the threshold of the Renaissance. Lorenzetti is expressing the new concern for individual experience and expression that will mark the future Renaissance in church art.

Enclosed in a reception hall, the scene presents an encounter between Jesus and the Roman procurator, Pontius Pilate. At left stands a Jewish leader with a cadre of Roman soldiers in the background. The soldiers hold spears and large shields, painted in the vivid Roman red, in front of them. Their shields and heavy helmets make them appear closed and menacing. The Jewish leader appears anxious and his raised right hand connotes his wish to be part of the proceedings.

Pilate, sitting enthroned, looks at an angle down directly into Jesus' eyes. With his right thumb and forefinger he nervously twists a golden tassel on his ornamented mantle, thus exhibiting the uncertainty, ambivalence, even fear regarding this situation that is suggested in the gospel account. He seems to have completed a statement uttered to Jesus, probably his question, "What is truth?"

The artist has emphasized the empty, silent space between Pilate and Jesus, not only by the open space in the overall composition between them, but also by painting the vertical line of a corner of the room as a divider of their space. Jesus is in the center of the picture, standing in a comfortable posture with his arms crossed at the wrists because they are tied. With his head in a thoughtful, perhaps quizzical, tilt, he stares in silence back into Pilate's eyes. The picture captures this moment of silence—the moment of truth—between Jesus and Pilate.

trut

A PARTICULAR TRUTH

A particular truth can be stated in words—that life is better than death and love than hate, that there is a god or is not, that light travels faster than sound and cancer can sometimes be cured if you discover it in time. But truth itself is another matter, the truth that Pilate asked for, tired and bored and depressed by his long day. Truth itself cannot be stated. Truth simply is, and is what is, the good with the bad, the joy with the despair, the presence and absence of God, the swollen eye, the bird pecking the cobbles for crumbs. Before it is a word, the gospel that is truth is silence, a pregnant silence in its ninth month, and in answer to Pilate's question, Jesus keeps silent, and even with his hands tied behind him manages somehow to hold silence out like a terrible gift.

Frederick Buechner

h

. . . for this I came
into the world,
to testify to the truth

Jesus, in John 18:37b

If twentieth-century Christians are to speak the truth for their sociohistorical situation, they cannot merely repeat the story of what Jesus did and said in Palestine, as if it were self-interpreting for us today. Truth is more than the retelling of the biblical story. Truth is the divine happening that invades our contemporary situation, revealing the meaning of the past for the present so that we are made new creatures for the future. . . . Our commitment to the divine truth . . . requires us to investigate the connection between Jesus' words and deeds . . . and our existence today. This is the crux of the christological issue that no Christian theology can avoid.

James H. Cone

ADVENT

Franz Pourbus the Elder, *Sermon of St. John the Baptist*

We continually

experience incompleteness

and await, hope, expect.

We wait for some

realization, fulfillment,

salvation.

The four weeks preceding Christmas comprise the season of Advent, whose liturgical color is purple or blue. The association of the color purple with Jesus Christ began very early in the visual expressions of Christianity. In catacomb paintings as early as 250 C.E., Jesus is presented as a shepherd who wears shepherd's clothing typical of the time and region where the art is found. But the artists proceeded further in their interpretation: the shepherd's garments were white with purple stripes or borders; purple was associated with high position or royalty. Only a few hundred years later, Jesus Christ sometimes was portrayed dressed entirely in royal purple as the Chosen One of God.

Life is filled with times of waiting; often a time of waiting overlaps with other periods of expectancy. Though many people today do not want to have to wait for anything if it can be avoided, everyone has such experiences of waiting. We learn that times of incubation are necessary for the truly significant to come to fruition. Amidst all the small waitings of mundane life experience are those most significant times of marked transitions, small or great transformations, goal fulfillments, culminations of processes and learnings. We continually experience incompleteness and await, hope, expect. We wait for some realization, fulfillment, salvation.

The season of Advent can be artful waiting. The lectionary readings variously proclaim the preparation, the expectation of the coming together of the Transcendent and the Earth, the divine fully present in the fully human. Almighty God deigns to be imminent, accessible, knowable. Paradox abounds in the scriptural readings of this season; in Advent we await the greatest mystery to be realized.

WAITING,   EXPECTANTLY . . .

j esus said, "There will be signs in the sun, the moon, and the stars, and on the earth distress among nations confused by the roaring of the sea and the waves. People will faint from fear and foreboding of what is coming upon the world, for the powers of the heavens will be shaken."

Luke 21:25-26

Luke 21:25-36

We can be reconciled to life
in its severest aspects
if we are confident
that the disasters
are not meaningless,
and that the valley
can be made a place of springs.

Charles Allen Dinsmore,
Atonement in Literature and Life

Paul Chesley, *Forked Lightning Reflected in Lake* (opposite)
David Austen, *Forest Fire at Night* (right)
Dennis Oda, *Kilauea Volcano Erupting* (far right)

And This Shall Be a Sign unto You

God speaks to us in [God's] own special sign language—a baby. Not much. A small December child. A baby is birth, beginnings, potential without guarantee. A baby is helpless but not hopeless. A baby is someone to watch. A baby is the future appearing now. Are there baby-signs from God signaling hope to us watchers on the hillsides?

Robert A. Raines

The Spirit is Breathing

The spirit is breathing.

All those with eyes to see,
women and men with ears for hearing
detect a coming dawn;
a reason to go on.

They seem small, these signs of dawn,
perhaps ridiculous.

All those with eyes to see,
women and men with ears for hearing
uncover in the night
a certain gleam of light;
they see the reason to go on.

Dom Helder Camara

The rare moment

is not the moment when there is something worth looking at but the moment when we are

capable of seeing.

Joseph Wood Krutch, *The Desert Year*

God's dream
and destination
is a day
when all flesh
in all places
is sensitive
receptive
welcoming
to torrents
freshets
cataracts
floods
and deluges
and inundations
of the Spirit.

Thomas John Carlisle

Naul Ojeda, *Untitled*, detail

Naul Ojeda's engraving depicts a surrealistic reality, that is, objects are placed in an out-of-"realistic" context; three-dimensional perspective is flattened into a two-dimensional slice. The sizes of objects defy conventional Western use of diminishing perspective. Through this style, Ojeda calls for viewers to discern a revelation in their midst that may be hidden by conventional "seeing" of history, of reality.

The word of God came to John son of Zechariah in the wilderness. He went into all the region around the Jordan, proclaiming a baptism of repentance for the forgiveness of sins, as it is written in the book of the words of the prophet Isaiah, "The voice of one crying out in the wilderness: 'Prepare the way of the Lord, make the paths of the Lord straight.'"

Luke 3:2b-4

Luke 3:1-6

Franz Pourbus the Elder, *Sermon of St. John the Baptist*

Painting in the latter half of the 1500s, a time when the reformation of the church was having great effect throughout Christendom, the artist Franz Pourbus the Elder reflects the northern, Flemish interest in each person's *experience* of faith. Using a rich range of blended colors, he reflects the gospel references that suggest the wide range of people who responded to John's preaching. The scene of persons gathered around John includes children, adolescents, young adults, couples of varying ages, and older persons. They seem to come from various vocations as well. Even a soldier is included. They seem engrossed in their own way with what he has to say. One younger man (upper right corner) looks out at us and draws us into the activity of the moment. In the foreground, at far left, a very tall man who fills the entire height of the picture stares at John with a studied and skeptical expression on his face. On the band of his hat are Hebrew characters that may suggest that he is a scholar who has some question about the subject of John's teaching.

In the center of the painting, the figure of John the Baptist exhibits a powerful presence. His posture is active, his gestures ardently expressive, and his facial features suggest the deep conviction with which he speaks.

Jesus possesses

significance

for us only

to the extent

that this significance

is inherent in himself,

in his history,

and in his person

constituted by this history.

Only when this

can be shown

may we be sure

that we are not merely

attaching our questions,

wishes, and thoughts

to his figure.

Wolfhart Pannenberg

In the Wilderness

John came out of the
desert
to preach in the
wilderness.

. . .

The wilderness
he preached in
was his own country.
A wilderness
not coming
from the hands of God,
but a jungle
caused by innumerable
human decisions
that were
    wrong,
    shortsighted,
    and selfish.
Decisions
that had created havoc
in the lives
of the many.
    It was in that
    jungle
    that John preached
    and baptized.
As long
as we think
about John
like that
—preaching
in his own country
two thousand years ago—
his preaching
remains distant
and very far
away.
Let us try
to get that wilderness
and also John's word
nearer home,
so that it can cut us
to the bone.

Let us speak
about the wilderness
in which we live.
And let us think
not only of sin
but of the world
we are accustomed
to.

. . .

It is in that forest,
in that jungle
that the word of God
sounds
through John,
saying that once
justice and integrity
are victorious,
the whole of humankind
will be saved,
that Jesus, the savior,
is going to bring
a total difference.
But indicating also
where we come in and
what we should do:
    straightening the paths
    we are walking now,
    preparing a way for the Lord,
    filling the valleys and potholes,
    leveling the mountains and
        obstacles in us
    and in the lives
    we live. . . .

Joseph G. Donders

Welcome the Wild One

Words: Brian Wren, 1986

Music: Sue Mitchell-Wallace, 1986

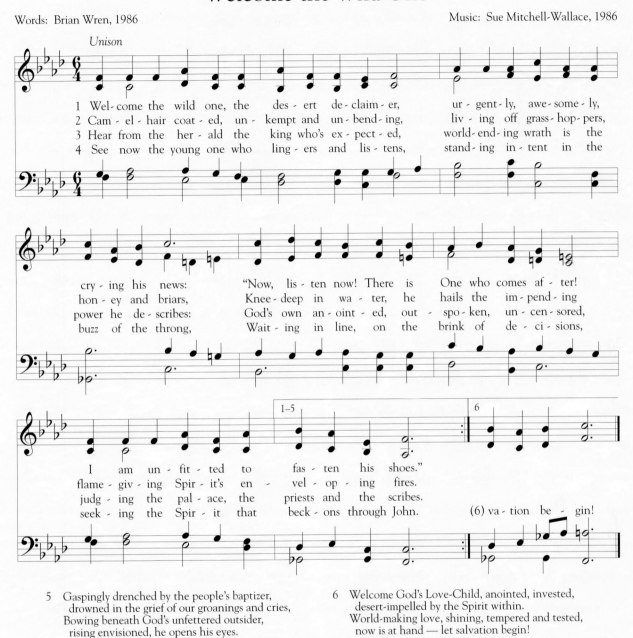

1 Wel-come the wild one, the des-ert de-claim-er, ur-gent-ly, awe-some-ly, cry-ing his news: "Now, lis-ten now! There is One who comes af-ter! I am un-fit-ted to fas-ten his shoes."

2 Cam-el-hair coat-ed, un-kempt and un-bend-ing, liv-ing off grass-hop-pers, hon-ey and briars, Knee-deep in wa-ter, he hails the im-pend-ing flame-giv-ing Spir-it's en-vel-op-ing fires.

3 Hear from the her-ald the king who's ex-pect-ed, world-end-ing wrath is the power he de-scribes: God's own an-oint-ed, out-spo-ken, un-cen-sored, judg-ing the pal-ace, the priests and the scribes.

4 See now the young one who ling-ers and lis-tens, stand-ing in-tent in the buzz of the throng, Wait-ing in line, on the brink of de-ci-sions, seek-ing the Spir-it that beck-ons through John.

(6) va-tion be-gin!

5 Gaspingly drenched by the people's baptizer,
drowned in the grief of our groanings and cries,
Bowing beneath God's unfettered outsider,
rising envisioned, he opens his eyes.

6 Welcome God's Love-Child, anointed, invested,
desert-impelled by the Spirit within.
World-making love, shining, tempered and tested,
now is at hand — let salvation begin!

Prepare the way of the Lord

R

ejoice in the Lord always; again I will say, Rejoice.

Let your gentleness be known to everyone.

The Lord is near.

Philippians 4:4-5

Philippians 4:4-7

Hildegard of Bingen, *Lucifer's Fall*

This image is a twelfth-century manuscript illumination.

This vision, with its wonderful colors of silver and gold, its riverlike outpourings in blue and white, its green valleys and hills, celebrates even in the midst of Lucifer's dark fall, the overpowering grace and goodness of creation. Even at the bottom, the darkest spot, a sparkle is to be seen, hope is to be realized.

Matthew Fox

First Coming

God did not wait till the world was ready,
till . . . nations were at peace.
God came when the Heavens were unsteady,
and prisoners cried out for release.

God did not wait for the perfect time.
God came when the need was deep and great.
God dined with sinners in all their grime,
turned water into wine. God did not wait

till hearts were pure. In joy God came
to a tarnished world of sin and doubt.
To a world like ours, of anguished shame
God came, and God's Light would not go out.

God came to a world which did not mesh,
to heal its tangles, shield its scorn.
In the mystery of the Word made Flesh
the Maker of the stars was born.

We cannot wait till the world is sane
to raise our songs with joyful voice,
for to share our grief, to touch our pain,
God came with Love: Rejoice! Rejoice!

Madeleine L'Engle

SHOUT FOR JOY

I have little patience for the blind joy of those who fail to see the sufferings of the world. I am skeptical of those whose joy seems forced, happy no matter what befalls them. But there is another joy — deeper than the good times and bad times life metes out, stronger than our best attempts and sorest failings — a joy that lifts us when we cannot lift ourselves, a peace that grasps us and returns us renewed.

This is the joy Paul proclaims as he writes to the Philippians from prison. Rejoice in the Lord, for our deepest joy lies not in our circumstances, but in God. Let all . . . know your forbearance. To know the joy that comes from God is not to be carried away in blissful happiness, but to be strengthened and deepened in our love for the world.

Barbara Gerlach

Jacob Lawrence, *Harriet Tubman Series No. 4*

The wilderness
and the dry land
shall be glad,
the desert shall
rejoice and blossom;
. . . it shall
blossom abundantly,
and rejoice with
joy and singing.

Isaiah 35:1-2a

Litany

One: **Surely God is our Salvation!**

People: We will trust and not be afraid!

       For God is our Strength and Song—and our only Salvation.

One: **With joy we will draw water from the Wells of Salvation.**
       And we will say in that day—

People: "Give thanksgiving to God!

       Call upon God's Name!

       Make known God's deeds among all the nations—

       Proclaim the Power of God!"

One: **"Sing praises to God for all the marvelous things—**
       let them be known in all the earth."

ALL: "Sing and shout for Joy, O People of God!

       For great in our midst

       Lives

       The Holy One of God."

Jann Cather Weaver, based on Isaiah 12:2-6

BLESSED

n those days Mary set out and went with haste to a Judean town in the hill country, where she entered the house of Zechariah and greeted Elizabeth. When Elizabeth heard Mary's greeting, the child leaped in her womb. And Elizabeth was filled with the Holy Spirit and exclaimed with a loud cry, "Blessed are you among women, and blessed is the fruit of your womb."

Luke 1:39-42

Luke 1:39-55

Visitation

Each woman listens.

Each speaks:

Ah! the life within you, within me—

a new revelation:

God's saving love

impregnates the universe

in woman . . .

joy . . .

Magnificat!

Again today

women tell their

stories to each other—

magnificat!

Listen sisters, listen brothers,

A new outpouring.

This time:

resurrection!

Mary Southhard

Giotto di Bondone
The Meeting of the Virgin and Elizabeth

Giotto, one of the undisputed master painters of the end of the medieval era and called by many the herald of the Renaissance, painted this fresco soon after 1306. It is one of a cycle of paintings with biblical subjects, especially the life and ministry of Jesus Christ. The painting cycle appears on the walls of a rather small family chapel in Padua, Italy. The several bands of pictures, which completely encircle the room, each present an arrested moment of action in an important incident or a statement of meaning centered on the event of Christ in human history.

Though the fresco paintings inevitably are damaged by moisture in the walls and by aging surfaces, the strength and power of the encounter depicted is not diminished. The setting the artist provides is rather simple. The architecture is only a suggestion, a porch and entrance. As was often the case in medieval church art, the environment for an event of significance was only like a stage set. Evidently, from their perspective this was sufficient to cue the viewer about the setting. The important matter was to bring forth the *significance* of the image in a direct, accessible manner.

With others, including an attendant at left, looking on, Mary and Elizabeth encounter each other for the first time since each of them became aware that they were expecting babies. The moment is both tender and intense. Giotto captures the moment when their arms begin to interlock as they approach each other for an embrace. The powerful expression on the face of Elizabeth and the tender gaze of Mary bespeak the wonder and astonishment of both women with what is happening to them and what their roles may be in the future. Imagine Elizabeth saying "Blessed are you among women, and blessed is the fruit of your womb" as they move toward each other.

Advent is the waiting season,

hoping to be rediscovered.

She is seasoned waiting,

wishing wisdom

and pregnant with promised life.

She is a season conceived each day.

. . .

Joseph J. Juknialis

We must be careful with the representation of Mary and Elizabeth. Certainly we are not meant to recognize pregnancy as the only divine role for women. In the hidden her-story of the gospel, women fulfilled their discipleship in an abundance of ways: by materially supporting Christ's ministry, by defying fear of death to stand beneath the Cross, and by being the first witnesses to the Risen Christ.

. . .

The expected births of both Mary and Elizabeth were ambiguous and troublesome. Both women understood their pregnancies as a time of question—rejection—and doubt. After the scorn of barrenness, Elizabeth remained secluded for five months; after the scorn of unexpected pregnancy, Mary stood to lose her legal and social rights as Joseph considered ending his betrothal to her. Mary and Elizabeth were women living in a time when, not unlike aspects of today, religion had become fossilized, seeking to control society rather than transform society. They, however, sought to live radically faithful lives in response to the call from their God. Not unexpectedly, these women lived lives like those of their soon-to-be-born sons. Do we think John and Jesus just "knew" how to live radically faithful lives? how to be preachers? how to be as eloquent as the Magnificat? how to be healers? John and Jesus knew how to live radically faithful lives because they were sons of two women who had faithfully faced a terrifying yet expectant reality.

Jann Cather Weaver

My Soul Gives Glory to My God

Melody from *Kentucky Harmony*, 1816
Harm. C. Winfred Douglas, 1940

Words by Miriam Therese Winter, 1987; rev. 1993

1. My soul gives glo - ry to my God. My heart pours out its praise. God lift - ed up my low - li - ness in ma - ny mar - vel - ous ways.
2. My God has done great things for me: yes, ho - ly is God's name. All peo - ple will de - clare me blessed, and bless - ings they shall claim.
3. From age to age, to all who fear, such mer - cy love im - parts, dis - pens - ing jus - tice far and near, dis - miss - ing self - ish hearts.
4. Love casts the might - y from their thrones, pro - motes the in - se - cure, leaves hun - gry spir - its sat - is - fied, the rich seem sud - den - ly poor.
5. Praise God, whose lov - ing cov - e - nant sup - ports those in dis - tress, re - mem - ber - ing past prom - is - es with pres - ent faith - ful - ness.

Words copyright © 1987 Medical Mission Sisters. Used by permission.
Music harmonization copyright © 1940 The Church Pension Fund. Used by permission.

Käthe Kollwitz, *Maria and Elizabeth*

Born in 1867 in Prussia, Käthe Kollwitz moved to Berlin in 1891. Later, for her denunciation of fascism, she was threatened with internment in a concentration camp. Further, thirty of her sketches were burned in the 1939 bonfire of anti-Nazi art for being "distorted" and "un-German." By the beginning of World War II, any references to her art had been removed from all Nazi books on art.

Considered by many a great artist, Kollwitz has left artistic renderings of her acquaintance with sorrow or grief which probe the particular, the political, and the biblical. Her sensitive crayon draw-ing of 1928, *Maria and Elizabeth*, suggests the astonished, tender moment of encounter of the two who have exchanged astounding news and anticipate an extraordinary future.

Liturgy

All the way to Elizabeth
and in the months afterward,
she wove him, pondering,
"This is my body, my blood!"

Beneath the watching eyes
of donkey, ox, and sheep
she rocked him, crooning,
"This is my body, my blood!"

In the moonless desert flight
and the Egypt-days of his growing,
she nourished him, singing,
"This is my body, my blood!"

Under the blood-smeared cross
she rocked his mangled bones,
remembering him, moaning,
"This is my body, my blood!"

When darkness, stones, and tomb
bloomed to Easter morning,
she ran to him, shouting,
"This is my body, my blood!"

And no one thought to tell her:
"Woman, it is not fitting
for you to say those words.
You don't resemble him."

Irene Zimmerman

CHRISTMAS

Domenico Ghirlandaio, *Adoration of the Shepherds*

"Glory to God in the highest heaven, and on earth peace among those whom God favors!" Silent night, holy night. Finally, the Earth and the Transcendent meet. Waiting ends. And it happens where we least expect it. The story tells of a makeshift barn with manger. In a humble human family, in humble surroundings, in an out-of-the-way place, a child is born, like every other human, albeit in difficult circumstances. But that child, despite the humble circumstances, will be adored.

Purity and divinity are present in the color of the season, white.

Though adored by the humble shepherds who are filled with awe, the readings for Christmas suggest the child grows as any other. Yet he will amaze the teachers in his youth. And he will have to confront the realities of the human situation and make choices. In time, he will be recognized as one fully human in whom God is fully present: Emmanuel, God with us. We celebrate his coming. And soon his family will flee with him from Herod. He will confront the realities of the human situation and respond to the challenge.

JOY TO THE WORLD!

AMAZED

So they went with haste and found Mary and Joseph, and the child lying in the manger. When they saw this, they made known what had been told them about this child; and all who heard it were amazed at what the shepherds told them. But Mary treasured all these words and pondered them in her heart.

Luke 2:16-19

Luke 2:15-20

Domenico Ghirlandaio
Adoration of the Shepherds

In 1485, the Renaissance was in full flower in Florence, Italy. The artist Domenico Ghirlandaio completed a painting commissioned to hang in the Church of the Holy Trinity there. The painting says much about the Nativity of Jesus.

The setting is rural, outside the town of Bethlehem as Ghirlandaio imagined it. The stable where Jesus was born is makeshift, a shed roof installed over ancient Roman ruins. In the lower center foreground, the infant Jesus lies nude, with thumb in mouth, emphasizing his full humanity. The halo at his head, however, represents the full presence of divinity in him, even at birth. Both, together, suggest a full orthodox Christian conception of the full humanity and divinity of Jesus. Mary is idealized as an image of feminine beauty and maternity. Joseph, shielding his eyes, looks at an angel figure hovering in the distant sky. Shepherds with their flocks receive the announcement of Jesus' birth. At far right, three shepherds view the child with quiet pleasure, respect, even adoration. The kneeling shepherd points with one hand at the child and indicates himself with the other. The gestures are clear: this child is his savior.

Behind the child rests an ornate Roman coffin symbolizing the irony of Jesus' future sacrificial death. Yet, the lid is gone suggesting that death will not hold him, that resurrection awaits.

Isn't it exciting to see that God can work through all kinds of people? The shepherds were the common people of their day; they were not of the ruling class. They were dutiful people with strange hours! At least during this time of year, they had to be out all night in order to keep the sheep from harm. They worked hard and were probably not dressed in fine clothes or were not even very clean for that matter.

. . .

Imagine their amazement! The angel had been absolutely right! The shepherds were privileged to see the One whom God had chosen to save their nation. These simple people from the hillside—unlearned, dirty, but wide-eyed and able to be inspired—were the first to see the Christ Child. How their hearts must have burned within them!

Muriel Tarr Kurtz, *Prepare Our Hearts: Advent and Christmas Traditions for Families*

Christ Climbed Down

Christ climbed down
from His bare Tree
this year
and ran away to where
there were no rootless Christmas trees
hung with candycanes and breakable
stars

Christ climbed down
from His bare Tree
this year
and ran away to where
there were no gilded Christmas trees
and no tinsel Christmas trees
and no tinfoil Christmas trees
and no pink plastic Christmas trees
and no gold Christmas trees
and no black Christmas trees
and no powderblue Christmas trees
hung with electric candles
and encircled by tin electric trains
and clever cornball relatives

. . .

Christ climbed down
from His bare Tree
this year
and ran away to where
no Bing Crosby carollers
groaned of a tight Christmas
and where no Radio City angels
iceskated wingless
thru a winter wonderland
into a jinglebell heaven
daily at 8:30
with Midnight Mass matinees

Christ climbed down from His bare
Tree
this year
and softly stole away into
some anonymous Mary's womb again
where in the darkest night
of everybody's anonymous soul
He awaits again
an unimaginable
and impossibly
Immaculate reconception
the very craziest
of Second Comings

Lawrence Ferlinghetti

For Christmas Eve

LEADER: Come away, come away, come today to Bethlehem.

PEOPLE: Come adore on bended knee, one whose birth the angels sing.

LEADER: Come away, come away, from your noisy celebration, to place of quietness and peace.

PEOPLE: Come with wonder, come with awe. Take your place among sheep and cattle.

ALL: Sing with joy, praise God, for the time of promise has come.
Sing the good news of Emmanuel: god-with-us! The Christ has come!

LEADER: Come away, come away, come today to Bethlehem.

Ruth C. Duck, ed., *Bread for the Journey*

Holy Center of this most holy season, Jesus, child and ruler, all our stars point to your birth; all our wanderings come home to you; all our griefs and delights find a place in the stable where you choose to transform poverty and pain and loneliness and rejection. Your light shines in our lives; your peace embraces our anger, sorrow, and loss; your life opens us to new discovery of our most intimate selves and of our neighbors, however we may find them—as poor as shepherds, as foreign as magi, as thoughtless as innkeepers, as helpless as infants. In your humble birth we discover your everlasting majesty and grace. We welcome you and offer you our thanks and praise, in your glorious name. Amen.

Ruth C. Duck and Maren C. Tirabassi, eds., *Touch Holiness*

Prayer of Confession

God, we confess that ours is still a world

in which Herod seems to rule:

the powerful are revered,

the visions of the wise are ignored,

the poor are afflicted,

and the innocent are killed.

You show us that salvation comes

in the vulnerability of a child,

yet we hunger for the "security" of weapons and walls.

You teach us that freedom comes in loving service,

yet we trample on others in our efforts to be "free."

Forgive us, God, when we look to the palace

instead of the stable,

when we heed politicians more than prophets.

Renew us with the spirit of Bethlehem,

That we may be better prepared for your coming.

Amen.

Keith Watkins, ed., *Thankful Praise:
A Resource for Christian Worship*

GLORY TO GOD!

And suddenly there was with the angel a multitude of the heavenly host, praising God and saying, "Glory to God in the highest heaven, and on earth peace among those whom God favors!"

Luke 2:13-14

Luke 2:(1-7)8-20

Henry Ossawa Tanner, *Angels Appearing Before the Shepherds*

From the perspective of the heavenly host, the African-American artist Henry Tanner paints the angels' appearance to the shepherds. The shepherds in the right foreground are only a small portion of God's creation who hear the song. The hillside, indeed the entire earth, hears the news. From the heavenly perspective, the viewer is invited to join the angels in the song to the waiting world.

The angels came down from the sky like birds. Their voices were bells. They sounded like flutes. "Praise God in heaven, alleluia."

They came flying out of the sky, singing, "Peace on earth, alleluia."

Sweet-smelling song-flowers were scattering everywhere, falling to earth in a golden rain. "Let's scatter these golden flowers, alleluia."

The flowers are heavy with dew, and the dew is filled with light, shining like jewels in Bethlehem. "Alleluia."

Heart flowers, plumelike bell flowers, red cup flowers. They're beaming with dawn light, they're shining like gold. "Alleluia."

Emeralds, pearls, and red crystals are glowing. They're glistening. It's dawn. "Alleluia."

Jewels are spilling in Bethlehem, falling to earth. "Alleluia."

Aztec story of the Nativity

In the Middle of the Night

In the middle of the night,
When stark night was darkest,
then You chose to come.

God's resplendent first-born
sent to make us one.

The voice of doom protest:
"All these words about justice,
love and peace—
all these naive words
will buckle beneath the weight of a reality
which is brutal and bitter, ever more bitter."
It is true, Lord, it is midnight upon the earth,
moonless night and starved of stars.
But can we forget that You,
the Son of God,
chose to be born precisely at midnight?

Dom Helder Camara

ALLELUIA!

Christmas Poem

When the song of the angels is stilled,

When the star in the sky is gone,

When the magi and the shepherds

    have found their way home,

The work of Christmas begins:

    To find the lost and lonely one,

    To heal the broken soul with love,

    To feed the hungry children

       with warmth and good food,

    To feel the earth below,

       the sky above!

    To free the prisoner from all chains,

    To make the powerful care,

    To rebuild the nations

       with strength of good will,

    To see God's children everywhere!

    To bring hope to every task you do,

    To dance at a baby's new birth,

    To make music in an old person's heart,

    And sing to the colors of the earth!

Jim Strathdee, in response to a Christmas poem by Howard Thurman

Our Lady of Vladimir

This twelfth-century Russian icon is also known as *Our Lady of Tenderness* and is one of the most venerated of icons.

One hand supports the child while the other remains free in an open gesture of invitation. At first I thought the Virgin pointed to Jesus with her open hand. I now realize that the word "point" misrepresents the true meaning of her gesture. She is not simply asking attention to her Son, nor is she directing us to him. That would be too external, manipulative, and controlling. I have slowly come to see the Virgin's gesture as a gentle invitation to move closer to Jesus and discover in that movement the God to whom we belong.

Henri Nouwen, *Behold the Beauty of the Lord: Praying with Icons*

JESUS, AMAZING CHILD

After three days Mary and Joseph found Jesus in the temple, sitting among the teachers, listening to them and asking them questions. And all who heard him were amazed at his understanding and his answers.

Luke 2:46-47

Luke 2:41-52

Jesus now claims for himself that special relation to God which was the real meaning of his dedication as an infant. To this point all signs of Jesus' special nature of mission have been to or through others: the angel, Mary, Elizabeth, Zechariah, shepherds, Simeon, and Anna, but now he claims it for himself.

Fred B. Craddock

Duccio, *Dispute with the Doctors*

Between 1308 and 1311, the Italian Duccio painted this panel for the altarpiece at the Cathedral of Siena. The panel makes the childhood of Jesus a significant event to meditate upon while at prayer and at the celebration of the Mass. Here Jesus is the Christ. Rather than the ordinary dress of a Galilean lad, he is dressed in a resplendent robe and, along with Mary, graced with a halo. He is enthroned—with all amazed. Rather than questioning him, Mary and Joseph revere the amazing child.

Hughie Lee-Smith, *Boy on the Roof*

Why?

Dear God—
Why do religious people
Always know they
Are so right
When they don't give
Us a chance to talk?

Treat Me Cool, Lord: Prayers
of Kids from City Streets

Children Are Faith

Faith is not unconditional acceptance or compliance to a set of doctrines. One can *believe* in doctrines, yet faith is no more the result of these doctrines than the color of a child's eyes is the result of their favorite stories.

When I watch children encounter and confront the objects of their attention, I am struck by their embodiment of the "stuff" of faith: perpetual motion, infinite curiosity, exacting questions, anguishing disappointments and doubts. Children daringly tackle the task of understanding their particular place in this rather curious and discordant scheme we call the world. Each day a child encounters immediate fears and joys—and harsh realities; each day these experiences become markers of their emerging sense of humanity.

Children embody faith. They are the place where I see, sometimes most clearly, God and faith meet and mingle. They are our elders. They are my teachers.

Jann Cather Weaver

Scared

God—
I'm scared
I feel funny
On my insides
I wish you wus here.

Maybe if I could help somebody
I'd feel better on the insides
Just doing one good thing
For a change—
Help me do it, God.

Treat Me Cool, Lord: Prayers of Kids
from City Streets

A Sense of Wonder

Linda lies on the garage floor
totally absorbed
experimenting
trying to burn a leaf with the sun's
rays shining through glass.
She is exploring reality
testing how it works
caught up in its mystery.
Her total absorption suggests something of
a child's capacity
to be captivated by reality
to wonder at its mysterious workings
to want to get involved with its
creative processes.
Growing older, we lose that childlike
openness and wonder.
Why do we live only on the
surface of things
hurried, preoccupied,
dulled to the marvels of the world,
no longer entranced by the power of
sunrays and glass to spark
a dead leaf?

James Evans McReynolds

And all who heard him were

at his understanding and his answers.

Luke 2:47

EPIPHANY

Byzantine mosaic, *The Transfiguration*

The infant Jesus

has become the human

in whom the people

begin to recognize the

very presence of God.

Now the Advent–Christmas–Epiphany celebration is completed. Celebrated on the twelfth day of Christmas, January 6, Epiphany is the day when Christians celebrate the manifestation that Jesus is the messiah. The visit of the Magi, coming from far places and representing diverse peoples, serves to confirm this. The liturgical color for Epiphany day and Epiphany Sunday (which celebrates Jesus' baptism) is white. Green is the color of all the other days of the season except the last Sunday, Transfiguration day, when the color returns to celebratory white.

Now the cycle is complete. The other side of the paradox, the Christian claim about Jesus, is manifested. In the mosaic from a Byzantine monastery near Athens, some of Jesus' disciples finally perceive who he really is. Their sudden awareness overwhelms them. For the man they have known, and with whom they have experienced so much, is transfigured. And they are transformed by their insight. Now, instead of the tiny child in the manger, the image suggests that Jesus is also the universal Savior, the incarnation of God.

Throughout the days following Epiphany, the selected lectionary readings present a series of events, from Jesus' baptism and the miracle at the wedding at Cana to the teaching of the Beatitudes. In these moments Jesus is revealed as the Christ. The infant adored has become the human in whom the people begin to recognize the very presence of God. These manifestations each suggest something about what it means to be a disciple of Jesus.

Transfiguration Sunday marks this realization of some followers of Jesus, and as they all depart for the great festival of Passover at the capital of Jerusalem, there is anxiety about what will happen in the days ahead. Jesus is prepared to meet whatever will come in order to complete the task that he set for himself. And we are invited the join him.

E P I P H A N I A — M A N I F E S T A T I O N , R E V E L A T I O N

LONG AWAITED

On entering the house, they saw the child with Mary his mother; and they knelt down and paid him homage. Then, opening their treasure chests, they offered him gifts of gold, frankincense, and myrrh. And having been warned in a dream not to return to Herod, they left for their own country by another road.

Matthew 2:11-12

Matthew 2:1-12

Peter Paul Rubens,
The Adoration of the Magi

The Dutch painter Rubens, active in the period after the Reformation called the Baroque (late 1500s, 1600s), brilliantly interprets the adoration of the infant Jesus by the magi. The contrast between light and shadow enhances the sense of drama and the artist's message.

In the center foreground, one of the magi kneels, thoroughly engrossed, staring open-mouthed into the face of the infant. Mary contentedly steadies Jesus on her lap. The infant Jesus, clearly fascinated with the nearby magus, wriggles in his direction, his right hand outreached. In the center of the picture, a turbaned magus leans back on his heels, places a hand on his hip, and rolls his eyes in recognition of the importance they assign this child. The third magus, far left, more aged than the others, presents his gift with a posture and facial expression that evidence a perception of the importance and gravity of this occasion.

In deep shadow, at far right center, behind Mary and Jesus, a balding Joseph looks at no one, occupied within himself, waiting patiently. Curious travelers with the kings crowd in to look at the child. Shirtless servants sitting atop camels crane forward toward the opening of the makeshift stable to catch a glimpse. One camel, open mouthed, brays, adding commotion to an already excited encounter. Ruined walls and columns suggest a stable constructed in a collapsing Roman building. By the time Rubens painted this picture, it was common to present the stable in this way, suggesting that the old Roman world was disappearing and a new Christian one was being established.

This exuberant, warmly human, at times amusing, image becomes a renewed celebration of the profound significance of the epiphany, the manifestation of the Christ to the Gentiles, who are represented by the magi.

Peter Paul Rubens,
The Adoration of the Magi, detail

When we read the story of the [Magi], we are caught up again in the mystery and wonder of their amazing expedition. All kinds of honest questions pop into our minds: How did they know? Where did they get the courage to travel such a long, long way? What happened to them after they met Mary, Joseph, and the Christ Child? Do you suppose they ever heard of Jesus again? Did this visit touch their lives in any special way?

. . .

It would be interesting to know all the different responses people have made to the birth of Jesus through the ages. We are told that the composer Handel wrote the "Hallelujah Chorus" from the oratorio, the Messiah in a very short time. Something obviously touched him in such a way that all his energies and enthusiasm could be put into his work in a magnificent way.

A story is told of St. Francis of Assisi, who lived in the thirteenth century. He worked in the church at a time when very few people could read, so they were deprived of the privilege of reading the story for themselves each holiday season. As a result, many did not really understand the beauty of the Christmas event. When Francis noticed a cavelike formation at the back of the church, his joy was great! He would arrange for people to see the Christmas story by putting his friends and neighbors in the cave with live animals and costumes to enliven the scene! . . . Seven hundred years later, we still set up scenes in our homes to remind us of the story. . . .

Muriel Tarr Kurtz, *Prepare Our Hearts, Advent and Christmas Traditions for Families*

I Am Waiting

I am waiting for my case to come up

and I am waiting

for a rebirth of wonder

and I am waiting for some

to really discover America

and wail

and I am waiting

for the discovery

of a new symbolic western frontier

and I am waiting

for the American Eagle

to really spread its wings

and straighten up and fly right

and I am waiting

for the Age of Anxiety

to drop dead

and I am waiting

for the war to be fought

which will make the world

safe for anarchy

and I am waiting

for the final withering away

of all governments

and I am perpetually awaiting

a rebirth of wonder

    . . .

and I am waiting

for the Salvation Army to take over

and I am waiting

for the human crowd

to wander off a cliff somewhere

clutching its atomic umbrella. . .

and I am waiting

for the meek to be blessed

and inherit the earth

without taxes. . .

and I am waiting

for a way to be devised

to destroy all nationalisms

without killing anybody

    . . .

and I am awaiting

perpetually and forever

a renaissance of wonder

Lawrence Ferlinghetti

A Psalm of Longing

My spirit hungers for your love,

O Divine Maker of hearts,

for the taste of your joy

and the aroma of your peace.

May this time of prayer

fill me with the whisper of your presence

and let me feel the touch

of your hand upon my heart.

How I long for the depths of your love,

to know your quiet constancy,

the feast of your friendship

that feeds me without end.

Oh, how my soul longs for you.

You elude all names we give you

and dwell beyond the grasp of brilliant minds.

Your essence pulses within every atom

yet extends beyond the far frontiers of space,

unscanned by the strongest telescopes.

Awaken me to your presence,

now, this moment,

in my heart.

Edward Hays

JESUS BAPTIZED

Now when all the people were baptized, and when Jesus also had been baptized and was praying, the heaven was opened, and the Holy Spirit descended upon him in bodily form like a dove. And a voice came from heaven, "You are my Child, the Beloved; with you I am well pleased."

Luke 3:21-22

Luke 3:15-17, 21-22

Pheoris West, *The Baptism of Jesus Christ*

This extraordinary contemporary painting, by North American artist Pheoris West, interprets Jesus standing in water as his baptism begins. The artist suggests a series of actions, the passage of time, even possible ambiguities in the image.

Not only the face of Jesus looking forward toward the viewer is presented, but a number of faces. Especially significant is the sharp angular silhouette of John the Baptist on the far right. Also notable is the face of shadow as it merges with the light to the left of Jesus. Clearly observable is how the artist indicates Jesus' movement to a centered commitment by the depiction of movement with his head.

Mary: *after the baptism*

Yes, of course. On many days I doubted.

My faith grew out of doubt . . . And I was waiting,

remembering in my heart the very things

that caused my doubt: the angel's first appearing

to me and then to Joseph; shepherds, kings,

the flight to Egypt. Remembering was fearing;

doubt helped. I had to face it all as true

the day John baptized him. Then he knew.

Madeleine L'Engle

You are
Amazing
Grace.
You are a
Precious
Jewel.
You—
Special,
Miraculous,
Unrepeatable,
Fragile,
Fearful,
Tender,
Lost.
Sparkling
Ruby
Emerald
Jewel
Rainbow
Splendor
Person.

Joan Baez

Like Jesus,

through

In the Silence, Name Me

Holy One,

untamed

by the names

I give you,

in the silence

name me,

that I may know

who I am,

hear the truth

you have put into me,

trust the love

you have for me,

which you call me to live out

with my sisters and brothers

in your human family.

Ted Loder

Orthodox Baptistery (Neonian) of Ravenna, *Baptism of Jesus*

This remarkable mosaic, created in the fifth century for the interior dome of the Orthodox Baptistery of Ravenna, Italy, has survived about 1500 years of dramatic change in the world.

Jesus is presented nude, standing in the Jordan River, as John the Baptist pours water over him from a bowl. The symbol of the Holy Spirit of God descends in the form of a dove. At right, a bearded figure awaits completion of the ceremony with a cloth extended toward Jesus for his use. The background is formed of gold mosaics. By this time, such backgrounds began to be used to connote the precious sanctity of an event depicted. From the floor below the dome, this glistening image projects the stunning power of this moment in Jesus' life.

baptism
we are named God's own.

THE WEDDING AT CANA

When the steward tasted the water that had become wine, and did not know where it came from (though the servants who had drawn the water knew), the steward called the bridegroom and said to him, "Everyone serves the good wine first, and then the inferior wine after the guests have become drunk. But you have kept the good wine until now." Jesus did this, the first of his signs, in Cana of Galilee, and revealed his glory; and the disciples believed in Jesus.

John 2:9-11

John 2:1-11

IF JESUS COULD

If Jesus could transform
common water
   into wedding wine
spit and dirt
   into new sight
troubled sea
   into a pathway
well water
   into living water
Could Christ transform
   the waters of my life
shallow
murky
polluted
stagnant
sour
   into a shower
   of blessing?

Tom Lane

At Cana Jesus Turns Water into Wine, Vie de Jesus Mafa.

As is the case with the overwhelming majority of efforts to communicate and interpret the Christian gospel throughout the history of the church, the communicator employs forms and media which make the statement lively and clear within his or her own context. This artist, from North Cameroon, Africa, has made engaging and lively this interpretation of this frequently told story from John's gospel. In a setting of village life, the happy diners share the festive event; one seated in the foreground with back to the viewer reaches for a jug (which leans, suggesting that it is empty), while continuing to look toward friends in conversation. At center left, Jesus' mother Mary is speaking, indicating to her son that the wine supply is exhausted. The substance of her statement is suggested by her hand gestures. With his back to the viewer, Jesus listens to her and will respond.

It is not by accident that the Gospel of John weaves into the very earliest period of Jesus' public life this human-interest story of the wedding that comes across with the lilt of springtime. The intention is to depict a contrast with the winter of his austerities in the forbidding wilderness of Judea. The story shows in bold relief how Jesus had survived the shortcomings of the wilderness and how he had moved beyond the ill-humored image of God upheld by the sectarians there. Jesus thoroughly enjoyed the wedding party of the young lovers.

It is worth our while to compare his laughing face . . . with the face of John the Baptist, the man . . . haranguing people forever about the wrath of God. This story discovers to us [sic] the beaming *joie de vivre* of Jesus, who had moved beyond the wilderness and beyond the religious brotherhood of John. . . .

". . . The preaching of John was a burden heavy with the old-time threat of utter destruction. But the preaching of Jesus is a song of joy." To paraphrase a certain verse in Mark, the face of John the Baptist's disciples personified sobriety itself, whereas the disciples of Jesus were like guests at a wedding party (Mark 2:18).

Shusaku Endo

THE WEDDING AT CANA

ERNESTO: In the Old Testament the messianic era had often been described as an epoch of great abundance of wine. The prophet Amos had said that when the Messiah came there would be great harvests of wheat and grapes, and that the hills would distill wine. By this miracle Christ is making it clear that he is the promised Messiah.

MARCELINO: He was coming to bring unity and brotherhood among people. That's the wine he brought. If there's no brotherhood among people there's no joy. A person's birthday or saint's day is not a happy party if there's division.

TERESITA, William's wife: But it wasn't at any old party that he performed the miracle. It was at a wedding party.

ERNESTO: It had often been prophesied also that the messianic era would be like a wedding with God.

FELIPE: No one will be excluded from that wedding. That will be true social justice.

Esperanza Guevara

Esperanza Guevara, *Untitled (The Wedding at Cana)*

Jesus did this,
the first of his signs,
in Cana of Galilee, and
revealed his glory.

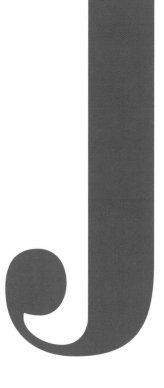

Jesus stood up to read, . . . "The Spirit of God is upon me, because God has anointed me to bring good news to the poor, and God has sent me to proclaim release to the captives and recovery of sight to the blind, to let the oppressed go free, to proclaim the year of God's favor." And Jesus rolled up the scroll, gave it back to the attendant, and sat down. The eyes of all in the synagogue were fixed on Jesus, who began to say to them, "Today this scripture has been fulfilled in your hearing."

Luke 4:16c, 18-21

Luke 4:14-21

Rembrandt, *Christ Preaching*

I Thank You for Those Things That Are Yet Possible

. . .

Thank you

for work

    which engages me in an internal debate

      between right and reward

    and stretches me toward responsibility

      to those who pay for my work,

        and those who cannot pay

          because they have no work;

for justice

    which repairs the devastations of poverty;

for liberty

    which extends to the captives of violence;

for healing

    which binds up the broken bodied

    and the broken hearted;

for bread broken

    for all the hungry earth;

for good news

    of love which is stronger than death;

and for peace

    for all to sit under fig trees

      and not be afraid;

for my calling . . . my life.

. . .

Ted Loder

What is hunger?

One Day

One day, youngsters will learn words they will not understand.

Children from India will ask:

What is hunger?

Children from Alabama will ask:

What is racial segregation?

Children from Hiroshima will ask:

What is the atomic bomb?

Children at school will ask:

What is war?

You will answer them.

You will tell them:

Those words are not used any more

like stage coaches, galleys or slavery

Words no longer meaningful.

That is why they have been removed from dictionaries.

Martin Luther King, Jr.

I, Too, Sing America

I, too, sing America.

I am the darker brother.
They send me to eat in the kitchen
When company comes,
But I laugh,
And eat well,
And grow strong.

Tomorrow,
I'll sit at the table
When company comes.
Nobody'll dare
Say to me,
"Eat in the kitchen,"
Then.
Besides,
They'll see how beautiful I am
And be ashamed,—

I, too, am America.

Langston Hughes

What is

What is racial segregation?

what

the atomic bomb?

Christ Will Come Again

Christ will come again,
God's justice to complete,
to reap the fields of time
and shift the weeds from wheat;
then let us passionately care
for peace and justice here on earth,
and evil's rage restrain with love,
till Christ shall come again.

Brian Wren

What is war?

ACCEPT OR REJECT

nd Jesus said, "Truly I tell you, no prophet is accepted in the prophet's hometown." . . . When they heard this, all in the synagogue were filled with rage. They got up, drove Jesus out of the town, and led him to the brow of the hill on which their town was built, so that they might hurl him off the cliff. But passing through the midst of them, Jesus went away.

Luke 4:24, 28-30

Luke 4:21-30

Rejection

Luke's report brings the starry-eyed Christian
    down to earth with a thud.
It previews something
that will take place often in Jesus' lifetime:
his words will fall on deaf ears.
Nor is rejection of Jesus' message
a phenomenon peculiar to his day alone.
Many centuries later, Thomas Carlyle wrote:
If Jesus were to come today,
people would not crucify him.
They would ask him to dinner,
hear what he had to say,
and make fun of him.
Why haven't 2,000 years changed things?
A high-school boy volunteered his answer:
Why don't I take Jesus' words more seriously?
I guess because if I did,
most of my friends would reject me,
just as many of Jesus' friends rejected him.
And I guess I couldn't take that just now.
Jesus left Nazareth with a deeper awareness of
not only what lay ahead of him,
but also what it meant to be a prophet.
To be a prophet meant to expose himself to rejection —
even death.

Mark Link

Henry Ossawa Tanner, *The Saviour*

Henry Ossawa Tanner's painting, *The Saviour*, now in the National Museum of American Art in Washington, was completed about 1900-1905. This picture is only one of many of his works of religious art, in which he united his powerful religious sensibilities and cultivated artistic qualities. Tanner's *Saviour* was painted during an era when a number of images of Christ were rather sentimental in character. By contrast, this interpretation may suggest to the viewer a more complex image, one of intense reflection or prayer, perhaps even perplexity.

Reassurance

I must love the questions
themselves
as Rilke said
like locked rooms
full of treasure
to which my blind
and groping key
does not yet fit.

and await the answers
as unsealed
letters
mailed with dubious intent
and written in a very foreign
tongue.
and in the hourly making
of myself
no thought of Time
to force, to squeeze
the space
I grow into.

Alice Walker

Georges Rouault, *Ecce Homo*

Georges Rouault was a devout Roman Catholic Christian whose life's efforts primarily were religious artworks such as *Ecce Homo*. He was an expressionist painter, one who chose to make visual statements of inner emotion, and thus at times distort shapes and colors in order to project that emotion.

In response to Georges Rouault's *The Holy Face*, an even more tragic crucified Jesus, Paul Tillich said: "Here you have a face in which there is nothing sentimental. Here Jesus is completely adequate to the situation of extreme agony. He looks beyond the agony but is not beyond it: he is seriously and realistically in it. For this reason I think this head of Christ should be in many churches in our time, showing that the cross is not a sentimental nicety but is in Christ and in all of us in the terrible reality of existence."

CONFESSION

You asked for my hands

   that you could use them for your purpose.

I gave them for a moment

   and then withdrew for the work was hard.

You asked for my mouth

   to speak against injustice.

I gave you a whisper

   that I might not be accused.

You asked for my eyes

   to see the pain of poverty.

I closed them

   for I did not want to know.

You asked for my life

   that you might work through me.

I gave you a fractional part

   that I might not get involved.

God, forgive me for calculated efforts to serve you only

   when it is convenient to do so,

   only in places where it is safe to do so.

Creator God, forgive me, renew me,

   and send me out as a usable instrument,

   that I may take seriously the meaning of Your Cross.

From the annual meeting of the United Methodist Women's Caucus, 1976.

"Truly I tell you,

no prophet

is accepted

in the prophet's

hometown."

DO NOT BE AFRAID

But when Simon Peter saw the boats filled with fish, he fell down at Jesus' knees, saying, "Go away from me, Lord, for I am a sinful person!" . . . Then Jesus said to Simon, "Do not be afraid; from now on you will be catching people." When they had brought their boats to shore, they left everything and followed Jesus.

Luke 5:8, 10b-11

Luke 5:1-11

Jesus, you have come to the lakeshore looking for neither wealth nor wise ones; You only asked me to follow humbly.

Tú Has Venido a la Orilla

Raphael (Raffaello Sanzio), *Miracle of the Fishes*, detail

As the companions of Peter and Andrew continue to draw fish from the water, Peter has fallen to his knees in his boat now filled with fish. Peter implores Jesus to leave him. In reply, Jesus raises his hand, "Do not be afraid." Behind Peter stands an astonished Andrew, gesturing with his outstretched hands at the gift of Christ's abundance.

Raphael's mastery of reflection is evident in this tapestry; even the face of one of the disciples is found among the fish. The artist also places doves moving over the water (between Andrew, Peter, and Jesus), pointing to the Hebrew image of God's Creation in Genesis, as well as foreshadowing the future Pentecost experience (Acts 2) of these disciples.

Tú has venido a la orilla,
no has buscado ni a sabios ni a ricos,
tan sólo quieres que yo te siga.

Tú necesitas mis manos
mi cansancio que a otros descanse,
amor que quiera seguir amando.

Cesareo Gabarain

Tony Festa, *Caring Hands*

What shall we say to you, our God —

...

You have called us

from far and near.

You have made us —

great and small,

each one of us different

in heart and face,

but all of us your people.

We ask you, then,

make new people of us

who hear your voice

with living hearts.

Do this today

and never take your hands

away from us.

...

Huub Oosterhuis

Tú has venido a la orilla
(You Have Come Down to the Lakeshore)

Music: Cesáreo Gabaraín, 1979
Harm. Skinner Chávez-Melo, 1987

Spanish words: Cesáreo Gabaraín, 1979; alt.
Trans. Madeleine Forell Marshall, 1989; alt.

1 Tú has venido a la orilla, no has buscado ni a sabios, ni a ricos, tan sólo quieres que yo te siga.
2 Tú sabes bien lo que tengo: en mi barca no hay oro ni espadas; tan sólo redes y mi trabajo.

1 You have come down to the lakeshore, seeking neither the wise nor the wealthy, But only asking for me to follow.
2 You know full well my posessions. Neither treasure nor weapons for conquest, Just these my fishnets and will for working.

Estribillo (Refrain)

Jesús, me has mirado a los ojos; sonriendo, has dicho mi nombre; en la arena he dejado mi barca; junto a tí buscaré otro mar.

O Jesus, you have looked into my eyes; kindly smiling, you've called out my name. On the sand I have abandoned my small boat; now with you, I will seek other seas.

3 Tú necesitas mis manos,
  mi cansancio que a otros descanse,
  amor que quiera seguir amando.
  Estribillo

3 You need my hands, my exhaustion,
  working love for the rest of the weary—
  A love that's willing to go on loving.
  Refrain

4 Tú, Pescador de otros mares,
  ansia eterna de almas que esperan.
  Amigo bueno, que así me llamas.
  Estribillo

4 You who have fished other waters;
  you, the longing of souls that are yearning:
  As loving Friend, you have come to call me.
  Refrain

When they had brought their boats to shore, they left everything and followed Jesus.

Jesus came down with them and stood on a level place, with a great crowd of the disciples and a great multitude of people from all Judea, Jerusalem, and the coast of Tyre and Sidon. . . . Jesus looked up at the disciples and said: "Blessed are you who are poor, for yours is the dominion of God. Blessed are you who are hungry now, for you will be filled. Blessed are you who weep now, for you will laugh."

Luke 6:17, 20-21

Luke 6:17-26

Marina Silva, *The Beatitudes*, detail

Rest in My Wings

Don't be afraid, I'm holding you close in the darkness.
                    . . .
So rest in my wings and put all your fears to flight.

Tho you be burdened, I will cradle you deep in my nest.

Tho you be weary, my wings will enfold you in rest.

Tho you be desert, my rivers will flow deep inside.

Tho you be barren, I'll fill out your womb with new life.

Tho you be orphaned, I'll always be here at your side.

Tho you be empty, I'll bring forth new fruit on the vine.

Tho you be thirsty, you'll drink from the well of my side.

Tho you be hungry, the finest of bread I'll provide.

Colleen Fulmer

Jesus and the crowds! This is where God's secret for the world is revealed. But it is not the size of the crowd that inspired Jesus. . . .
It was their sorrow and hunger that moved him.

C. S. Song

133

BLESS

In those moments of self-giving, inmost desire and outward deed overflow together. Our divided selves are made whole, and we experience God's blessing.

It is when we are pushed to the edge of human possibility by our poverty or our grief, by our thirst for righteousness or our search for peace, by our suffering or our love that God meets us. In these moments, which are our perfection and our peace, God comes to us as sure as the taste of salt on our tongues.

Barbara A. Gerlach,
The Things That Make For Peace

ED

Blessed

Blessed are those who are . . . emptied of all that doesn't matter, those for whom the riches of this world just aren't that important.
The reign of heaven is theirs.

Blessed are those who wear compassion like a garment . . .
For they too shall receive comfort.

. . .

Blessed are the creators of peace, those who build roads that unite rather than walls that divide, those who bless the world with the healing power of their presence.
For they shall be called children of God.

Blessed are those whose love has been tried, like gold, in the furnace and found to be precious, genuine, and lasting, those who have lived their belief out loud, no matter what the cost or pain.

. . .

Macrina Wiederkehr

"Fortunate are the poor in spirit."

That means:

> Fortunate are those who are willing
> to let themselves be censured by the word of God,
> to re-examine their views,
> to believe they haven't yet understood a thing,
> to be taken by surprise,
> to have their mind changed,
> to see their convictions,
> their principles,
> their tidy systems
> and everything they took for granted
> swept out from under them,
> and to face the fact, once for all,
> that there's no such thing as a matter of course
> and that God can ask anything.

Louis Evely

NO STRINGS ATTACHED

7hen Joseph said to his brothers, "Come closer to me." And they came closer. He said, "I am your brother, Joseph, whom you sold into Egypt. And now do not be distressed, or angry with yourselves, because you sold me here; for God sent me before you to preserve life.

Genesis 45:4-5

Genesis 45:3-11, 15

I've Been Scolded

I'm sorry.
Why, Lord, is that so hard to say?

First I said: it's not my fault.
Then I said: my sister made me.
I was angry all afternoon,
with my sister, with everybody,
with myself.

Then I said: I'm sorry.
Now I'm happy with everybody,
with myself,
and with you, Lord.
Amen.

Madeleine L'Engle

Marc Chagall, *Joseph Recognized by His Brothers*

For one human being
to love another:
that is perhaps
the most difficult
of all our tasks,
the ultimate,
the last test and proof,
the work for which
all other work
is but preparation.

Rainer Maria Rilke

Bob Galbraith, *Los Angeles, May 6 Gang Summit*, AP/Wide World Photos, Inc.

Members of rival Los Angeles street gangs greet one another upon arrival at a summit in South Central Los Angeles. The city's notorious Blood and Crip gangs have joined forces in a solidarity move with leaders saying the recent riots have proven inner-city blacks cannot continue killing their brothers.

Love is not fundamentally . . . a matter of sentiment, attachment, or being "drawn toward." Love is active, effective, a matter of making reciprocal and mutually beneficial relation with one's friends and enemies. Love creates righteousness, or Justice, here on earth. To make love is to make justice. . . .

We are not automatic lovers of self, others, world, or God. Love does not just happen. . . . Love is . . . a willingness to be present to others without pretense or guile. Love is a conversion to humanity—a willingness to participate with others in the healing of a broken world and broken lives.

Carter Heyward, *Our Passion for Justice*

God wants to be thought of
as our Lover.
I must see myself so bound in love
as if everything that has been done
has been done for me.
That is to say,
The Love of God makes such a unity
in us
that when we see this unity
no one is able to separate oneself
from another.

Julian of Norwich, Medieval English mystic

Love is full
of such yearning
such adamant
insistence for
right-relation
such compassion
such rage
And it is absolutely
irrepressible

Carter Heyward

TRANSFIGURED

Jesus took with him Peter and John and James, and went up on the mountain to pray. And while Jesus was praying, the appearance of his face changed, and his clothes became dazzling white. . . . Then from the cloud came a voice that said, "This is my Child, my Chosen; to this one you shall listen!" When the voice had spoken, Jesus was found alone. And they kept silent and in those days told no one of the things they had seen.

Luke 9:28b-29, 35-36

Luke 9:28-36 (37-43)

O Virtus Sapientiae

O virtus sapientiae,
quae circuiens circuisti
comprehendendo omnia
in una via, quae ha bet vitam,
tres alas habens,
quarum una in altum volat,
et altera de terra sudat,
et tertia uniduqe volat
Laus tibi sit, sicut te decet,
    o sapientia.

O moving force of Wisdom,
encircling the wheel of the cosmos,
Encompassing all that is,
all that has life,
in one vast circle.

You have three wings:
The first unfurls aloft
in the highest heights.
The second dips its way
dripping sweat on the Earth.
Over, under, and through
all things whirls the third.
Praise to you,
O Wisdom,
worthy of praise!

Hildegard of Bingen

Livan Kudriashev, *Luminescence*

It was Jesus of Nazareth all right, the man they'd tramped many a dusty mile with, whose mother and brothers they knew, the one they'd seen as hungry, tired, footsore as the rest of them. But it was also the Messiah, the Christ, in his glory. It was the holiness of the man shining through his humanness, his face so afire with it they were almost blinded.

Even with us something like that happens once in a while. The face of a man walking his child in the park, of a woman picking peas in the garden, of sometimes even the unlikeliest person listening to a concert, say, or standing barefoot in the sand watching the waves roll in, or just having a beer at a Saturday baseball game in July. Every once and so often, something so touching, so incandescent, so alive transfigures the human face that it's almost beyond bearing.

Frederick Buechner, *Transfiguration*

Transfiguration is living by vision: standing foursquare in the midst of a broken, tortured, oppressed, starving, dehumanizing reality, yet seeing the invisible, calling to it to come, behaving as if it is on the way, sustained by elements of it that have come already, within and among us. In those moments when people *are* healed, transformed, freed from addictions, obsessions, destructiveness, self worship or when groups or communities or even, rarely, whole nations glimpse the light of the transcendent in their midst, there the New Creation has come upon us. The world for one brief moment is transfigured. The beyond shines in our midst—on the way to the cross.

Walter Wink, *Interpretation*

The play's not done, Oh, not quite,
For life never ends in the moonlit night.
And despite what pretty poets say,
The night is only half the day.

So we would like to truly finish
What was foolishly begun,
For the story is not ended
And the play is never done
Until we've, all of us, been burned a bit
And burnished by the sun.

Jerry Schmidt and Tom Jones, *The Fantastiks*

This is my Child,

to this

Byzantine mosaic, *The Transfiguration*

This Byzantine mosaic of c. 1100, from the Monastery of Daphni near Athens, interprets the overwhelming experience of Peter, James and John when they recognized Jesus transfigured in their midst.

Litany

In the midst of hunger and war
we celebrate the promise of plenty and peace.

In the midst of oppression and tyranny
we celebrate the promise of service and freedom.

In the midst of doubt and despair
we celebrate the promise of faith and hope.

In the midst of fear and betrayal
we celebrate the promise of joy and loyalty.

In the midst of hatred and death
we celebrate the promise of love and life.

In the midst of sin and decay
we celebrate the promise of salvation and renewal.

In the midst of death on every side
we celebrate the promise of the living Christ.

Celebration of Life

my Chosen

one you shall listen!

LENT

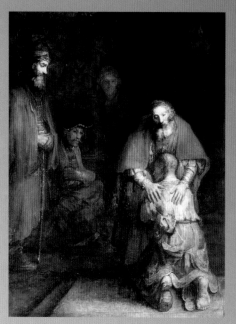

Rembrandt van Rijn,
The Return of the Prodigal Son

Lent focuses on

a journey in which

one realizes

the complete gift of

Jesus Christ for others.

Purple is the liturgical color employed during Lent. And on Ash Wednesday, the first day of Lent, the colors are black or gray. On Palm Sunday, the beginning of Holy Week before Easter, the color is red. For Maundy Thursday, the day that Jesus and his disciples celebrated Passover and shared what would be their last meal together, the color returns to purple. On the following day, Good Friday, the day of crucifixion, the color is black.

In the painting by Rembrandt, the prodigal son has repented and returns to his father. The penitence of the son is deep, complete; and the parent receives the son back into his arms with great relief, compassion, and quiet joy. Their reuniting is poignantly powerful as their forms intertwine. Thus does God receive those who genuinely search themselves, seek restoration and renewal in penitence, and "return home."

Lent is a journey, for both the church and individuals, of intense self-examination, of penitence for alienation from God and one's fellow creatures, and for preparation for restoration. The season is focused on a journey in which one realizes the complete gift of Jesus Christ for others. It is a journey that requires facing the cross. As the season approaches its climax, it is remembered that Jesus was determined to complete his mission and that he suffered greatly. Finally he gave himself in complete trust to God as he submitted to crucifixion. In the Crucifixion rests the basis for claiming that indeed he was what he taught. When Jesus prayed on the cross that God would forgive his executioners and those who betrayed him, he exhibited the complete union of himself with that central characteristic of God, unqualified love.

To confront that complete and unqualified love is to be judged as one falls short of it. Yet, as those who betrayed or left Jesus in fear return, they are forgiven, even as contemporary followers seek that same forgiveness and restoration.

To Easter there are no shorter routes. One passes through and remembers that the Last Supper and Crucifixion precede the victory of Easter.

FORGIVENESS AND RESTORATION

GIVE ME JESUS

I heard my Mother say,
Give me Jesus.
Dark midnight was my cry,
Give me Jesus—
You may have all this world—
Give me Jesus!

WHERE YOUR HEART IS

Beware of practicing your piety before others in order to be seen by them; for then you have no reward from God in heaven. . . . For where your treasure is, there your heart will be also."

Matthew 6:1, 21

Matthew 6:1-6, 16-21

Aminah Brenda Lynn Robinson, *Give Me Jesus* (opposite)

Lenten Psalm of Awakening

Come, O Life-giving Creator,
    and rattle the door latch
    of my slumbering heart.
Awaken me as you breathe upon
    a winter-wrapped earth,
    gently calling to life virgin Spring.

Awaken in these fortified days
    of Lenten prayer and discipline
    my youthful dream of holiness.
Call me forth from the prison camp
    of my numerous past defeats
    and my narrow patterns of being
    to make my ordinary life extra-ordinarily alive,
    through the passion of my love.

Show to me during these Lenten days
    how to take the daily things of life
    and by submerging them in the sacred,
    to infuse them with a great love
    for you, O God, and for others.
Guide me to perform simple acts of love and prayer,
    the real works of reform and renewal
    of this overture to the spring of the Spirit.

O Father of Jesus, Mother of Christ,
    help me not to waste
    these precious Lenten days
    of my soul's spiritual springtime.

Edward Hays

Let Us Pray

LEADER: **Let us pray.**

PEOPLE: Most holy and merciful God:

We confess to you and to one another,

and to the whole communion of saints

in heaven and on earth,

that we have sinned by our own fault

in thought, word, and deed,

by what we have done,

and by what we have left undone.

LEADER: **We have not loved you**

with all our heart, and mind, and strength.

We have not loved our neighbors as ourselves.

We have not forgiven others

as we have been forgiven.

PEOPLE: Have mercy on us, O God.

LEADER: **We have been deaf to your call**

to serve as Christ served us.

We have not been true

to the mind of Christ.

We have grieved your Holy Spirit.

PEOPLE: Have mercy on us, O God.

LEADER: **We confess to you, O God,**

all our past unfaithfulness.

The pride, hypocrisy, and impatience in our lives.

PEOPLE: We confess to you, O God.

LEADER: **Our self-indulgent appetites and ways**

and our exploitation of other people,

PEOPLE: We confess to you, O God.

LEADER: **Our anger at our own frustration**

and our envy of those more fortunate than ourselves,

PEOPLE: We confess to you, O God.

LEADER: **Our intemperate love of worldly goods and comforts**

and our dishonesty in our daily life and work,

PEOPLE: We confess to you, O God.

LEADER: **Our negligence in prayer and worship**

and our failure to commend the faith that is in us,

PEOPLE: We confess to you, O God.

LEADER: **Accept our repentance, O God,**

for the wrongs we have done.

For our neglect of human need and suffering

and our indifference to injustice and cruelty,

PEOPLE: Accept our repentance, O God.

LEADER: **For all false judgments,**

for uncharitable thoughts toward our neighbors,

and for our prejudice and contempt

toward those who differ from us,

PEOPLE: Accept our repentance, O God.

LEADER: **For our waste and pollution of your creation**

and our lack of concern for those who come after us,

PEOPLE: Accept our repentance, O God.

LEADER: **Restore us, O God,**

and let your anger depart from us.

PEOPLE: Favorably hear us, O God, for your mercy is great.

Amen.

United Church of Christ, *Book of Worship*

Did'st Thou give me
this inescapable loneliness
so that it would be easier
to give Thee all?

Dag Hammarskjöld, *Markings*

Ann Marie Rousseau, *A Day in the Life of Darian Moore*

J esus, full of the Holy Spirit, returned from the Jordan and was led by the Spirit in the wilderness, where for forty days he was tempted by the devil.

Luke 4:1-2a

Luke 4:1-13

The choice between God and every other god is a real choice. Both make promises, both demand loyalty. It is possible to live by both. If there were no real alternative to God, all [humanity] would choose [God]. Indeed, God is the more difficult choice to justify in terms of provable results.

The chief difficulty is that God demands of us that we live by faith: faith in [God], [God's] sovereignty over the future, [God's] sufficiency for the present; while, on the other hand, the various other gods whom we can serve appeal to us in terms of the things which we can see and the forces which we can calculate. The choice between the life of faith and the life of sight is a choice between a God whom only faith can apprehend and gods whom one has only to see to understand.

D. T. Niles in *The Bible Through Asian Eyes*

No Christian escapes

a taste of the wilderness on the way

to the Promised Land.

Evelyn Underhill, *The Fruits of the Spirit*

An Dong-Sook, *Temptation of Christ*

In An Dong-Sook's *Temptation of Christ*, the devil is presented in clearly human form, though only portions of the torso, arms, and face (upper right segment of the picture) can be seen. Traditional images of Mephistopheles (the devil) in the history of art, most of which give the figure the sinister qualities suggested here, influence this visual interpretation of the evil one. Jesus, shown as a young man, squatting and with his back to us, seems to ponder the stone and return it as he finds within his own faith the strength to meet and resist temptation. Even though the face of Jesus is not visible, the almost vertical line of his back confirms the perception of strength in the face of temptation.

Master LCZ (Lorenz Katzheimer),
Temptation of Christ

Master LCZ presents Jesus and the evil one in a foreboding natural setting. The craggy rock outcropping directly behind the devil reinforces a negative response to this figure, while the trees behind Jesus are intended to add to his appeal. The artist has drawn the evil one as a combination of creatures, real and imagined, making it easier to reject the otherwise seductive offers of immediate gratification. Jesus raises his right hand in a gesture rebuking the devil. Choices between God and gods might not be always so clearly delineated. For example, in T. S. Eliot's verse drama, *Murder in the Cathedral,* the main character, Archbishop Thomas á Becket, also is tempted as he considers his allegiance to God or the king of England. In his response to the fourth temptation, Thomas answers,

16 לֹא תְנַסּוּ אֶת־יְהֹוָה אֱלֹהֵיכֶם

כַּאֲשֶׁר נִסִּיתֶם בַּמַּסָּה׃

Deuteronomy 6:16

Do not put the Lord your God to the test!

כִּי לֹא עַל־הַלֶּחֶם לְבַדּוֹ יִחְיֶה הָאָדָם

Deuteronomy 8:3

One shall not live by bread alone!

12 וְעַתָּה יִשְׂרָאֵל מָה יְהֹוָה אֱלֹהֶיךָ שֹׁאֵל מֵעִמָּךְ כִּי אִם־לְיִרְאָה
אֶת־יְהֹוָה אֱלֹהֶיךָ לָלֶכֶת בְּכָל־דְּרָכָיו וּלְאַהֲבָה אֹתוֹ

וְלַעֲבֹד אֶת־יְהֹוָה אֱלֹהֶיךָ בְּכָל־לְבָבְךָ וּבְכָל־נַפְשֶׁךָ׃

13 לִשְׁמֹר אֶת־מִצְוֺת יְהֹוָה אֱלֹהֶיךָ

Deuteronomy 10:13

You shall worship the Lord your God, and serve only God!

"The last temptation is the greatest treason:

To do the right deed for the wrong reason."

A Prayer

God in heaven, you have helped my life to grow like a tree. Now something has happened. Satan, like a bird, has carried in one twig of his own choosing after another. Before I knew it he had built a dwelling place and was living in it. Tonight, my Father, I am throwing out both the bird and the nest.

"Nigerian Prayer," *Morning, Noon and Night*

Whether we gaze
with longing into the garden
or with fear and trembling
into the desert, of this
we can be sure—God walked
there first! And when we
who have sinned and despoiled
the garden are challenged
now to face the desert, we do not
face it alone. Jesus has gone
there before us to struggle with
every demon that has ever
plagued a human heart. Face the
desert we must if we would
reach the garden, but Jesus has
gone there before us.

James Healy, *"Starting Point"*

Charles Burchfield, *Sun and Rocks*

The artist here invites the viewer into an ominous wilderness where the very forces of nature seem to be in conflict. In what might seem to be a place without the presence of God, the brilliant sun and its surrounding nimbus in the form of a cross are inescapable. Even in the most trying of situations, the times of greatest conflict, God is present.

jesus said, "Jerusalem, Jerusalem, the city that kills the prophets and stones those who are sent to it! How often have I desired to gather your children together as a hen gathers her brood under her wings, and you were not willing!"

Luke 13:34
Luke 13:31-35

During the season of Lent, we are challenged by our memory of what is to come. We know that Good Friday is ahead and that crucifixion comes before resurrection. We know what is to come because we already have been this way. Jesus challenges our notions of who God is and our visions of God's reign. We also are challenged to expand our understanding of God to include images of a strong, nurturing presence alongside those of judge. Our ideas of what constitutes justice and mercy are complicated by the words and deeds of Jesus.

Why?

Why do the babies starve

When there's enough food to feed the world

Why when there're so many of us

Are there people still alone

Why are the missiles called peace keepers

When they're aimed to kill

Why is a woman still not safe

When she's in her home

Love is hate

War is peace

No is yes

And we're all free

But somebody's gonna have to answer

The time is coming soon

Amidst all these questions and contradictions

There're some who seek the truth

But somebody's gonna have to answer

The time is coming soon

When the blind remove their blinders

And the speechless speak the truth

Tracy Chapman

Käthe Kollwitz, *Seed Corn Must Not Be Ground*

Morris Graves, *Hold Fast to What You Have Already and I Will Give You the Morning Star*

In this painting, Morris Graves suggests the process of transformation through a continuing action. In the image, from the most base, rough rock, all the way to ethereal light, a series of chalices moves upwards in a strong vertical line from lower to upper center of the panel. Some interpreters have identified an elevated eucharistic (communion) host with the disk of light which radiates outward and downward, breaking into the shadows around it. This image suggests the challenge of holding fast while knowing that truth is not always welcomed by those who hear it.

Redemption

Jesus is going to Jerusalem to fulfill his destiny. He knows it. From the beginning he has before his eyes all our sins which he will redeem. Now, little by little, day by day, their weight lies on him more heavily, for the moment approaches when he must pay. The cross. And he alone; all the others are busy with silly dreams. We too; there's our business and the stock exchange which is not going well and which is worrying us. Or else it is working out all right and our worries are no less. There are clients and there is the price of butter. All that is so much more important than the cross of Jesus.

Jacques LeClerq, *A Year with the Liturgy*

Once on the Great Sabbath (before the Passover) the rabbi of Roptchitz came home from the house of prayer with weary steps. "What made you so tired?" asked his wife. "It was the sermon," he replied. "I had to speak of the poor and their many needs for the coming Passover. Unleavened bread and wine and everything else is terribly high this year."

"And what did you accomplish with your sermon?" his wife asked.

"Half of what is needed," he answered. "You see, the poor are now ready to take. As for the other half, whether the rich are ready to give—I don't know about that yet."

William B. Silverman,
Rabbinic Wisdom and Jewish Values

You have to be critical and see the world and persons with your own judgment, and Christians must learn to sharpen their distinctive Christian judgment.

The rich must be critical amid their own surroundings of affluence: why they are wealthy and why next door there are so many poor. A wealthy Christian will find there the beginning of conversion, in a personal questioning: Why am I rich and all around me so many that hunger?

Oscar Romero, *The Violence of Love*

Now Jesus was teaching in one of the synagogues on the sabbath. And just then there appeared a woman with a spirit that had crippled her for eighteen years. She was bent over and was quite unable to stand up straight. When Jesus saw her, he called her over and said, "Woman, you are set free from your ailment." When he laid his hands on her, immediately she stood up straight and began praising God.

Luke 13:10-13

Luke 13:10-17

Jean Antoine Houdon, *Jesus Healing*

Judith Oelfke Smith, *Jesus Freeing Crippled Woman*

Coulton Waugh, *Swing Low Sweet Chariot*

Jean Antoine Houdon, *Jesus Healing,* also identified as *John the Baptist*

The museum catalog identifies John the Baptist as the subject of this sculpture. However, the authors agree, after consultation with other scholars, that the composition of the work and its attributes more strongly suggest Jesus as subject.

In this life-size sculpture, the artist presents Jesus in midstride, moving forward, with his right arm and hand extended. His mouth is open as if to speak. His eyes, half-closed, look down. It is as though he actively seeks to reach out, to touch, free, or heal. The open mouth and the outstretched hand combine two scriptural images of healing: *touch* and *breath*. The power of touch as a healing force is more familiar as scientific study and personal experience demonstrate that physical touching is necessary for healthy human emotional development. Some writers even have quantified the amount of touching an individual needs. Probably less familiar is the notion of breath as a healing agent. In Genesis, the word translated as *Spirit* also can be translated as *wind* or *breath*. In Genesis 2, in reference to God's creation of humankind, the text states, ". . . and *breathed* into his nostrils the breath of life. . . ." The connection between breath and life is more than physiological; it is spiritual. In this sculpture, Jesus' mouth is open, perhaps either to speak a word of healing and freedom, or to breathe afresh on us.

We raise our eyes in prayer
through the bars, darkly.

Together with a thousand prisoners in their cells
and with many more thousands in the larger
prison of our country.

We pray for freedom
and even more urgently, for life.

As nameless executioners salvage
those whom they used to merely torture and detain
and both children and parents
slowly but surely die
of sickness that has many names
and only one name.

We ask for faith
to see that death and prison are not forever
that life and freedom will prevail.

We ask for faith to celebrate even while we mourn
knowing that death and prison
are already signs of a people's struggle
for freedom and life.

We raise our voices in prayer
through the bars, boldly
believing there will be an answer
as our people awaken.

Amen.

Edicio de la Torre, in *The Bible Through Asian Eyes*

O Glad, Exulting, Culminating Song!

A vigor more than earth's is thy notes . . .
A reborn race appears—a perfect world, all joy!
Women and men in wisdom, innocence and health - all joy!
Riotous laughing bacchanals fill'd with joy!

War, sorrow, suffering gone—
    the rank earth purged-nothing but joy left!

The ocean fill'd with joy—the atmosphere all joy!

Joy! joy in freedom, worship, love!
    joy in the ecstasy of life!

Enough to merely be! enough to breathe!

Joy! joy! all over joy!

Walt Whitman

So the younger son set off and went to his father. But while he was still far off, his father saw him and was filled with compassion; he ran and put his arms around him and kissed him.

Luke 15:20

Luke 15:1-3; 11b-32

Leaving home

is much closer

to my spiritual experience

than I might have thought.

Henri J. M. Nouwen,
The Return of the Prodigal Son

Rob Roth, *Leaving Home*

Leavetaking

After you board the train, you sit & wait,

to begin your first real journey alone.

You read to avoid the window's awkwardness,

knowing he's anxious to catch your eye,

loitering out in never-ending rain,

to wave, a bit shy, another final goodbye;

you are afraid of having to wave too soon.

And for the moment you think it's the train

next to you has begun, but it is yours,

and your face, pressed to the windowpane,

is distorted & numbed by the icy glass,

pinning your eyes upon your father,

as he cranes to defy your disappearing train.

Both of you waving, eternally, to each other.

Greg Delanty, *Southward*

Before returning,

there is departure.

Before forgiveness,

there is estrangement.

Rembrandt van Rijn, *The Return of the Prodigal Son*

In this Rembrandt painting, the powerful experiences of returning and re-establishing community are exhibited as they were suggested in the biblical parable. The aged father almost lunges forward to embrace the returning son, as others observe the reunion. The son, following the ordeal of his own spiritual journey of self-discovery and, as suggested in the scripture, God-discovery, kneels and leans into the powerful release of his father's embrace.

Wherever I may wander,
Wherever I may be,
I'm certain of my Maker's love;
God's care is over me.

Ann B. Snow,
Wherever I May Wander, hymn

More than any other story in the Gospel, the parable of the prodigal son expresses the boundlessness of God's compassionate love. And when I place myself in that story under the light of that divine love, it becomes painfully clear that leaving home is much closer to my spiritual experience than I might have thought....

Leaving home is . . . much more than an historical event bound to time and place. It is a denial of the spiritual reality that I belong to God with every part of my being, that God holds me safe in an eternal embrace, that I am indeed carved in the palms of God's hands and hidden in their shadows. Leaving home means ignoring the truth that God has "fashioned me in secret, moulded me in the depths of the earth and knitted me together in my mother's womb." Leaving home is living as though I do not yet have a home and must look far and wide to find one.

Henri J. M. Nouwen,
The Return of the Prodigal Son

HE CAME TO HIMSELF

Lent is a time for coming to ourselves, of realizing the

distance we have put between ourselves and God. It is a

time for recovering our "desire for God." In a lecture at

Scarritt-Bennett Center, Henri J. M. Nouwen said,

"The spiritual life starts at the place where you can hear

God's voice." As Jesus so wisely said, it takes ears

ready to hear to really listen, and eyes ready to see to

really perceive. Coming to ourselves prepares us to

return home, regardless of how home is understood.

Listen to what God is saying to us:

You are my child.

You are written in the palms of my hand.

You are hidden in the shadow of my hand.

I have molded you in the secret of the earth.

I have knitted you together in your mother's womb.

You belong to me.

I am yours. You are mine.

I have called you from eternity and you are the one who is held safe

and embraced in love from eternity to eternity.

You belong to me. And I am holding you safe and I want you to

know that whatever happens to you, I am always there. I was

always there; I am always there; I always will be there and hold you

in my embrace.

You are mine. You are my child. You belong to my home. You

belong to my intimate life and I will never let you go. I will be

faithful to you.

Henri J. M. Nouwen, "Lecture"

The various changes introduced . . . into the liturgical life . . . reveal and communicate the spirit of Lent, they make us see, feel and experience that bright sadness which is the true message and gift of Lent. "Sad brightness": the sadness of my exile, of the waste I have made of my life; the brightness of God's presence and forgiveness, the joy of the recovered desire for God, the peace of the recovered home. Such is the climate of lenten worship; such is the first and general impact on my soul.

Alexander Schmemann, *Great Lent*

mary took a pound of costly perfume made of pure nard, anointed Jesus' feet, and wiped them with her hair. The house was filled with the fragrance of the perfume. But Judas Iscariot, one of the disciples (the one who was about to betray Jesus), said, "Why was this perfume not sold for thousands of dollars and the money given to the poor?" . . . Jesus said, "Leave her alone. She bought it so that she might keep it for the day of my burial. You always have the poor with you, but you do not always have me."

John 12:3-5, 7-8

John 12:1-8

Jacopo Bassano, *Christ in the House of Mary, Martha, and Lazarus*

Awaiting Jesus in this warm, domestic scene is a kitchen dining room filled with the goods of a plentiful household and populated with people busily engaged in the preparation of a meal for an honored guest. Jesus calmly enters the room, followed by other men in the arched doorway in the middle left of the picture. Martha graciously bows to her friend while the inclination of her head and extension of her inviting left arm create a direct line from Jesus' face to the table being prepared. Overflowing with deep feelings and more outgoing than her sister, Mary kneels at the left of Jesus and soon will anoint his feet "with costly perfume," provoking an admonishment from Judas Iscariot (behind Jesus).

Gracious God, we come before you a people too nearly conformed to this world and its values. We fail to develop our God-given abilities, then envy those who do. Too busy for the care of our bodies or the development of our minds and spirits, we neglect the nurture of our own best selves. We serve, but sometimes with resentment, because we say "Yes" to the most insistent caller more than to you. Expecting too much of ourselves, we resent others who seem not to do their share. We waffle between weakness which allows others to walk all over us, and defensiveness which ignores the rights of others. We spend our money on that which is not bread and turn our eyes away from images of those who have no bread. Yet we ignore our own hunger and thirst for you and your righteousness. Transform us by your Spirit and renew our minds. May we find the joy and peace that come from seeking your will, through Jesus, your faithful servant. Amen.

Ruth C. Duck, *Touch Holiness*, adapted

Jimilu Mason, *The Servant Christ*

Placed in front of an inner-city clinic for the homeless, Christ House in Washington, D.C., this sculpture immediately confronts anyone who approaches the building entrance. The sculptor, Jimilu Mason, has written, "Many have questioned me about placing this beautiful work in a place where it will surely be abused. My response has been, there is very little they could do to HIM (the man) that hasn't already been done."

This life-size figure is of a man wearing jeans and a workshirt with the sleeves rolled up. He kneels on his left knee with his hands poised over a shallow basin. The space between his hands is inviting, waiting. His face is turned upwards, looking into the eyes of anyone who stops long enough to ponder this figure frozen in time and space. Inspired by the story of Jesus washing the feet of his disciples (John 13:1-16), this sculpture goes beyond the simple illustration of a single text. Instead it presents for contemplation a model of servanthood embodied in the life and teachings of Jesus of Nazareth.

Oh, to Be So Poor

She lived life out of a wheelchair.

Barely hearing. Almost blind.

At worship today

Christ's Supper was offered to her,

but she thought the plate of broken bread was the

offering plate.

Bewildered, she said a bit too loud,

"I don't have anything to give."

Poor woman, they all thought.

Not so.

Through any disorientation, we have everything

in the Christ who gives his life for us.

Through our deafness, he hears for us.

Through our blindness, he sees for us.

Through our trembling hands, he will take the bread

and cup for us.

We hear Christ's words:

> Let not your heart be troubled.

> I will hold it.

> I will feed you.

> I will drink the cup for you.

> I will fill you.

> I will be your world.

Oh, to be so poor.

Robert W. Guffey, Jr.

Said Judas to Mary

Words and music: Sydney Carter, 1964; alt.

1 Said Judas to Mary, "Now what will you do with your oint-ment so rich and so rare?" "I'll pour it all o-ver the feet of the Christ, and I'll wipe it a-way with my hair," she said, "I'll wipe it a-way with my hair." (2 "Oh)

2 "Oh Mary, oh Mary, oh, think of the poor. This oint-ment, it could have been sold; And think of the blan-kets and think of the bread you could buy with the sil-ver and gold," he said, "you could buy with the sil-ver and gold." (3 "To–)

3 "To-mor-row, to-mor-row, I'll think of the poor; to-mor-row," she said, "not to-day; For dear-er than all of the poor in the world is my love who is go-ing a-way," she said, "my love who is go-ing a-way." (4 Said)

4 Said Jesus to Mary, "Your love is so deep, to-day you may do as you will. To-mor-row, you say, I am go-ing a-way, but my bod-y I leave with you still," he said, "my bod-y I leave with you still." (5 "The)
(6 –way.")

"The poor of the world are my bod-y," he said,
  "to the end of the world they shall be.
The bread and the blan-kets you give to the poor
  you will know you have giv-en to me," he said,
  "you'll know you have giv-en to me."

"My bod-y will hang on the cross of the world
  to-mor-row," he said, "not to-day.
And Mar-tha and Mar-y will find me a-gain
  and wash all my sor-row a-way," he said,
  "and wash all my sor-row a-way."

PALM BRANCHES AND A CROSS

Christ humbled Christ's self and became

obedient to the point of death—even

death on a cross. Therefore God also

highly exalted Jesus and gave Jesus the

name that is above every name.

Philippians 2:8-9

Philippians 2:5-11

Blessing of the Palms

O God, who in Jesus Christ

triumphantly entered Jerusalem,

heralding a week of pain and sorrow,

be with us now

as we follow the way of the cross.

In these events of defeat and victory,

you have sealed the closeness

of death and resurrection,

of humiliation and exaltation.

We thank you for these branches

that promise to become for us

symbols of martyrdom and majesty.

Bless them and us

that their use this day may announce in our time

that Christ has come

and that Christ will come again.

Amen! Come, Christ Jesus!

UCC Book of Worship

Chartres Cathedral, France, *Christ's Entry into Jerusalem*

The medieval sculptors' guild of Chartres, France, interpreted in abstract relief sculpture the great stories of faith from Hebrew and Christian Scriptures for all to see. Many people who were unable to read literature learned to interpret the visual arts that were so much a part of the church's communication and education in the Middle Ages. Often this art was relatively abstract and symbolic rather than realistic in order to make the meaning of the stories or statements quickly accessible.

In this detail from the Royal Portal or entryway of the cathedral, Jesus rides on the back of a colt as a row of individuals line his path, facing outward, waving long, slender palm branches. At far right, someone places a garment on the path before the donkey. Over the figures, arches of an imagined architectural setting suggest that this event is known through the source of faith and salvation, the church. The image portrays the progress of Jesus' journey into Jerusalem, a journey that ultimately will lead to Golgotha.

Hosanna

Hosanna! Blessed is the one who comes in the name of the Lord.

Today we enter Holy Week, with its cycle of life, death, and new life.

Hosanna! Blessed is the one who comes in the name of the Lord.

Jesus, the holy one, the whole one, enters Jerusalem as he rides on the back of a donkey colt. Crowds wave palm branches and cry out,

Hosanna! Blessed is the one who comes in the name of the Lord.

Jesus, holy one, enter the gates of our hearts today as we join you in this time of your Passion. With you, let us remember and celebrate your birth, your calling, your ministry.

Hosanna! Blessed is the one who comes in the name of the Lord.

Jesus, our mentor of wholeness, guide us through the streets of our journey. Open our eyes and our ears to the guiding of God's spirit who calls us to costly faithfulness and to joyous wholeness. Let us sing with all our selves.

Hosanna! Blessed is the one who comes in the name of the Lord. Hosanna in the highest heaven. Amen.

Beth Richardson, "Passion Sunday"

James Ensor, *Christ Entering Brussels in 1889*

The *Super Star* lyrics may seem visibly represented in James Ensor's *Christ Entering Brussels in 1889*. Measuring nearly 8-1/2 by 14 feet, this painting can have a powerful impact on the viewer. While this physical impact is weakened in a photo reproduction, the intent of the artist remains clear.

An enormous crowd, complete with military escort, surges forward. In the front rows a variety of costumes appears, yet two arrest the viewer's attention. In the lower left segment of the picture is a figure in a horrifying mask beside a representation of "Death," a skull with top hat. Only upon close examination is the figure of Jesus on a donkey visible in the painting. He is presented as a small figure in the crowded setting, about in the middle of the painting. The perspective draws our eyes to that place, a location of the least activity.

The shadow of death is present, even in the excitement of a celebrative entry.

Twentieth-century artists interpret the entry of Jesus into Jerusalem through a "rock opera," *Jesus Christ, Superstar*.

CAIAPHAS

Tell the rabble to be quiet we anticipate a riot

This common crowd is much too loud

Tell the mob who sing your song

that they are fools and they are wrong

They are a curse, they should disperse

CROWD

Hosanna Heysanna Sanna Sanna Ho

Sanna Hey Sanna Ho Sanna

Hey JC, JC you're alright by me

Sanna Ho Sanna Hey Superstar

SIMON ZEALOTES

Christ you know I love you

Did you see I waved?

I believe in you and God

So tell me that I'm saved

Jesus I am with you

Touch me touch me Jesus

Jesus I am on your side

Kiss me kiss me Jesus

Tim Rice, from *Jesus Christ, Superstar*

These words by British lyricist Tim Rice demonstrate the variety of responses to Jesus, both at the time of his own ministry and into the modern era. Some people have feared the radical new message of God's love and the consequences of living in that spirit of love. Others have responded with a superficial acceptance, hearing the appealing message of the inclusion of all in God's realm, but discovering that the requirements of that love exceed their enthusiasm. Still others have responded with humble joy, discovering in Jesus and his message the healing of body, mind, and spirit.

For I received from the Lord what I also handed on to you, that the Lord Jesus on the night when he was betrayed took a loaf of bread, and when he had given thanks, he broke it and said, "This is my body that is for you. Do this in remembrance of me." In the same way he took the cup also, after supper, saying, "This cup is the new covenant in my blood. Do this, as often as you drink it, in remembrance of me." For as often as you eat this bread and drink the cup, you proclaim the Lord's death until he comes.

I Corinthians 11:23-26

I Corinthians 11:23-26

Holy Thursday

Is this a holy thing to see
In a rich and fruitful land,
Babes reduc'd to misery,
Fed with cold and usurious hand?

Is that trembling cry a song?
Can it be a song of joy?
And so many children poor?
It is a land of poverty!

And their sun does never shine,
And their fields are black & bare,
And their ways are fill'd with thorns:
It is eternal winter there.

For where-e'er the sun does shine,
And where'e'er the rain does fall,
Babe can never hunger there,
Nor poverty the mind appall.

William Blake

Tintoretto (Jacopo Robusti), *Last Supper*

Prepared for the Church of San Georgio Maggiore in Venice during the years 1592-1594, Tintoretto's *Last Supper* was an attempt to capture the mystical and emotional nature of faith.

The atmosphere of the room is shadowy, causing the illuminated figures and objects to stand out in bold relief. The angels near the ceiling denote the presence of God. All the figures around the table, except Judas, exude a subtle light, a halo, symbolizing their sanctity.

Unaware of the import of these proceedings, the serving staff go about their familiar tasks. Several watch the table to ascertain needs. At the far left one inquires of a diner. This disciple raises his hand to halt the servant's speech so that he may hear Jesus' words, "This is my body broken for you."

Invitation

This table is open to all who confess Jesus as the Christ

and seek to follow Christ's way.

Come to this sacred table

not because you must,

but because you may.

Come not because you are fulfilled,

but because in your emptiness

you stand in need of God's mercy and assurance.

Come not to express an opinion,

but to seek a presence

and to pray for a spirit.

Come to this table, then,

sisters and brothers, as you are.

Partake and share.

It is spread for you and me

that we might again know

that God has come to us,

shared our common lot,

and invited us to join the people of God's new age.

United Church of Christ, *Book of Worship*

Pietro Annigone, *Jesus in the Garden of Gethsemene*

And after their last meal together, Jesus went to the Garden of Gethsemene and prayed earnestly and in great anxiety. The hours of the night languidly moved on in the darkness as the dread of what he sensed would happen came ever closer. Finally, his friends fell asleep in the garden while he continued to pray, and gained the strength and composure to face the coming day.

Pietro Annigone, a contemporary Italian painter, attempted to express these experiences in a fresco in the little church called Santuario di Maria Santissima del Buon Consiglio in the town of Pistoia, Italy.

We have all had our private terrors,
Our particular shadows, our secret fears.
But now a great fear is upon us, a fear not of one but
of many,
A fear like birth and death, when we see birth and
death alone
In a void apart. We
Are afraid in a fear which we cannot know, which we
cannot face, which none understands,
And our hearts are torn from us, our brains unskinned
like the layers of an onion, our selves are lost, lost
In a final fear which none understands.

T. S. Eliot, *Murder in the Cathedral*

in REMEMBRANCE
of Me

BETRAYED AND ARRESTED

jesus went out with his disciples across the Kidron valley to a place where there was a garden, which he and his disciples entered. Now Judas, who betrayed him, also knew the place, because Jesus often met there with his disciples. So Judas brought a detachment of soldiers together with police from the chief priests and the Pharisees, and they came there with lanterns and torches and weapons. Jesus asked them, "Whom are you looking for?" And they said, "Jesus of Nazareth." Jesus answered, "I told you that I am he. So if you are looking for me, let these men go." This was to fulfill the word that he had spoken, "I did not lose a single one of those whom you gave me." Then Simon Peter, who had a sword, drew it, struck the high priest's slave, and cut off his right ear. The slave's name was Malchus. Jesus said to Peter, "Put your sword back into its sheath. Am I not to drink the cup that God has given me?" So the soldiers, their officer, and the Jewish police arrested Jesus and bound him.

John 18:1-3, 7-12

John 18:1-19:42

Valentin de Boulogne, *The Taking of Christ*

Valentin de Boulogne, a French painter in the early Baroque era, reflects here the strong emphasis on individual emotional experience that was typical of the church during and soon after the Reformation.

In the lower right of the painting, Peter reacts in defense of Jesus and pushes down one of the men sent to make the capture. Peter raises his knife to cut off the man's ear. Near the center of this active, violent scene, two soldiers with armor struggle to take hold of Jesus. The soldier farthest left grabs at the neckline of Jesus' garment. The other soldier, with his back to the viewer, reaches out with his right hand in front of Jesus to grasp Jesus' left shoulder or arm. Judas' left hand is placed on the center of Jesus' chest while his right arm is around Jesus' neck. He is ready to identify Jesus by kissing him in a supposed gesture of friendly greeting.

Jesus' hands are calmly clasped in front of him in sharp contrast to the others. His head is turned away from the bawling, bright light of the torch and he faces Judas very close at hand and gazes directly into his face. Judas appears unnerved by the direct encounter. Thus Jesus has accepted the betrayal of his supposed friend, understanding the motivations that drive the man and the confusion of his other followers. He accepts the burden he must bear in order to express unqualified love. This moment exalts the presence of God's love in Jesus as he gives of himself completely so that others might show that same love in their lives.

Life only demands from you
the strength you possess.
Only one feat is possible—
not to have run away.

Dag Hammarskjöld

R. Must I sacrifice in order to be happy?

D. "Sacrifice" is a big word. Let us say "identify" in a way that would include sacrifice but not limit it to that. And the business of identification works both ways. There are no limits to [human] ability to respond to appeals made to [one's] natural goodness, just as [one] has an enormous capacity for response to sacrifices made by others for [oneself]. In fact, it is doubtful whether there is any greater power in human affairs than is exerted through the example of [one's] love for [another].

R. What specific examples are you thinking of?

D. All the world's great spiritual leaders have derived their power largely by making the supreme identification; namely, by offering their lives in the cause of human need or ennoblement. When we study the lives of these leaders, we see that each of them was aware that the example of renunciation and sacrifice awakens powerful forces in human beings.

Norman Cousins

"Treat others as ends,

And myself as an end only in my capacity as a means: to shift the dividing line in my being between subject and object to a position where the subject, even if it is in me, is outside and above me — so that my *whole* being may become an instrument for that which is greater than I.

Dag Hammarskjöld

CALL TO CONFESSION

LEADER: Judas, slave of jealousy, where are you?

PEOPLE: I am here.

LEADER: Peter, slave of fear, where are you?

PEOPLE: I am here.

LEADER: Thomas, slave of doubt, where are you?

PEOPLE: I am here.

LEADER: Men and women of Jerusalem, enslaved to mob rule, where are you?

PEOPLE: I am here.

LEADER: Pilate, slave of expediency, where are you?

PEOPLE: I am here.

LEADER: The story of Christ's passion and death mirrors for us much of our own weakness and sin. We all come *here* as men and women who have missed the mark and who are alienated from God and our neighbor near and far.

Richard N. Eick

never as means."

EASTER

Paul T. Granlund, *Resurrection*

Death could not

contain him.

Love incarnate is

the victory,

and history is forever

changed because of

God's gift through

the Savior.

The walls of death are not strong enough to prevail against the power of God. Almost birdlike, this figure is breaking free of earth's gravity, no longer under the sway of ordinary time and space. This is the power of resurrection. The somber, contemplative emphasis of Lent culminated in the deepening gloom after the crucifixion and entombment of Jesus. Then so silently it came, Easter morn bathed in the soft light of dawn. Death could not contain him. Love incarnate is the victory, and history is forever changed because of God's gift through the Savior.

> Jesus said to Mary Magdalene, "Woman, why are you weeping? Whom are you looking for?" Supposing Jesus to be the gardener, she answered, "Sir, if you have carried Jesus away, tell me where you have laid him, and I will take him away." Jesus said to her, "Mary!" She turned and responded in Hebrew, "Rabbouni!" (which means Teacher).
>
> John 20:15-16

The liturgical color for the Easter season is celebratory white, and this mood permeates not only Easter Day but is part of the fifty days of Easter, culminating in the triumph of Pentecost. A quiet dawn issues into the great jubilation of Easter morning worship. The lectionary readings marking the continuing weeks of Easter initially possess a quieter pace of dawning. The followers of Jesus at first do not recognize him, or they require proof of this incredible event. They begin with a more gradual realization. The scripture readings of the season challenge Christians to live in a new and changed reality. This reality finally becomes the startling realization of the presence of the Holy Spirit at Pentecost.

Jesus said to Mary Magdalene, "Woman, why are you weeping? Whom are you looking for?" Supposing Jesus to be the gardener, she answered, "Sir, if you have carried Jesus away, tell me where you have laid him, and I will take him away." Jesus said to her, "Mary!" She turned and responded in Hebrew, "Rabbouni!" (which means Teacher).

John 20:15-16
John 20:1-18

This is the day of God;

let us rejoice and be glad in it.

Love, I thought, is stronger
than death or the fear of death.
Only by it, by love,
life holds together and advances.

Ivan Turgenev

Paul T. Granlund, *Resurrection*

Art representing the crucifixion and the risen Christ is commonly seen, but art which attempts to present the moment of resurrection is rare. In a smaller-than-life representation, Paul Granlund has attempted to interpret that moment. The figure of Christ is shown bent over, knees and head nearly touching. The arms are outstretched in a position of crucifixion. The figure is bound on three sides by slabs of the tomb and on the fourth by the earth. Close examination reveals holes in the top and in the right side-panel where the arm would have protruded when the panels were tightly closed around the body.

The movement of the body is not downward, but upward and out. The outstretching of the arms and the propelling tension in the legs emphasize the surging strength of this Christ as the lid of the tomb is thrown off. The walls of death are not strong enough to prevail against the power of God. Almost birdlike, this figure is breaking free of earth's gravity, no longer under the sway of ordinary time and space.

This is the power of resurrection.

Albert P. Ryder, *Christ Appearing to Mary*

The shock of recognition is clearly visible in Mary's face and body as she looks into the face of the risen Christ in this painting. It represents a transforming moment in the life of a woman so drastically changed by her earlier encounters with Jesus; ". . . and the former things shall not be remembered or come into mind" (Isaiah 65:17b).

Easter

Rise heart; thy Lord is risen. Sing his praise
      Without delays,
Who takes thee by the hand, that thou likewise
      With him mayst rise;
That, as his death calcined thee to dust,
His life may make thee gold, and much more just.

Awake, my lute, and struggle for thy part
      With all thy art.
The cross taught all wood to resound his name,
      Who bore the same.
His stretched sinews taught all strings, what key
Is best to celebrate this most high day

Consort both heart and lute, and twist a song
      Pleasant and long;
Or since all music is but three parts vied
      And multiplied;
O let thy Spirit bear a part,
And make up our defects with his sweet art.

George Herbert

In this time before the full realization of the realm of God, often we experience the pain of loss or death through social neglect or disease. Faith sustains us in anticipation of that time of complete joy.

Ryan White Panel,
AIDS Memorial Quilt, NAMES Project

God will wipe
away every tear,
neither shall there be
mourning nor crying nor
pain any more.

Revelation 21:4a

Piero della Francesca, *Resurrection*

In this powerful image from the early Italian Renaissance, Piero della Francesca interprets the eternal significance of Jesus' resurrection. Jesus stands in a grand posture with one foot still in the sarcophagus (stone coffin) and the other resting atop its open edge. Christ's gaze falls on the viewer no matter where one stands in relation to the painting. In his right hand, Christ holds the staff for a triumphal banner of victory over death. (The flag with a white field and deep red cross upon it became a symbol popularly used in this era of the church's history.) The vertical staff emphasizes Christ's stature. The sleeping soldiers, unaware of what has happened, emphasize the silent wonder of it all, while the arrangement of the soldiers in relation to Christ presents a perfect symmetry to the scene. Although the background landscape contains trees devoid of foliage (a symbol for death), the landscape at right is verdant with life, with the figure of Christ representing the transition from death to life. The soft light of the coming dawn bathes the figures and environment.

Neither the cross nor death could contain him. Love incarnate is the victory, and history is forever changed because of God's gift through the Savior. The artist celebrates the eternal Savior.

PEACE BE WITH YOU

When it was evening on that day, the first day of the week, and the doors of the house where the disciples had met were locked for fear of the religious authorities, Jesus came and stood among them and said, "Peace be with you."

John 20:19

John 20:19-31

O, give thanks to God, for God is good;

God's steadfast love endures forever!

Psalm 118:29

Michael Smither, *Doubting Thomas*, mural

Contemporary artist Michael Smither interprets a later appearance of the resurrected Jesus to followers gathered in a room. Though the mural is large, the number of figures crowded together in a room where there is strong contrast between light and deep shadow suggests not only their anxiety but their intimacy. Among the disciples, there are women, children, and pets present. The strongly contrasting colors of clothing and the many sharp angles caused by the movement of the figures create an atmosphere of excitement around that electric moment. Lit only by three candles, the scene focuses on the interaction between Thomas and Jesus. The wounds of crucifixion are apparent as is the pierced side of Jesus as he responds to the doubt of Thomas. Thomas is awestruck and appears on the verge of exclaiming, "My Lord and my God!" The man just behind and to the left of Thomas both participates in the action and observes the viewers. The viewer thus confronts both the possibility of doubt and the opportunity to enter vicariously into the peace that Jesus brought to his followers.

Vessel of Wholeness

Fractured

cracked

held together

in wholeness

completeness

by the air of the Spirit

the putty of trust

the glue of friendship

the cement of Scripture.

Serving a purpose

Beautifying the world

Testifying

to the power,

strength,

and possibilities

of limitations embraced.

Imelda Cooper

A Litany

LEADER   Jesus Christ, the Passover
Lamb who was slain, lives!

OTHERS   Worthy is the Lamb to receive
power and wisdom and glory
and blessing!

LEADER   Myriads of the faithful, freed
and called to be a nation of
priests of God, sing praise:

ALL   Blessing and honor, glory and
power be unto God, forever
and ever. Amen!

Ruth C. Duck, "Fourth Sunday in
Eastertide," adapted

peace

Heal Me, Hands of Jesus

Heal me, hands of Je - sus, and search out all my pain; re - store my hope, re - move my fear, and bring me peace a - gain.
Cleanse me, blood of Je - sus, take bit - ter - ness a - way; let me for - give as one for - given and bring me peace to - day.
Know me, mind of Je - sus, and show me all my sin; dis - pel the mem - o - ries of guilt and bring me peace with - in.
Fill me, joy of Je - sus; anx - i - e - ty shall cease, and heaven's se - ren - i - ty be mine, for Je - sus brings me peace!

Shalom
Peace be with you!

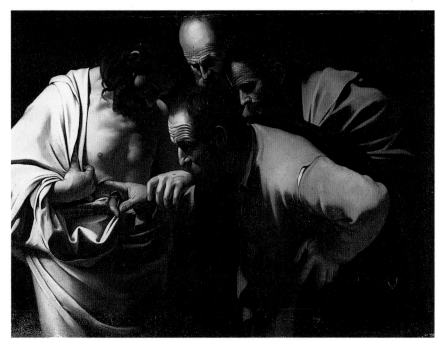

Michelangelo Merisi da Caravaggio, *The Incredulity of St. Thomas*

In a contrasting interpretation of Thomas's meeting with the risen Christ, the great Baroque painter Caravaggio eliminates all detail from the background of the room so that complete attention may focus on the close encounter between the two. Strong natural light illuminates portions of the figures to heighten the drama. In this excruciatingly realistic interpretation of his determination to satisfy his skepticism, Thomas raises his brows and peers with almost squinted eyes into the open wound in Jesus' side. Patiently submissive, Jesus pulls back his garment to expose his chest and guides Thomas' hand as he inserts his finger into the wound. The gaze of two other followers is utterly fixed upon the action. In any age Christians may desire some form of proof in their reticence to invest their faith, and thus Thomas becomes a figure with whom later members of the church community may identify.

COME, HAVE BREAKFAST

When they had gone ashore, they saw a charcoal fire there, with fish on it, and bread. Jesus said to them, "Bring some of the fish that you have just caught." So Simon Peter went aboard and hauled the net ashore, full of large fish, a hundred fifty-three of them; and though there were so many, the net was not torn. Jesus said to them, "Come and have breakfast."

John 21:9-12a

John 21:1-19

Gabriel Axel, *Babette's Feast*

The film *Babette's Feast* sensuously explores the complex relationship between physical and spiritual needs. Babette, a French expatriot, lives in Denmark and works for room and board in the household of two sisters. The sisters are the spiritual leaders of a small religious sect established by their father. Fourteen years after her arrival, Babette learns that she has won a lottery. Out of gratitude for their generous hospitality in the form of community, Babette asks permission of the sisters to cook a "real French dinner" to celebrate the anniversary of their father's birth. Permission received, Babette imports everything necessary—food, wine, dishes, and linens. Since this small religious community has adopted an austere lifestyle, they agree among themselves to allow Babette this one evening of luxury, but that they will not comment on the feast.

A special invited guest, the nephew of one of the members of the community, speaks of the spiritual nature of the meal and the care with which it has been prepared and served. Not realizing that Babette is the chef to whom he refers, the general tells about a chef in Paris who "had the ability to transform a dinner into a kind of love affair—a love affair that made no distinction between a bodily appetite and a spiritual appetite."

Do you

Follow

love me?

Feed my sheep.

They met Him again after
they had seen Him killed.
And then after they
had been formed into
a little society or community,
they found God somehow
inside them as well,
directing them,
making them able to do things
they could not do before.

C. S. Lewis, *Mere Christianity*

me.

Bread-Breaking Prayer

As bread that was scattered on the hillside,
was gathered together and made one,
so too, we, your people,
scattered throughout the world,
are gathered together around your table
and become one.

As grapes grown in the field
are gathered together and pressed into wine,
so too are we drawn together
and pressed by our times to share a common lot
and are transformed into your life-blood for all.

So let us prepare to eat and drink
Jesus taught us:
inviting the stranger to our table
and welcoming the poor.
May their absence serve to remind us
of the divisions this Eucharist seeks to heal.
And may their presence help transform us
into the Body of Christ we share.

Janet Schaffran and Pat Kozak, *More Than Words*

God is my shepherd, I shall not want.

Psalm 23:1

Psalm 23

Eternal and everlasting God,
Source of all happiness,
we praise you for making known
our Shepherd and Defender.
Grant that as we cast
away all fear and terror of
death, we may embrace and confess
your truth revealed in your Son,
our sovereign Master, Christ Jesus. Amen.

Daily Prayer

You watch over your creation,

a shepherd

with whom all living things are safe.

You know us all

and keep us

wherever we move.

O God, do this,

we ask you,

all the days of our lives—

may we never want

and may we enter your rest

and know your peace.

Today and every day

of our lives.

Huub Oosterhuis

The Good Shepherd, fresco painting, c. 250 C.E.

This very ancient image from the ceiling of a family tomb room (cubiculum) in a Roman catacomb presents Jesus as shepherd of the flock (the church). He wears a shepherd's tunic and short skirt (for ease in pursuing straying sheep). His clothing is that of an ordinary shepherd, yet it is white with purple stripes, a color design reserved for persons of great authority. This extraordinary representation probably refers to Jesus as fully human and divine. His right hand and arm are extended in an open and welcoming gesture. Strapped across one shoulder is a leather pouch for provisions he will distribute. He carries also the sheep that strayed and was rescued, and on either side of him stand sheep (symbolizing the church). Also to the right and left are sketches of trees in which doves are perched holding olive branches in their beaks. The birds represent God's peace and the salvation the shepherd brings. The scene is encircled, suggesting the eternal significance of the shepherd, the Savior.

Luke, age 11, *Smiling Shepherd*

To *want for* refers to lacking something, feeling as though something important is missing from one's life. This psalm, possibly the best known and loved of all, suggests that because God is like God is, we shall not want for anything. Even though most of us are not shepherds and have not even seen a shepherd, we understand that a shepherd provides for the needs of the ones in her/his care. The young artist here seems to understand God as a caretaker and explains, "That's the world on his T-shirt. If this is the only planet with life on it, then God thinks this is the most important place. He cares. He's got his sleeves rolled up for work."

Luke, age 11, from *Innocent Wisdom*

We shall not want.

Bobby McFerrin,

a singer/songwriter/poet,

uses this psalm

to honor the

shepherd-like caring

of his mother.

The 23rd Psalm

The Lord is my Shepherd, I have all I need,
She makes me lie down in green meadows,
Beside the still waters, She will lead.

She restores my soul, She rights my wrongs,
She leads me in a path of good things,
And fills my heart with songs.
Even though I walk, through a dark and dreary land,
There is nothing that can shake me,
She has said she won't forsake me,
I'm in her hand.

She sets a table before me, in the presence of my foes
She anoints my head with oil,
And my cup overflows.

Surely, surely goodness and kindness will follow me,
All the days of my life,
And I will live in her house,
forever, forever and ever.

Glory be to our Mother, and Daughter
And to the Holy of Holies,
As it was in the beginning, is now and ever shall be
World, without end. Amen.

Dedicated to my Mother
Bobby McFerrin

Thomas Hart Benton, *The Lord Is My Shepherd*

Thomas Hart Benton suggests in his painting that *want* and fulfillment may have connotations other than physical. This elderly couple sits at a bare table in a sparse setting. While the man looks forward at something unseen by the viewer, the woman turns to look at him. Her left hand and arm very nearly touch his. They do not want for companionship. The painting perhaps suggests that the restoration of one's soul may have more to do with such intimacy and companionship than with a great supply of material goods.

then I saw a new heaven and a new earth; for the first heaven and the first earth had passed away, and the sea was no more. . . . And I heard a loud voice from the throne saying, "See, the home of God is among mortals. God will dwell with them as their God; and they will be God's peoples, and God will indeed be with them and will wipe every tear from their eyes. Death will be no more; mourning and crying and pain will be no more. For the first things have passed away." And the one who was seated on the throne said, "See, I am making all things new."

Revelation 21:1, 3-5a

Revelation 21:1-6

"O Holy City, Seen of John"

Give us, O God, the strength to build the city
    that has stayed too long a dream, whose laws are love,
    whose ways are God's own ways,
    And where the sun that blazes is God's grace for all our days.

Walter Russell Bowie

When I Wake Up in the Morning

When I wake up in the morning I had a pair of Good Glasses. I saw a woman and she told me her name was Miss Gilbert. She brought ice cream and a lot of things like dress shoes. I also saw a angel in the sky. She help me out with things. She told me to imagine what was in my head so I said a lot things like Candy, ice-cream, cake also childrens playing with toys and dancing.

But then I drop my Good Glasses and when I pick my Good Glasses up they had bad things written all over them. I saw that Miss Gilbert took all my Good that she gave me, and the Angel turn into a monster and my ice cream melt. My shoes had a hole, and the sky turn into smoke and my cake disappeared before my very eyes. I like my Good Glasses.

Amalia G., age 14

Choi Hyun-Joo, age 10, *Jerusalem*

In 1976, children from around the world were invited to paint the city of Jerusalem to celebrate the unification of the many faiths in the city. Each child drew the city as she imagined it. Each Jerusalem was his own. Here a young South Korean girl draws a new Jerusalem where the world's children dance together and doves of peace watch over the city.

We, Without a Future

We, without a future,
Safe, defined, delivered
Now salute you, God,
Knowing that nothing is safe,
Secure, inviolable here.
Except you,
And even that eludes our minds at times.

We did not want it easy, God,
But we did not contemplate
That it would be quite this hard
This long, this lonely.

So, if we are to be turned inside out,
And upside down,
With even our pockets shaken
Just to check what's rattling
And left behind,
We pray that you will keep faith with us,
And be with us,
holding our hands as we weep,
Giving us strength to continue,
And showing us beacons
Along the way
to becoming new.

Anna McKenzie

Lucas Cranach, *New Jerusalem*

This woodcut was created to illustrate Revelation 21 for Martin Luther's Bible of 1522.
Cranach etched into wood a new city, German in appearance, and had an angel present
the city to John of Patmos. The woodcut suggests that the German Reformation itself
brought newness to Europe, inviting common folk to seek direct access to God.

For what's the use
of a utopian dream
if we're stuck
with the same old
men and women? . . .
Unless we can be
changed we'll dream
a Holy City but
end with death
and pain and a warring
of nations, everytime.
"A new heaven and
a new earth"? My God!
What we need
is nothing less than
a whole new human race.

David Buttrick

We anticipate

what is not yet

and practice now

your future

we say and sing

that all you have made

your creation is good

laboriously

so very slowly

we work out your promise

in hope and fear

and strive to build

a city of peace

a new creation

where you will

be our light, our all.

Give us strength, O God,

to persevere

and bring us to

a happy end.

Huub Oosterhuis

Making New; That's What's Going On

Now, do you want to know a secret? *Making new; that what's going on in the world; that's what's happening.* The Holy City is not future perfect, it's present tense. (Check out the Greek verbs in the text!) Now the Holy City is descending. Now God is making things new. Right now God is wiping tears and easing pain and overcoming the power of death in the world.

Now! There's nothing otherworldly about the vision; it's happening now in the midst of our worn, torn, broken world. And with the eyes of faith, you can see it happening.

David Buttrick

OPEN HEART, OPEN HOME

A certain woman named Lydia, a worshiper of God, was listening to us; she was from the city of Thyatira and a dealer in purple cloth. God opened her heart to listen eagerly to what was said by Paul. When she and her household were baptized, she urged us, saying, "If you have judged me to be faithful to the Savior, come and stay at my home." And she prevailed upon us.

Acts 16:14-15

Acts 16:9-15

Meinrad Craighead, *Lydia*

COME

AND STAY

AT MY HOME

Unto me?

"I do not know you—
 Where may be your house?"

"I am Jesus—late of Judea—
 Now of Paradise."

"Wagons have you to convey me?
 This is far from thence—"

"Arms of mine sufficient phaeton,
 Trust Omnipotence."

"I am spotted."
"I am Pardon."
"I am small."

"The least
 Is esteemed in Heaven
 the chiefest.
 Occupy my House."

Emily Dickinson

Abraham Welcoming the Three Visitors, detail

Hospitality is a gift;

one to be given and received.

In both instances,

one becomes vulnerable;

one trusts and is trusted.

First and foremost, I felt a sense of being home, a place where "they have to take you in," but also, a place where they *want* to take you in. In the ideal experience of it, home is a place for healing wounds and celebrating fulfillment. It's an environment which welcomes you to kick off your shoes, sink into an armchair, and put your feet up. You can be yourself. The masks are down, and you become as comfortable and vulnerable as a sleepy puppy. How I wished the church could be such a place for me!

Chris Glaser, *Come Home!*

But it is a special blessing to play your position *willingly*, because then your heart is able to feel the tenderness and supportiveness of my angels and Spirit Guides who surround the world in eagerness to help. "We know that all things [even your 'errors'] work together for good for those who love God [i.e., who willingly open themselves to channel Her love into the world], who are called according to [Her] purpose" [Rom. 8:28, NRSV; that is, everyone is called to come home to a kingdom of mutuality and peace-with-justice, but some remain alienated at this time and cannot sense or enjoy the benefits of loving God. They too will eventually come home; but those who offer God their willingness will become *awakened* and *consciously aware* that they are part of God's purpose—a truly beautiful and blessed state of mind!]. (Journal 10, 10-130)

Virginia Ramey Mollenkott, *Sensuous Spirituality*

In the late 400s and the 500s C.E., mosaic art began to be used in churches frequently to interpret stories, scripture, symbols, and religious experiences. In this mosaic from the Church of San Vitale in Ravenna, Italy, several important figures and stories from Hebrew Scripture are presented on the wall of the building and in a *tympanum* (in this case, an arch above an arcade with capitals and columns). Focus attention on the center and left portion of the tympanum arch (the right portion depicts another story). In this particular image, the viewer is reminded of another time when a home was opened in hospitality to visitors. For, in the early church, it was a common practice to interpret events from Hebrew Scripture as parallels to events in Christian Scripture. Here, Abraham greets the three visitors (Genesis 18:1-15) and offers them refreshment. The visitors reveal to Abraham and Sarah what God is prepared to do for them and for their children. Yet the parallel goes further. By placing this scene near the altar in this church, this meal is interpreted as preceding the communion meal of Christian worship. This is the hospitality of God: opening the divine heart to all and welcoming all into the household of God, the church.

One day, as we were going to the place of prayer, we met a slave-girl who had a spirit of divination and brought her owners a great deal of money by fortune-telling. . . . But when her owners saw that their hope of making money was gone, they seized Paul and Silas and dragged them into the marketplace before the authorities.

Acts 16:16, 19

Acts 16:16-34

Susan McCord, *Random*

In what many of us have come to expect to be a highly structured medium, Susan McCord introduces the notion of random connections.
In her quilt shown here, the design appears at first as chaos, something without order. Eventually it reveals itself to be a pattern of successively smaller rectangular "frames," each one consisting of random textures, colors, and forms. Everything in the quilt is connected to everything else in it; the threads, cloth types, forms, all are related. But these connections are not obvious upon first examination. Extended viewing and reflection are required for the connections to come to one's awareness.

In his novel, *Howard's End*, E. M. Forster also weaves a story of connections, intricate in detail and subtle in development. Very near the end of the story, Helen inquires of Meg concerning her husband, "Meg, is or isn't he ill? I can't make out." Margaret responds, "Not ill. Eternally tired. He has worked very hard all his life, and noticed nothing. Those are the people who collapse when they do notice a thing." Becoming aware of just how closely connected we are to each other, and how intimately our values and our faith are connected to everyday occurrences in our life can be a revealing and powerful experience.

The interconnected

responsibility to support

the state community

while retaining

one's ultimate loyalty

to God is suggested.

The story/image suggests

a delicate path.

But Jesus indicates where

the priority lies.

As frequently was so clearly exhibited in the visually evocative lines of Shakespearean drama, the Bard makes a quintessential statement about the interconnected quality of our inner experience and social behavior:

The web of our life is of a mingled yarn, good and ill together: our virtues would be proud if our faults whipped them not; and our crimes would despair if they were not cherished by our virtues.

William Shakespeare, *All's Well That Ends Well*, 4.3

The fresco (opposite), painted in about 1425 by Masaccio, is in a small Renaissance chapel in the Church of Santa Maria del Carmine in Florence, Italy. The picture presents a continuous narrative in which we witness Jesus (near the center) confronted by tax collectors and questioned about paying taxes. In this story recounted in the Gospel According to Matthew (17:24-27), Jesus asks Simon Peter what he thinks about the matter. "From whom do kings of the earth take toll. . .? From their children or from others?" When Peter said, "From others," Jesus said to him, "Then the children are free. However, so that we do not give offense to them, go to the sea and cast a hook; take the first fish that comes up; and when you open its mouth, you will find a coin; take that and give it to them for you and me." In Masaccio's image, the narrative is continuous from the initial encounter in the center, to Peter extracting the coin from the mouth of the fish at left, and finally at far right, Peter pays the required tax. Masaccio even dresses the figures of Jesus, Peter, and the disciples in imagined clothing of ancient Israel while the questioner and tax collector are clothed in garments of the "modern" era of the artist's own time.

Our knowledge of God *is* in and through each other. Our knowledge of each other *is* in and through God. We act together and find our good in each other and in God, and our power grows together, or we deny our relation and reproduce a violent world where no one experiences holy power.

Beverly Wildung Harrison, *Making Connections*

Beverly Wildung Harrison reminds us that connections and relationships have to do with more than threads and cloth. We are connected one to the other because of who we are and who God is. The Italian early Renaissance artist, Masaccio, depicts an occasion at which Jesus dealt with the relationships between faith, money and power.

Always connect

Masaccio, *The Tribute Money*

PENTECOST

(CYCLE C)

Jonathan Green, *The Congregation*

The Spirit of God,

fiery, sweeping,

enters Jesus' followers,

enabling them to *embody*

the ministry that

Jesus had begun.

Jesus' followers, many having fled on the day of his crucifixion, steadily had become aware of his resurrection, and finally had gathered together fifty days afterward. The lectionary reading for Pentecost Sunday uses powerful imagery to describe their experiences on that day. Acts 2 refers to the *Spirit* of God descending upon them and infusing them with power. The very word *spirit* is defined by *Random House Webster's College Dictionary* in ways that characterize this all-important day: "the animating principle of life; an attitude or principle that pervades thought, stirs one to action; a vigorous, courageous, or optimistic attitude; vigorous sense of membership in a group; to encourage; urge on or stir up."

Thus, the Spirit of God, fiery, sweeping, enters Jesus' followers individually and collectively, raising them to ecstatic heights, enabling them *to embody* themselves the ministry that Jesus had begun. Now they could go forth and live out the love they had experienced through Jesus Christ. Now they could be his vicars, together and scattered. The formation of the church had begun through the power of the Spirit. The strong, assertive quality of the color red makes it the liturgical color for Pentecost.

The energy that the disciples had found enabled them to grow in faith and to be aware of God acting in the past, being redeemingly incarnate in Jesus Christ; and now they experienced God's presence among them. This spirit is captured in the painting *The Congregation*.

Thus, the Sunday following Pentecost is called Trinity Sunday and celebrates God as Creator, Redeemer, and Spirit ever present. The liturgical color for Trinity Sunday is white and for all the weeks after Pentecost, green.

The nucleus of Christians at Pentecost now had the inner strength to *nurture* the growth of the church. They would meet life and proclaim and interpret the Word. They would seek to transform the world, in the name of the one who embodied unqualified love.

FIERY POWER

When the day of Pentecost had come, all were together in one place. And suddenly from heaven there came a sound like the rush of a violent wind, and it filled the entire house where they were sitting. . . . All of them were filled with the Holy Spirit and began to speak in other languages, as the Spirit gave them ability.

Acts 2:1-2, 4

Acts 2:1-21

O wind that sways
no branches,
fire that does not burn,
unimaginable light
that does not blind,
fountain of life
that has no end,
infinite river of joy,
flawless mirror
of God's power,
kind laughing agent
of God's mirth,
gentle consolation
of God's mercy,
O Holy Spirit of God,
abide with your people;
come to us now. . . .

Garth House, *Litanies for All Occasions*

Artist unknown, *Pentecost*

The transformations of fear into power, of confusion into clarity, of silence into communication, are present in this painting from Indonesia. The bright colors enhance the surprise and excitement one can observe in the faces and bodies of these who experience Pentecost. In the extreme foreground, lower center of the painting, is an observer figure who looks back at the viewer, drawing one into the action of this amazing story.

To me who am but black cold charcoal

grant, O Lord,

that by the fire of Pentecost,

I may be set ablaze.

After a Prayer of St. John of Damascus, in
With All God's People: The New Ecumenical Prayer Cycle

Emil Nolde, *The Pentecost,* © Nolde Stiftung Seebüll

In this twentieth-century interpretation, Emil Nolde presents the experience of Pentecost through a group of people crowded together, confined by the very definite border of the canvas of the painting. "Divided tongues, as of fire, appeared among them, and a tongue rested on each of them. All of them were filled with the Holy Spirit. . . ." (Acts 2:3ff, NRSV). A flame appears above the heads of each of the figures facing the viewer, indicating the presence of the Holy Spirit of God in their midst and in each of them, while those figures in the foreground with backs toward the viewer seem to be observers, not so blessed. The observers draw the viewer into the moment of extraordinary experience. Contrast the facial expression of the foreground figure at left with that of the figure directly facing the viewer with hands in a prayerful position. The contrast may suggest the difference between the downcast follower of Jesus immediately after the crucifixion and that of the witness of the resurrected Christ.

We remember that your church

was born in wind and fire,

not to sweep us heavenward

like a presumptuous tower,

but to guide us down

the dusty roads of this world

so that we may lift up the downcast,

heal the broken,

reconcile what is lost,

and bring peace amidst unrest.

Garth House, *Litanies for All Occasions*

HOPE GIVEN

HOPE

ope does not disappoint us, because

God's love has been poured into

our hearts through the Holy Spirit

that has been given to us.

Romans 5:5

Roman 5:1-5

John Biggers, *Shotgun, Third Ward #1*

John Biggers grew up in the Third Ward of Houston, Texas. This painting depicts a row of "shotgun-style" buildings, one a church, the others, homes. Of five adult figures in the foreground, three have their backs to the viewer. In the middleground stands a group of children with an older adolescent or adult. Three of the adults gaze at the fire-gutted church. A male cleric holding a lantern with a burning candle and a woman with a small child face the viewer as they look away from the scene. According to Elton Fox in *Seventeen Black Artists*, the lighted candle is a recurring motif of hope, as are children, in Biggers's works. The way to a new future already is illuminated. The group of children are playing, apparently unaware of the tainted present. At right, the woman holding a child seems to turn to face that future. She holds hope in her arms as the clergyperson brings light.

AN ALABASTER JAR

7hen turning toward the woman, Jesus said to Simon, "Do you see this woman? I entered your house; you gave me no water for my feet, but she has bathed my feet with her tears and dried them with her hair. You gave me no kiss, but from the time I came in she has not stopped kissing my feet. You did not anoint my head with oil, but she has anointed my feet with ointment. Therefore, I tell you, her sins, which are many, have been forgiven; hence she has shown great love. But the one to whom little is forgiven, loves little." Then Jesus said to her, "Your sins are forgiven."

Luke 7:44-48

Luke 7:36-8:3

The Anointing

She saw the feet,

bruised and dusty,

stretched out behind him—

worn, working feet.

Audacity and need coalesced.

A single impulse

precipitated her into

a precarious moment of hope.

A dam of saline grief burst,

making clear rivulets in a grimy flesh

wiped clean with hair.

Elizabeth J. Canham

Wu Yuen-kwei, *Her Sins Are Forgiven*

Jesus behaved in unorthodox ways for a Jewish man of his day. His attitude of friendship and acceptance of the despised and rejected people in society must have made a strong impression on this woman who entered the Pharisee's home to anoint Jesus' feet. Knowing how upright citizens denounced prostitutes, she nevertheless had the courage to enter, uninvited, to perform a sacrificial act of love—pouring out expensive ointment upon the feet of Jesus and drying them with her hair, oblivious or uncaring of the disapproval of the other people present.

Masao Takenaka and Ron O'Grady, *The Bible Through Asian Eyes*

orgi

She spoke nothing.

In silence she looked

intently on Jesus.

Soon the tears

that formed in her eyes

began to overflow.

The tears alone bespoke

the sorrow she knew.

The tears told Jesus everything.

God rejoiced to welcome her.

Shusake Endo, *A Life of Jesus*

Tentatively, she entered.
She knew she was not welcome here.
She could care less about their kind,
the unkind way they ogled her.
She had her own world,
her own dreams,
her own enveloping despair.
And then she saw him sitting there.
Smashing her alabaster jar,
she poured its fragrance on his feet
and wept in defiance, not defeat,
as he caressed her hair.
"What a waste!" they said.
He knew they meant her life.
They meant the money spent,
the times they went
to sleep one hour with her.
She did what she had to.
Stay alive.
She and her child and her guilt survived
on the lust and disgust of the likes of them.
The poor who are always with us
would do things differently
if they could.
She knew he knew and understood.
Jesus looked at her,
looked right through her,
and saw that she was good.

Miriam Therese Winter

Anointing
. . .
We too have alabaster boxes
to be broken in the trust
that what we share will not be judged
in terms of vain conceit.
Rejoiced in rather
in the open way of One
who poured the precious oil
his own life to make
all other gifts complete.

J. Barrie Shepherd

veness

ONE IN CHRIST

As many of you as were baptized into Christ have clothed yourselves with Christ. There is no longer Jew or Greek, there is no longer slave or free, there is no longer male and female; for all of you are one in Christ Jesus. And if you belong to Christ, then you are offspring of Abraham and Sarah, heirs according to the promise.

Galatians 3:27-29

Galatians 3:23-29

Norman Rockwell,
The Golden Rule, detail
© The Curtis Publishing Company

Norman Rockwell, the
American master illustrator
who was able to present
us to ourselves,
both as we strive to be
and as we are ordinarily,
shows us a portrait
of our family, the human race.
Even in this honest,
sensitive attempt at inclusion,
some stereotypes
of cultures and religions
tend to persist.

Being one in Christ
indicates the eradication
of dehumanizing images
and perceptions.
Jesus did not see a prostitute;
he saw Mary Magdalene.
He did not see a tax collector;
he saw Matthew.

More Light Statement

As a community of faith, the congregation of the First Presbyterian and Trinity Church of South Orange, New Jersey, welcomes all who believe in Jesus Christ and acknowledge Him as Lord and Savior, denying no one full participation in its life and leadership on the basis of race, ethnic origin, worldly condition, age, sex, sexual orientation, or any other particular element of his or her total humanity. We believe that the errors of society which have resulted in oppression and despair are not the ways of God, and we seek not to assume judgement upon our sisters and brothers in our journey of faith. Instead we seek more light on the ways in which we can offer our support and our love to all the children of God.

In accordance with this total view, we join with "More Light" churches and others seeking fairness, openness, honesty, and the affirmation of all who declare their membership in the Body of Christ.

The First Presbyterian and Trinity Church,
South Orange, New Jersey

Soumya Mohanty, *No More*

The artist Soumya Mohanty interprets the Good News in his illustration-drawing *No More*. He interprets oneness in Christ as a new birth and an exultant reaching forth with stereotypical divisions of race and gender eradicated.

One
IN CHRIST

Like the Murmur of the Dove's Song

To the members of Christ's body,
to the branches of the Vine,
to the church in faith assembled,
to its midst as gift and sign;
Come, Holy Spirit, come.

With the healing of division,
with the ceaseless voice of prayer,
with the power to love and witness,
with the peace beyond compare;
Come, Holy Spirit, come.

Carl P. Daw, Jr.

"... and have not charity."
Isn't the fulfillment of
our duty towards our neighbor
an expression of our
deepest desire?
It very well may be.

Dag Hammarskjöld

Dag Hammarskjöld served for many
years as the Secretary General of the
United Nations. His contributions
were enormous as he did much to
shape this world organization.

or you were called to freedom, brothers and sisters; only do not use your freedom as an opportunity for self-indulgence, but through love serve one another. For the whole law is summed up in a single commandment, "You shall love your neighbor as yourself."

Galatians 5:13-14

Galatians 5:1, 13-18

El Greco (Domenikos Theotokopoulos),
St. Martin and the Beggar

Charity, the love of neighbor, is the theme of
El Greco's painting of St. Martin and the Beggar.
Tradition holds that Martin was a wealthy
Hungarian serving in the military near Amiens,
France. As a child, Martin converted to
Christianity and expressed a desire to enter a
monastery. His father forced him into a military
career, but his faith eventually led him back to
his first love—the church and service to the
poor. El Greco presents for our consideration the
chance meeting of Martin and a beggar. Upon
meeting this beggar on a cold winter day, Martin
used his sword to divide his cloak in two and gave
half to the poor man. According to Jordan,
Martin later reported that Christ appeared to him
that very night and said, "What thou hast done
for that poor man, thou hast done for me." Later,
Martin would serve as Bishop of Tours for thirty
years. And, he would be recognized as a saint of
the church.

Jacob Lawrence, *Men Exist for the Sake of One Another. Teach Them Then or Bear With Them*

In this painting, Jacob Lawrence depicts a seated adult figure with four children of varying ages standing nearby. In his hands, the adult holds a small tree with tendril roots. The very large arms and hands of the central figure suggest an emphasis on the service aspect of life. Here, the children are taught about the inter-relatedness of life. The figures are surrounded by new life, plants and birds. This visual statement and its verbal title are a unity. Through them, Lawrence implies that if these lessons are not taught, then the consequences of inaction must be borne.

To clasp the hands
in prayer
is the beginning
of an uprising
against the disorder
of the world.

Karl Barth

"Whoever wants to be first must be last of all
and servant of all."

Mark 9:35b

Goodness

in any form

has an all-

conquering

power to

call forth

a response of

the same kind.

David B. Noss
and John B. Noss

229

AS A MOTHER COMFORTS HER CHILD

*A*s a mother comforts

her child,

so I will comfort you;

you shall be comforted

in Jerusalem.

Isaiah 66:13

Isaiah 66:10-14

David Heller, author of *The Children's God,* talked with many children about God. Here is his conversation with nine-year-old Arthur:

Arthur: **God is a man, for sure.**

David: What if God was the other sex?

Arthur: **But God is a man!**

David: But could you play "What if"?

Arthur: **If God was a . . . huh! Well, I don't know [laughs anxiously]. I don't know. Well, I couldn't even imagine God being a lady— no sir [laughs nervously].**

David Heller, *The Children's God*

Mary Cassatt, *Margot Embracing Her Mother*

The root of the Hebrew word for compassion is most interesting. That root means womb. Originally, compassion referred to the deep love and empathy a mother has for her children and the accompanying love and empathy experienced by those who have shared the same womb. Jesus replaced the holiness code admonition, "You must be holy just as God is holy," with the Kingdom code, "You must be compassionate just as your Heavenly Father is compassionate." In Jesus' day, much of society was determined by that holiness orientation, which, of course, led to impatience with those who were not "holy." But where the emphasis on holiness excluded many, Jesus' focus on compassion embraced all: The womb that envelops us is stronger and greater than our sin or even justifiable divine impatience.

Ron Zorn, "Compassion, Patience and the Womb of God"

Strong mother God, working night and day,
planning all the wonders of creation,
setting each equation,
genius at play:
Hail and Hosanna,
strong mother God!

Brian Wren, *Bring Many Names*

S. K. Dutt, *A Frail Baby Enfolded in the Arms of Mother Teresa*

THESE ARE IMAGES OF COMFORT, INTIMACY, NURTURING, AND COMPASSIONATE WELCOME;
THESE ARE IMAGES OF GOD.

Mother and God

Words and music:
Miriam Therese Winter

Moth - er and God, to you we sing;

wide is your womb, warm is your wing.

In you we live, move, and are fed

sweet, flow - ing milk, life - giv - ing bread.

Moth - er and God, to you we bring

all bro - ken hearts, all bro - ken wings.

Consider how frequently Jesus referred to God as compassionate. Such reflection may cause one to include maternal traits among their perceptions/conceptions of the nature of God.

HARD WORDS

then Amos answered Amaziah,

"I am no prophet, nor a prophet's son;

but I am a herdsman, and a dresser of

sycamore trees, and the Lord said to me,

'Go, prophesy to my people Israel.'"

Amos 7:14-15

Amos 7:7-17

Because we have seen pain without
    being moved,
because we forget your love with
    solemn pride,
because we pass by happy before
    poverty and sadness,
Lord have mercy,
Lord have mercy,
have mercy on us.

For speaking of love without loving
    our sister or brother,
for speaking of faith without living
    your word,
because we live without seeing our
    personal evil, our sin,
Christ have mercy,
Christ have mercy,
have mercy on us.

For our tranquility in our affluent life,
for our great falseness in preaching
    about poverty,
for wanting to make excuses for
    injustice and misery,
Lord have mercy,
Lord have mercy,
have mercy on us.
Amen.

Book of Worship: United Church of Christ

Jacopo (da Ponte) Bassano, *The Good Samaritan*

From the passage in Luke, one of the Gospel readings for this week, the Italian painter Bassano, who worked in the period just following the beginning of the Reformation, found the source for this painting which interprets a moment in the Bible story.
The background provides a natural setting which suggests the length of the journey. In the immediate background at left, a man reading while walking and dressed in clothing to suggest a priest has passed by the injured man. Still further down the road is another passerby who ignored the plight of the victim. In the lower right foreground, two dogs sniff the ground (perhaps at the point of shed blood; note the streaks of blood on the figure of the victim). In the extreme lower center of the foreground, the Samaritan has placed a container of the wine or oil he used in dressing the victim's wounds. Intriguingly younger than his Samaritan rescuer, the victim is bandaged and is being lifted gently toward the saddled donkey, almost invisible in the deep shadows of the probable place of attack, a bluff beside the road. The bright red tunic of the Samaritan focuses attention on him and his quiet, reassuring efforts to support and lift the injured man onto the animal's back.

Although providing his own interpretation of the scriptural passage, Bassano is faithful to the story in bringing later followers of Christ into contact with the unexpected one who acts out God's will in the situation. Thus the artist continues the prophetic ministry of bringing the properly religious face to face with Amos' or Jesus' "hard words" that call for action.

Kyrie eleison

Kyrie eleison

The real exile of Christians in the First World is that we have learned to endure it. We do not consider our living in the affluent societies as being in captivity. We rather have adjusted ourselves so much to Egypt that we feel at home. We have adjusted ourselves to the Egyptian lifestyle. We have adopted the basic beliefs of the Egyptians. We see individualism as the measure of human development, and we share assumptions of history's caprice— sometimes this group on top, sometimes another group. We have learned to endure the exile so well that we no longer see ourselves as exiled people— as strangers in a strange land. . . . To learn to endure the exile is to suppress even our thirst for justice.

Dorothee Soelle, "Thou Shalt Have No Other Jeans Before Me (Levi's Advertisement, Early Seventies): The Need for Liberation in a Consumerist Society"

Dorothee Soelle
speaks of the diversion
of attention
from calls for justice
in modern consumerist societies.
It may be typical
to wish to align oneself
with the side of righteousness.
But confession may be
more appropriate.

Vincent Van Gogh, *The Good Samaritan*

More than 300 years after Bassano, the artist Vincent Van Gogh, who was the son of a Protestant Christian minister, presents another visual interpretation of the powerful verbal imagery present in Jesus' story of the good Samaritan. Brilliant light and color dominate the image. At left, two figures who have chosen not to become involved in the injured man's plight continue their journey on the road. The victim's travel bag, emptied by the assailant-robber, lies open and empty beside the road at left. The red-bearded Samaritan struggles to lift the injured man onto his horse. The victim attempts to assist by pushing and lifting his injured body onto the mount. The vibrant colors and lines comprising the background only emphasize further the activity of saving rescue.

Christe eleison

LEADER We praise the Spirit which unites us as one people. But the plenitude of our gifts disturbs us. We seek to know the truth, but trust only our own truth.

PEOPLE We seek to feed the hungry, but trust only the manna gathered by our own hands.

LEADER We seek to see the plumb line hanging in our midst, but tilt our heads and move our bodies to see the angle we want.

ALL **We have failed to celebrate the life gifts of all persons. We have failed, even in this community, to feed and be fed with those gifts. We have failed to work and to wait for justice.**

Wheadon United Methodist Church, Evanston, Illinois

JUSTICE FOR THE POOR

hen God said to me, "Hear this,
you that trample on the needy, and bring to ruin the poor
of the land, . . . buying the poor for silver and the needy for
a pair of sandals, and selling the sweepings of the wheat."
God has sworn by the pride of Jacob: Surely I will never
forget any of their deeds.

Amos 8:4, 6-7

Amos 8:1-12

Pinturicchio, *Amos and the European Sibyl*, detail

Amos is the first of the prophets whose words are collected and preserved in a book. He is certainly not the last, however. How contemporary some of his sayings are! Are there instances of religious hypocrisy in our society? How many people believe that prosperity must be the result of doing right in the religious sphere? Are there in our society examples of injustice in the courts, of extravagance in the face of hunger and want, of corrupt and deceitful business practices? A society with such elements cannot long survive because it will crumble from the weight of its own oppressions and the decay of its moral foundation. Amos did not believe that changes should be made simply because society would be better because of them or because people owed such conduct to each other as people; this is a humanistic understanding. Rather, the changes which Amos proposed, even demanded, were changes rooted in his understanding of God.

James M. Efird

Faith clearly tells us that where the poor person is, there Jesus Christ himself is; where God, there is justice.

Philip Guamán Poma de Ayala

Many of us are crucified with you—abandoned in jails, on trash heaps, in the streets, in cardboard shelters, under bridges, with nothing to eat but what others throw away.

May we say with you, "Father, forgive them, for they know not what they do."

At the same time, there are those among us who crucify you still. We weep at the thought of the cruel persons who crucified you; but we continue to do the same thing, when we abandon our children, or the elderly, when we enjoy our coffee with sugar while farm workers are being subjected to a cruel, unjust exploitation, when we make fun of the imaginary inferiority of blacks, the poor, or other races. Forgive us, Lord, for all the times we have lynched, scourged, tortured, and murdered the poor, blacks, or immigrants, when we have robbed them of their lands, despised them for their customs, and expelled them from our countries because we want no "foreigners" among us.

Lord, stir up in me a great sorrow and sense of scandal at having crucified you by abusing the weak in our country, and grant me a desire to change my life. Help me see the invisible wickedness of my people, that I may repent and begin to walk a new way.

Lord, do not permit us to pursue the paths that crucify whole populations. Help us crucify our false values, that we may rise to new values. Lord, I know not the way. But you can do all things. You can accomplish this in me and in my people. Amen.

José Oscar Beozzo, *Jesus Is Crucified*

When we are really honest
with ourselves,
we must admit that our lives
are all that really
belong to us.
So it is how we use our lives
that determines
what kind of people we are.

Cesar Chavez

Jesus of Montreal

The life of Daniel was changed. As a character in
the film *Jesus of Montreal*, Daniel is transformed by
portraying Jesus in a new interpretation of the Passion
narrative in a public presentation. He upsets the status quo when he experiences the truth of the Gospel.
During auditions for a beer commercial, the producer
and director humiliate one of the women in the cast,
and Daniel responds by overturning the tables and
smashing equipment. Daniel is transformed by his
encounter with Jesus and discovers contemporary situations where the call for justice must be answered.

Jesus was praying in a certain place, and after he had finished, one of the disciples said to him, "Lord, teach us to pray, as John taught his disciples." Jesus said to them, "When you pray, say: Father [and Mother], hallowed be your name. Your dominion come. Give us each our daily bread. And forgive us our sins, for we ourselves forgive everyone indebted to us. And do not bring us to the time of trial."

Luke 11:1-4

Luke 11:1-13

O Birther! Father-Mother of the Cosmos,
Focus your light within us—make it useful:
Create your reign of unity now -
Your one desire then acts with ours,
as in all light, so in all forms.
Grant what we need each day in bread and insight.
Loose the cords of mistakes binding us,
as we release the strands we hold
of others' guilt.
Don't let surface things delude us.
But free us from what holds us back.
From you is born all ruling will,
the power and the life to do,
the song that beautifies all,
from age to age it renews.
Truly—power to these statements—
may they be the ground from which all
my actions grow: Amen.

Neil Douglas-Klotz, *Prayers of the Cosmos*

Orant (Praying Figure), fresco

In this early Christian fresco painting in a family tomb located in a Roman catacomb, the central figure is in the early Christian stance of prayer, that is, standing, head upraised and eyes open, with arms outstretched and hands open with the palms upturned. In contrast to the more recent common position of bending over, with head bowed, eyes closed, and hands clasped, this position symbolically opens the one in prayer to the presence of God. The prayer Jesus taught the disciples calls for an openness to God. One might imagine Jesus and his followers standing together as they drew strength from God and each other.

LORD, TEACH US TO PRAY.

These hands are not closed;

rather, they are placed together

in a gesture of supplication

which would have been recognized

by people in the artist Dürer's time.

This same gesture, when

accompanied by a slight bow

of the upper torso of the body,

is used as a form of greeting

in many cultures.

Possibly the several perspectives

presented suggest, for some,

new ways of engaging God through

the prayer that Jesus still teaches

his disciples through the church.

Albrecht Dürer, *Study of Hands in Prayer*

Being able to say amen implies being able to trust and be confident and certain that everything is in the hands of [God]; [God] has already conquered mistrust and fear, despite everything. The Lord's Prayer has encompassed the whole path of humanity in its drive toward heaven and its rootage in the earth. One finds in it the motif of light and the motif of darkness. And to all of it we say "Yes, so be it!" And we can say yes and amen to the threat of evil, to the promptings of temptation, to the insults we receive, and to the onerous quest for bread, only if we retain our certainty that God is our [God], that we are consecrated to [the divine] holy name, that we are confident that [God's reign] will come, and that we are sure [God's] will is to be done on earth as it is in heaven.

Leonardo Boff, *The Lord's Prayer: The Prayer of Integral Liberation*

IN GOD'S ARMS

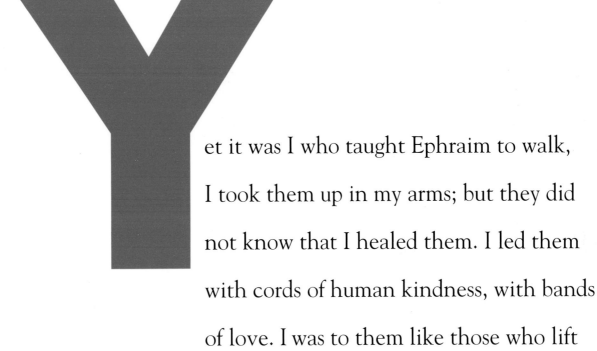

Yet it was I who taught Ephraim to walk, I took them up in my arms; but they did not know that I healed them. I led them with cords of human kindness, with bands of love. I was to them like those who lift infants to their cheeks. I bent down to them and fed them.

Hosea 11:3-4

Hosea 11:1-11

Still from Family Filmstrips

The image of a wild-eyed preacher with Bible in one hand and a condemning finger pointing at the viewer has become a bit like an icon in the late twentieth century U.S.A. Such images suggest wrath and judgment. It is clear from both Hebrew and Christian scriptures that judgment is *one* facet of God's relationship with humanity, but it is not the only nor even the primary one. In addition to the image suggested in the scripture presented at the beginning, Julian of Norwich, an English mystic, helps to understand the connection between love and judgment.

To the property of motherhood belong nature, love, wisdom and knowledge, and this is God. For though it may be so that our bodily bringing to birth is only little, humble and simple in comparison with our spiritual bringing to birth, still it is [God] who does it in the creatures by whom it is done. The kind, loving mother who knows and sees the need of her child guards it very tenderly, as the nature and condition of motherhood will have. And always as the child grows in age and in stature, she acts differently, but she does not change her love. And when it is even older, she allows it to be chastised to destroy its faults, so as to make the child receive virtues and grace. This work, with everything which is lovely and good, our Lord performs in those by whom it is done. So [God] is our Mother in nature by the operation of grace in the lower part, for love of the higher part. And God wants us to know it, for [God] wants to have all our love attached to [God].

Julian of Norwich, *Showings*

Strong mother God,
working night and day,
planning all the wonders of creation,
setting each equation,
genius at play:
Hail and Hosanna,
strong mother God!

Warm father God,
hugging every child,
feeling all the strains of human living,
caring and forgiving,
till we're reconciled:
Hail and Hosanna,
warm father God!

Brian Wren, *Bring Many Names*

William Taylor, *Mother and Child*

Out of a single block of wood, sculptor William Taylor captures in a visual text some of the same insights proposed by the verbal texts presented here. The intimate link between mother and child seems almost organic in character. Is the human relationship with God any less than that?

Consider the words of Brian Wren in another attempt to understand the seeming paradox of the *loving judgment* of God.

Romantic love is

blind to everything except

what is lovable and lovely,

but Christ's love sees us

with terrible clarity

and sees us whole.

Christ's love so wishes

our joy that it is ruthless

against everything

in us that diminishes our joy.

The worst sentence

Love can pass

is that we behold the suffering

which Love endured

for our sake,

and that is also our acquittal.

The justice and mercy

of the judge are ultimately one.

Frederick Buechner, *Wishful Thinking*

To be confronted by divine love involves . . . a judgment. . . .

That the judgment of God is a judgment of love means that no one will be rejected and separated except those who have refused to tolerate the presence of love.

Gustaf Aulén, *The Faith of the Christian Church*

I was to them like those
who lift their infants
to their cheeks.

Hosea 11:3b

BY FAITH

n

ow faith is the assurance of things hoped for, the conviction of things not seen.

Hebrews 11:1

Hebrews 11:1-3, 8-16

The future is always faced with uncertainty, even panic. The unknown is always seen as more terrifying than the known, for we are not certain our coping behaviors have developed to meet the new challenges. Besides, we get accustomed to dealing with the familiar. It's secure, like old bedroom slippers. Anything new might require us to reprogram ourselves altogether. And that we find a most threatening prospect. Again the question haunts us. Given the jostling and rapid change of today, with future discoveries a boggle to the imagination, how does one face tomorrow without fear? How does one develop an inner hold to meet the invading forces of the yet-to-be-born?

Roger Sizemore, *Keeping in Touch*

Why did the two old crocks laugh? They laughed because they knew only a fool would believe that a woman with one foot in the grave was soon to have her other foot in the maternity ward. They laughed because God expected them to believe it anyway. They laughed because laughing felt better than crying. They laughed because if by some crazy chance it just happened to come true they would really have something to laugh about, and in the meanwhile it helped keep them going.

Faith is "the assurance of things hoped for, the conviction of things not seen," says the Epistle to the Hebrews (11:1). Faith is laughter at the promise of a child called laughter.

Frederick Buechner,
Wishful Thinking: A Theological ABC

George Segal, *Abraham's Farewell to Ishmael*, © George Segal/VAGA, New York, 1994.

In this recent sculptural work by George Segal, *Abraham's Farewell to Ishmael*, both uncertainty and faith are suggested. At left, Abraham embraces the son who was to be the future; Hagar (in foreground) faces the unknown of desert-exile, her own empty arms mimicking Abraham's; and in the right background, Sarah, mother-to-be of yet a different future, watches in silence as one uncertain future is traded for another.

For Hagar, a servant, uncertainty is nothing new. Upon conceiving Ishmael, she was banished by Sarah, only to be told by God to return to that household. Now, exiled by Abraham because of Sarah's jealousy of Ishmael's importance as the eldest son, Hagar once again faces uncertainty. God honors the covenant with Abraham to bless Hagar and Ishmael. But we only know this because we know how the story unfolds. Here, in this sculpture, the artist suggests Abraham, Hagar, Ishmael and Sarah face uncertainty with conviction.

THE CLOUD OF WITNESSES

Therefore, since we are surrounded by so great a cloud of witnesses, let us also lay aside every weight and the sin that clings so closely, and let us run with perseverance the race that is set before us, looking to Jesus the pioneer and the perfecter of our faith, who for the sake of the joy that was set before him endured the cross, disregarding its shame, and is seated at the right hand of the throne of God.

Hebrews 12:1-2

Hebrews 11:29-12:1-2

David Roberts, *The Departure of the Israelites*

David Roberts' nineteenth century interpretation of the Israelites' departure from an Egyptian city for their journey to an unknown land emphasizes the great drama of this extraordinary event. Painted during a time of intense interest in increased Biblical scholarship and fascination with antiquity, the artist provokes the imagination. Suggested is the enormity of the decision, based on faith, of a whole subcultural group (the Hebrews in Egypt) to leave their now familiar life and follow Moses, who invoked their trust that God would lead them to a new, though unknown home.

Amidst the architectural and artistic splendor of Egypt, the figures of the Israelite families carry a few belongings and lead their animals down stairs and through the streets toward the desert sand storm in the distance. Moses would have them be a "cloud of witnesses," to the world, the covenant people of the one God. To be this, they must be pioneers of faith.

Let us praise faithful women,
random representatives
of all women
whose faithfulness mirrors
the God
who is faithful to us.

Mary of Magdala,
follower of Jesus,
first witness to the Resurrection,
leader of the early Church.

Hail, faithful woman!

All those *"many others,"*
women who followed Jesus,
whom scripture does not name:

Hail, faithful woman!

Hail, faithful woman!

Miriam Therese Winter

Henry Ossawa Tanner, *The Three Marys*

In the circle of life we each have a special gift, a special function. In the Native worldview there is no in or out; everyone in the circle is necessary. The gift and function of each person are necessary for the benefit of the whole family of human beings and those that walk, crawl, swim, and fly. We are all relatives. It is this wisdom of compassion, seeing things in their balance, that is so significant in turning aside illusions of scarcity and bringing peace to our own hearts.

The third creative fire is the fire of creative intelligence, building intelligence, that our dreams may succeed, that our works may actually manifest for the benefit of many.

Dhyani Ywahoo, *Voices of our Ancestors*

In the Bible, faith is never a matter simply for an isolated individual. It involves a community of persons that stretches back into the past, embraces people in the present, and anticipates a fellowship in the future. Faith involves a "cloud of witnesses" to God's continuing faithfulness.

Paul Hammer, *Word Among Us*

Lineage

My grandmothers were strong.
They followed plows and bent to toil.
They moved through fields sowing seed.
They touched earth and grain grew.
They were full of sturdiness and singing.
My grandmothers were strong.

My grandmothers are full of memories
Smelling of soap and onions and wet clay
With veins rolling roughly over quick hands
They have many clean words to say.
My grandmothers were strong.
Why am I not as they?

Margaret Walker

ALL THAT IS WITHIN ME — BLESS GOD

Bless God, O my soul, and all that is within me, bless God's holy name. . . . God is merciful and gracious, slow to anger and abounding in steadfast love.

Psalm 103:1, 8

Psalm 103

Often learning has less to do

with facts than with experience.

Eyes less conditioned

only by the oughts

or the shoulds of life

sometimes may see more clearly

than those preoccupied

with confirming old information.

Helen Keller

At times my heart cries out with longing to see these things. If I can get so much pleasure from mere touch, how much more beauty must be revealed by sight. Yet, those who have eyes apparently see little. The panorama of color and action which fills the world is taken for granted. It is human, perhaps, to appreciate little that which we have and to long for that which we have not, but it is a great pity that, in the world of light, the gift of sight is used only as a mere convenience rather than as a means of adding fullness to life.

Helen Keller

Phil Borges, *Young Girl with Lily*

Blessing of the Stew Pot

Blessed be the Creator

and all creative hands

which plant and harvest,

pack and haul and hand

over sustenance—

Blessed be carrot and cow,

potato and mushroom,

tomato and bean,

parsley and peas,

onion and thyme,

garlic and bay leaf,

pepper and water,

marjoram and oil,

and blessed be fire—

and blessed be the enjoyment

of nose and eye,

and blessed be color—

and blessed be the Creator

for the miracle of red potato,

for the miracle of green bean,

for the miracle of fawn mushrooms,

and blessed be God

for the miracle of earth:

ancestors, grass, bird,

deer and all gone,

wild creatures

whose bodies become

carrots, peas, and wild

flowers, who

give sustenance

to human hands, whose

agile dance of music

nourishes the ear

and soul of the dog

resting under the stove

and the woman working over

the stove and the geese

out the open window

strolling in the backyard.

And blessed be God

for all, all, all.

Alla Renée Bozarth

Luca della Robbia, *Singing Boys*, detail

Praises to God

On mah journey now,
Well I wouldn't take nothin' for mah journey now!
Praises to God—
One day I was walking along,
Well the elements opened an' de love come down—
Praises to God!
I went to de valley an' I didn't go to stay,
Well, my soul got happy an' I stayed all day!
Praises to God!
Praises to God!

Aminah Robinson

Bless God, O my soul!

Jonathan Green,
The Congregation, detail

Text Sources

Arts: Imaging the Faith

For a discussion of symbolism, see Erich Kahler, "The Nature of the Symbol," in *Symbolism in Religion and Literature*, ed. Rollo May (New York: George Braziller, 1960), 70; Paul Tillich, *Dynamics of Faith* (New York: Harper and Brothers, 1957), 42; and Robert C. Monk, Walter Hofheinz, Kenneth Lawrence, et al., "The Role of Symbols in Religion," in *Exploring Religious Meaning*, 4th ed. (Englewood Cliffs, N.J.: Prentice-Hall, 1993).

Masao Takenaka and Ron O'Grady, *The Bible Through Asian Eyes* (Auckland: Pace Publishing in association with The Asian Christian Art Association, 1991), 102.

Imagine That: An Introduction for the Young

Frederick Buechner, "Creation," in *Wishful Thinking: A Theological ABC* (San Francisco: Harper and Row, 1973), 18. © 1988 by Frederick Buechner. Used by permission of HarperCollins Publishers, Inc.

Pentecost 15

Gijs Okhuijsen and Cees van Opzeeland, *In Heaven There Are No Thunderstorms: Celebrating the Liturgy with Developmentally Disabled People* (Collegeville, Minn.: The Liturgical Press, 1992), 52, 53.

Wayne Saffen, "Ephphatha," in *The Third Season: Pentecost* (Philadelphia: Fortress Press, 1974), 41-42. Used by permission.

Thomas John Carlisle, "The Gift I Need," in "Journey with Job," *alive now!*, September/October 1982, 29. Used by permission.

Phil Porter, "Thousand Red Birds," in *Sermonettes and Scandals: The Book* (Oakland, Calif.: Phil Porter Studios, 1989). Used by permission.

Pentecost 16

Nelle Morton, *Journey Is Home* (Boston: Beacon Press, 1985), 41.

Marva Nettles Collins, quoted by Brian Lanker in Barbara Shummers, ed., *I Dream a World: Portraits of Black Women Who Changed America* (New York: Stewart, Tabori & Chang, 1989), 75.

Paulo Freire, *Pedagogy of the Oppressed*, trans. Myra Bergman Ramos (New York: Seabury Press, 1970), 58, 66.

Sting, excerpted from "They Dance Alone," in album *Nothing Like the Sun* (Hollywood: A&M Records, 1987). © 1987 Reggatta Music, Ltd./Illegal Songs, Inc. All rights reserved. Used by permission.

Pentecost 17

Excerpted from materials by Congregations Concerned for Children, as told to Magaly Rodriquez Mossman by Robin Van Doren, who heard it from elders of the Hopi Nation; quoted in Kathleen A. Guy, *Welcome the Child: A Child Advocacy Guide for Churches* (Washington, D.C.: Children's Defense Fund, 1991), 27.

Ann Weems, "Greenless Child," in *Reaching for Rainbows: Resources for Creative Worship* (Philadelphia: Westminster Press, 1980), 33. © 1980 Ann Weems. Used by permission of Westminster/John Knox Press.

Hans Rudi-Weber, *Jesus and the Children: Biblical Resources for Study and Preaching* (Atlanta: John Knox Press, 1979), 19-20.

Written for National Children's Day, June 1982, The Washington Cathedral, Washington, D.C., quoted in Kathleen A. Guy, *Welcome the Child: A Child Advocacy Guide for Churches* (Washington, D.C.: Children's Defense Fund, 1991), 25. Used by permission.

Fred Pratt Green, lyrics; Roy Hopp, music, "Little Children, Welcome" (Carol Stream, Ill: Hope Publishing Co.). Words © 1973 by Fred Pratt Green. Music © 1988 by Roy Hopp.
All rights reserved. Used by permission.

Pentecost 18

Rosa Parks, interview by Brian Lanker in *I Dream a World: Portraits of Black Women Who Changed America*, ed. Barbara Shummers (New York: Stewart, Tabori & Chang, 1989), 16.

Susan Savell, "Carry It On," from *The Power of My Love for You*, cassette, Heartlight Records, 1986. Used by permission.

Diann Neu, "In Praise of Hands: A Hand Blessing," *WATERwheel* 2, no. 1 (Winter 1989). Published by the Women's Alliance for Theology, Ethics and Ritual, 8035 13th Street, Silver Spring MD 20910 (301-589-2590). Used by permission.

John H. Westerhoff, III, *A Pilgrim People: Learning Through the Church Year* (Minneapolis: Seabury Press, 1984), 19.

Pentecost 19

Dorothy Hanson Brown, "The Eighth Song," *alive now!* 12, no. 3 (May/June 1982), 34. Used by permission.

Frederick Buechner, *Wishful Thinking: A Theological ABC* (San Francisco: Harper & Row, 1973), 18. © 1988 by Frederick Buechner. Used by permission of HarperCollins Publishers, Inc.

Ruth Duck, "Colorful Creator" (hymn), unpublished, © 1992 Ruth C. Duck. Used by permission.

Langston Hughes, "Dream Variations," in *Selected Poems* (New York: Alfred A. Knopf, 1926). © 1926 by Alfred A. Knopf, Inc., and renewed 1954 by Langston Hughes. Reprinted by permission of the publisher.

James Weldon Johnson, "The Creation," in *God's Trombones: Seven Negro Sermons in Verse* (New York: Viking Press, 1955), 17-20.

Catherine Cameron, "God, Who Stretched the Spangled Heavens," words © 1967 by Hope Publishing Co., Carol Stream, Ill. 60188. All rights reserved. Used by permission.

Pentecost 20

Abraham J. Heschel, *The Prophets: Part II* (New York: Harper & Row, 1962), 1, 5.

The Amistad Research Center, Preserving America's Ethnic Heritage, brochure (New Orleans: The Amistad Research Center, Tulane University). Used by permission.

Pentecost 21

Fourth-century desert disciple, quoted in *Welcome the Child: A Child Advocacy Guide for Churches* (Washington, D.C.: Children's Defense Fund, 1991), preface.

Francesco Bernardone (St. Francis of Assisi), *Prayer for All*, World Council of Churches.

Alan Paton, *Instrument of Thy Peace*, rev. ed. (New York: Seabury Press, 1982), 11-12.

Mother Teresa, quoted in Daphne Rae, *Love Until It Hurts* (San Francisco: Harper & Row, 1981), 8, 45, 47.

Allan Boesak, *Black and Reformed* (Maryknoll, New York: Orbis Books, 1984), 29. Used by permission.

Carter Heyward, *Our Passion for Justice: Images of Power, Sexuality, and Liberation* (New York: Pilgrim Press, 1984), 124.

Pentecost 22

Hyemeyohsts Storm, *Seven Arrows* (New York: Harper & Row, 1972), 4-5.

"Trail of Tears," in *In the Spirit of the Circle: A Christian Education Resource Created by Native American Episcopalians* (New York: The Episcopal Church Center, 1989). Used by permission.

Michael Pavlovsky, *Brochure of the National Civil Rights Museum*, Lorin Hotel, Memphis, Tennessee. Used by permission.

Masao Takenaka and Ron O'Grady, *The Bible Through Asian Eyes* (Auckland, New Zealand: Pace Publishing in association with The Asian Christian Art Association, 1991), 98. Used by permission.

Miriam Therese Winter, *Woman Prayer, Woman Song* (Oak Park, Ill.: Meyer-Stone Books, 1987), 160. © 1987 by the Medical Mission Sisters. Used by permission of the Crossroad Publishing Company.

Pentecost 23

"Preparation for the Shema," *Welcoming Shabbat: The Prayerbook of Chevrei Tikva* (Cleveland, Ohio: Friends of Hope—A Synagogue for Gay and Lesbian Jews). Used by permission.

Elie Wiesel, *Night*, trans. Stella Rodway (New York: Avon, 1969), 76.

George E. Elliott, "Things of This World," *Commentary*, December 1962, 342. Used by permission.

St. Patrick (attributed), as reprinted in *Hymns for the Family of God* (Nashville: Paragon Associates, 1976), no. 643, revised.

Psalm 119:1-3, *Inclusive Language Lectionary: Readings for Year A*, revised ed. (New York: The Pilgrim Press, 1986), 69. Used by permission.

All Saints' Day

William Shakespeare, *Julius Caesar*, 4.3., in *Shakespeare: The Complete Works*, ed. G. B. Harrison (New York: Harcourt, Brace and World, 1952), 839.

Chief Seattle of the Dwamish, "Words Upon Surrendering His Land," in *The Washington Historical Quarterly* 22, no. 4 (October 1931). Quoted in T. C. McLuhan, *Touch the Earth: A Self-Portrait of Indian Existence* (Outerbridge Dienstfrey, 1971; reprint, New York: Simon and Schuster, 1992), 27. Used by permission.

The Episcopal Church, *The Book of Common Prayer* (The Church Hymnal Corporation and Seabury Press, 1977), 194. Used by permission.

Wheadon United Methodist Church, Evanston, Ill., "The Corporate Confession," in *Flames of the Spirit: Resources for Worship*, ed. Ruth C. Duck (New York: The Pilgrim Press, 1985), 55. Used by permission.

William Walsham How, "For All the Saints" (lyrics), in *Hymnbook for Christian Worship*, ed. Charles Huddleston Heaton (St. Louis, Mo.: The Bethany Press, 1970), 279, vv. 1, 2, 6.

Pentecost 24

Richard Braunstein, in *The New Book of Christian Quotations*, comp. Tony Castle (New York: Crossroad, 1983), 9.

Toyohiko Kagawa, quoted in Masao Takenaka and Ron O'Grady, *The Bible Through Asian Eyes* (Auckland, New Zealand: Pace Publishing in association with The Asian Christian Art Association, 1991), 126. Used by permission.

Joseph G. Donders, "His Widow Complex," in *The Jesus Community: Reflections on the Gospels for the B-Cycle* (Maryknoll, NY: Orbis Books, 1981), 282-4. Used by permission.

G. A. Studdert-Kennedy, "Awake, Awake to Love and Work" (hymn), in *Unutterable Beauty* (London: Hodder & Stoughton, Ltd., 1921). Used by permission.

Pentecost 25

Ted Loder, "Ground Me in Your Grace," in *Guerrillas of Grace: Prayers for the Battle* (San Diego: LuraMedia, 1984), 5. © 1984 by LuraMedia, Inc., San Diego, Calif. Used by permission.

Carl F. Burke, ed., *Treat Me Cool, Lord: Prayers of Kids from City Streets* (New York: Association Press, 1968), 72. Used by permission.

Pentecost 26

Paul Hammer, "The Background Word," in *Word Among Us: A Worship-centered, Lectionary-based Curriculum for the Whole Congregation* Leader's Guides (Cleveland: United Church Press, 1994), Pentecost 26. Used by permission.

James H. Cone, *God of the Oppressed* (New York: Seabury Press, 1975), 108.

Frederick Buechner, *Telling the Truth: The Gospel as Tragedy, Comedy and Fairy Tale* (San Francisco: Harper & Row, 1977), 16.

Advent 1

Charles Allen Dinsmore, *Atonement in Literature and Life* (Boston: Houghton, Mifflin and Co., 1906), quoted in *alive now!* 15, no. 2 (March/April 1985), 22.

Joseph Wood Krutch, *The Desert Year* (New York: Sloane, 1956, © 1952), quoted in *alive now!* 10, no. 4 (July/August 1980), 6.

Robert A. Raines, *Living the Questions* (Waco, Texas: Word Books, 1976), 98. Used by permission.

Thomas John Carlisle, *alive now!* 12, no. 3 (May/June 1982), 57. Used by permission.

Helder Camara, *It's Midnight, Lord*, trans. Joseph Gallagher, Thomas Fuller, and Tom Contry (Washington, D.C.: Pastoral Press, 1984), 31. Used by permission.

Advent 2

Wolfhart Pannenberg, *Jesus—God and Man*, trans. L. L. Wilkins and D. A. Priebe (Philadelphia: Westminster Press, 1968), 48.

Joseph G. Donders, *The Jesus Community: Reflections on the Gospels for the B-Cycle* (Maryknoll, N.Y.: Orbis Books, 1981), 11-16. Used by permission.

Brian Wren, lyrics; Sue Mitchell Wallace, music, "Welcome the Wild One," as reproduced in Brian Wren, *Bring Many Names* (Carol Stream, Ill.: Hope Publishing Co., 1989), 31a. Words © 1986 and music © 1989 by Hope Publishing Co., Carol Stream, Ill. 60188. All rights reserved. Used by permission.

Advent 3

Matthew Fox, *Illuminations of Hildegard of Bingen* (Santa Fe, NM: Bear & Co., 1985), 62. Used by permission.

Madeleine L'Engle, "A First Coming," in *A Cry Like a Bell* (Wheaton, Ill.: Harold Shaw, 1987), 57. Revised by Jann Cather Weaver. Used by permission.

Barbara Gerlach, *The Things That Make for Peace* (New York: Pilgrim Press, 1981), 60-61. Used by permission.

Jann Cather Weaver, "Litany Based on Isaiah 12:2-6" (NRSV; RSV; Jerusalem) (Cleveland: United Church Press, 1994).

Advent 4

Joseph J. Juknialis, *When God Began in the Middle* (Saratoga, CA: Resource Publications, 1982), 42. © 1982 by Resource Publications, Inc., 160 E. Virginia St. #290, San Jose, CA 95112. Used by permission.

Mary Southhard, "Visitation," in Julia Ahlers, Rosemary Broughton, and Carl Koch, eds., *Womenpsalms* (Winona, Minn.: St. Mary's Press, 1992), 10. Used by permission.

Jann Cather Weaver, "On the Representation of Mary and Elizabeth" (Cleveland: United Church Press, 1994).

Irene Zimmerman, "Liturgy," in Julia Ahlers, Rosemary Broughton, and Carl Koch, eds., *Womenpsalms* (Winona, Minn.: St. Mary's Press, 1992), 55-56. Used by permission.

Miriam Therese Winter, *My Soul Gives Glory to My God*, harmonized by C. Winfred Douglas from melody "Kentucky Harmony." Text © 1987 Medical Mission Sisters. Music from *The Hymnal 1982*, © The Church Pension Fund. Used by permission.

Christmas/Nativity

Muriel Tarr Kurtz, *Prepare Our Hearts: Advent and Christmas Traditions for Families*, (Nashville: The Upper Room, 1986), 88-89. Used by permission.

Ruth C. Duck, ed., "For Christmas Eve," in *Bread for the Journey: Resources for Worship* (New York: The Pilgrim Press, 1981), 20. Used by permission.

Lawrence Ferlinghetti, "Christ Climbed Down," in *A Coney Island of the Mind: Poems by Lawrence Ferlinghetti* (Norfolk, Conn.: New Directions Books, 1958), 69-70. Used by permission.

Keith Watkins, ed., "Prayer of Confession," in *Thankful Praise: A Resource for Christian Worship* (St. Louis, Mo.: CBP Press, 1987), 68. Used by permission.

Ruth C. Duck and Maren C. Tirabassi, eds. *Touch Holiness: Resources for Worship* (New York: The Pilgrim Press, 1990), 12. Used by permission.

Christmas

John Bierhorst, trans., *Spirit Child: A Story of the Nativity* (New York: William Morrow and Company, 1984), 8.

Helder Camara, *It's Midnight, Lord*, trans. Joseph Gallagher, Thomas Fuller, and Tom Conry (Washington, D.C.: Pastoral Press, 1984), 47. Used by permission.

Jim Strathdee, in response to a Christmas poem by Howard Thurman, 1969, quoted in Ruth C. Duck and Michael G. Bausch, eds., *Everflowing Streams: Songs for Worship* (New York: The Pilgrim Press, 1981), 33. Used by permission.

Henri J. M. Nouwen, *Behold the Beauty of the Lord: Praying with Icons* (Notre Dame, Ill.: Ave Maria Press, 1991), 35.

Christmas 1

Fred B. Craddock, *Luke* (Louisville: John Knox Press, 1990), 42. Used by permission.

Jann Cather Weaver, "Children Are Faith" (Cleveland: United Church Press, 1994).

"Scared" and "Why?" in Carl R. Burke, ed., *Treat Me Cool, Lord: Prayers, Devotions, Litanies (Prayers of Kids from City Streets Spoken in Their Own Language)* (New York: Association Press, 1968), 30-31. Used by permission.

James Evans McReynolds, "A Sense of Wonder," in Joseph Wood Krutch, *The Desert Year* (New York: Sloane, 1956, © 1952). Used by permission of the Trustees of Columbia University in the City of New York. All rights reserved.

Epiphany

Muriel Tarr Kurtz, *Prepare Our Hearts: Advent and Christmas Traditions for Families* (Nashville: The Upper Room, 1986), 126-27.

Lawrence Ferlinghetti, "I Am Waiting," in *A Coney Island of the Mind: Poems by Lawrence Ferlinghetti* (Norfolk, Conn.: New Directions Books, 1958), 49, 50, 52. Used by permission.

Edward Hays, "A Psalm of Longing," in *Prayers for a Planetary Pilgrim: A Personal Manual for Prayer and Ritual* (Easton, Kans.: Forest of Peace Books, 1989), 172. Used by permission.

Baptism of Jesus/Epiphany 1

Madeleine L'Engle, "Mary: After the Baptism," in *A Cry Like a Bell* (Wheaton, Ill.: Harold Shaw, 1987), 66. © 1987 by Crosswicks. Used by permission of Harold Shaw Publishers, Wheaton, Ill.

Joan Baez, quoted on card 150-B016 (Van Nuys, Calif.: David M & Company, 1986). Used by permission.

Ted Loder, "In the Silence, Name Me," in *Guerrillas of Grace: Prayers for the Battle* (San Diego: Lura Media, 1984), 24. Used by permission.

Epiphany 2

Tom Lane, "Could I?" in *alive now!* 12, no. 3 (May/June 1982), 51. Used by permission.

Shusaku Endo, *A Life of Jesus*, trans. Richard A. Schuchert (New York: Paulist Press, 1973), 33. Used by permission.

Esperanza Guevara, "The Wedding at Cana," in *The Gospel in Art by the Peasants of Solentiname*, ed. Philip and Sally Scharper (Maryknoll, N.Y.: Orbis Books), 30. Used by permission.

Epiphany 3

Ted Loder, "I Thank You for Those Things That Are Yet Possible," in *Guerrillas of Grace: Prayers for the Battle* (San Diego: Lura Media, 1984), 43. Used by permission.

Martin Luther King, Jr., quoted in Kathleen A. Guy, *Welcome the Child: A Child Advocacy Guide for Churches* (Washington, D.C.: Children's Defense Fund, 1991), 113. Reprinted by arrangement with the Heirs to the Estate of Martin Luther King, Jr., c/o Joan Daves Agency as agent for the proprietor. All material copyright by Dr. Martin Luther King, Jr., and the Estate of Martin Luther King, Jr.

Langston Hughes, "I, Too," in *Selected Poems of Langston Hughes* (New York: Alfred A. Knopf, 1959). © 1926 by Alfred A. Knopf, Inc., and renewed 1954 by Langston Hughes. Used by permission.

Brian Wren, "Christ Will Come Again" (lyrics), in *Bring Many Names* (Carol Stream, Ill.: Hope Publishing Co., 1989), 10a. Words © 1989 by Hope Publishing Co., Carol Stream, Ill. 60188. All rights reserved. Used by permission.

Epiphany 4

Mark Link, "Rejection," from *The Seventh Trumpet: The Good News Proclaimed* (Niles, Ill.: Argus Communications, 1978), 70-71. Used by permission.

From the annual meeting of the United Methodist Women's Caucus, Burlingame, California, February 13-15, 1976. Used by permission.

Paul Tillich, *The Demonic in Art*, in John Dillenberger and Jane Dillenberger, eds., *Paul Tillich: On Art and Architecture* (New York: Crossroad, 1987), 110.

Alice Walker, "Reassurance," in *Revolutionary Petunias and Other Poems* (San Diego: Harcourt, Brace, Jovanovich, 1991), 195-96. © 1972 by Alice Walker. Used by permission of Harcourt, Brace and Co.

Epiphany 5

Cesáreo Gabaraín, "Tú has venido a la orilla" ("You Have Come Down to the Lakeshore"). Text and music (Pescador de Hombres) © 1979, 1987, Cesáreo Gabaraín. Trans. © 1989 Madeleine Forell Marshall. Harm. © 1987 Skinner Chávez-Melo. Published by OCP Publications, 5536 NE Hassalo, Portland, OR 97213. All rights reserved. Used by permission.

Huub Oosterhuis, *Open Your Hearts*, trans. David Smith (New York: Crossroad, 1971), 21, 23. Used by permission.

Epiphany 6

Colleen Fulmer, "Rest in My Wings," in *Cry of Ramah* (Albany, Calif.: Loretto Spirituality Network), cassette.

C. S. Song, *Tell Us Our Names: Story Theology from an Asian Perspective* (Maryknoll, N.Y.: Orbis Books, 1984), 97.

Barbara A. Gerlach, *The Things That Make for Peace* (New York: The Pilgrim Press, 1981), 37.

Louis Evely, *That Man Is You*, trans. Edmond Bonin (New York: Paulist Press, 1964), 64. Used by permission.

Macrina Wiederkehr, "Blessed," as quoted in Janet Schaffran and Pat Kozak, *More Than Words: Prayer and Ritual for Inclusive Communities*, rev. ed. (Oak Park, Ill.: Meyer-Stone Books, 1988), 75. Used by permission.

Epiphany 7

Madeleine L'Engle, "I've Been Scolded," in *Tambourines! Tambourines to Glory! Prayers and Poems*, selected by Nancy Larrick (Philadelphia: The Westminster Press, 1982), 650. Used by permission.

Carter Heyward, *Our Passion for Justice: Images of Power, Sexuality, and Liberation* (New York: The Pilgrim Press, 1984), 88, 186.

Rainer Maria Rilke, *Letters to a Young Poet*, rev. ed., trans. M. D. Herter Norton (New York: Norton & Company, 1954), 53-54. Used by permission.

Julian of Norwich, quoted in Brendon Byole, ed., *Meditations with Julian of Norwich* (Santa Fe, N.M.: Bear & Company, 1983), as quoted in Marilyn Sewell, ed., *Cries of the Spirit: A Celebration of Women's Spirituality* (Boston: Beacon Press, 1991), 245.

Transfiguration Sunday

Hildegard of Bingen (1098-1179), *O Virtus Sapientiae*, in *Hildegard of Bingen's Book of Divine Works*, edited by Matthew Fox (Santa Fe: Bear and Company, 1987), 368. © 1987 by Bear and Company, Inc., Santa Fe, NM. Used by permission.

Walter Wink, "Expository Article on Mark 9:2-8," *Interpretation: A Journal of Bible and Theology* 36 (1982): 63-67. Used by permission.

Jerry Schmidt and Tom Jones, *The Fantastiks*, Polygram Records. Used by permission of Music Theatre International, N.Y.

Frederick Buechner, "Transfiguration," in *Whistling in the Dark: A Theological ABC* (San Francisco: Harper & Row, 1988). © 1988 by Frederick Buechner. Used by permission of HarperCollins Publishers, Inc.

"Celebration of Life," in *Jesus Christ—The Life of the World: A Worship Book for the Sixth Assembly of the World Council of Churches*.

Ash Wednesday

Dag Hammarskjöld, *Markings*, trans. Leif Sjöberg and W. H. Auden (New York: Alfred A. Knopf, 1966), 166. Translation © 1964 by Alfred A. Knopf, Inc., and Faber & Faber Ltd. Used by permission.

Edward Hays, *Prayers for a Planetary Pilgrim: A Personal Manual for Prayer and Ritual*, (Easton, Kans.: Forest of Peace Books, 1989), 136. Used by permission.

United Church of Christ, *Book of Worship* (New York: United Church of Christ Office for Church Life and Leadership, 1986), 187-88. Used by permission.

Lent 1

D. T. Niles, in Masao Takenaka and Ron O'Grady, eds., *The Bible Through Asian Eyes* (Auckland, New Zealand: Pace Publishing in association with The Asian Christian Art Association, 1991), 90. Used by permission.

T. S. Eliot, *Murder in the Cathedral* (New York: Harcourt, Brace and World, 1963), 44.

Evelyn Underhill, *The Fruits of the Spirit* (London: Longmans, Green and Co., 1956), 69.

James Healy, "Starting Point," *National Catholic Reporter*, April 6, 1990, 2.

"Nigerian Prayer," in John Carden, ed., *Morning, Noon and Night*, quoted in J. Robert Baker, Evelyn Koehler, and Peter Mazar, eds., *A Lent Sourcebook: The Forty Days, Book Two* (Chicago: Liturgy Training Publications, 1990), 103. Used by permission of the Church Missionary Society, London.

Lent 2

Tracy Chapman, "Why?" (words and music). © 1988 EMI April Music and Purple Rabbit Music. All rights controlled and administered by EMI April Music, Inc. All rights reserved. International copyright secured. Used by permission.

Jacques LeClerq, *A Year with the Liturgy: Meditations and Prayers* (Dublin: Scepter, Ltd., 1959), quoted in J. Robert Baker, Evelyn Koehler, and Peter Mazar, eds., *A Lent Sourcebook: The Forty Days, Book One* (Chicago: Liturgy Training Publications, 1990), 161.

William B. Silverman, *Rabbinic Wisdom and Jewish Values* (New York: Union of American Hebrew Congregations, 1971), 84.

Oscar Romero, *The Violence of Love*, comp. and trans. James Brockman (New York: Harper Collins, 1988), 213.

Lent 3

Edicio de la Torre, in Masao Takenaka and Ron O'Grady, eds., *The Bible Through Asian Eyes* (Auckland: Pace Publishing in association with The Asian Christian Art Association, 1991), 176. Used by permission.

Walt Whitman, "O Glad, Exulting, Culminating Song," quoted in Mark Link, *In the Stillness Is the Dancing* (Niles, Ill.: Argus Communications, 1972), 119.

Lent 4

Greg Delanty, "Leavetaking," in *Southward* (Baton Rouge: Louisiana State University Press, 1992). © 1992 by Greg Delanty. Used by permission of Louisiana State University Press.

Henri J. M. Nouwen, *The Return of the Prodigal Son: A Meditation of Fathers, Brothers, and Sons* (New York: Doubleday, 1992), 33, 35.

Alexander Schmemann, *Great Lent* (Crestwood, N.Y.: St. Vladimir's Seminary Press, 1974), 34-36. © St. Vladimir's Seminary Press, 575 Scarsdale Road, Crestwood, NY 10707. Used by permission.

Henri J. M. Nouwen, "Lecture," cited in *alive now!* March/April 1992, 27, 26. A version of this appears in *Life of the Beloved: Spiritual Living in a Secular World* (New York: Crossroad, 1992).

Ann B. Snow, text from hymn, "Wherever I May Wander," in *Songs and Hymns for Primary Children* (Philadelphia: Westminster Press), 1963. Words © 1963 by W. L. Jenkins. Used by permission.

Lent 5

Sydney Carter, "Said Judas to Mary." Music © 1964 by Gilliard, Ltd. Sole agent in the USA: Galaxy Music Corp., Boston, Mass. Used by permission.

Robert W. Guffey, Jr., "Oh, to Be So Poor," in *alive now!*, May/June 1991, 55, lines 1-24. Used by permission.

Jimilu Mason, correspondence with Robert Mayhew, September 17, 1986. Copy provided to author by Robert Mayhew. Used by permission.

Ruth C. Duck, "A Prayer," in Ruth C. Duck and Maren C. Tirabassi, eds., *Touch Holiness: Resources for Worship* (New York: The Pilgrim Press, 1990), 197, adapted. Used by permission.

Palm/Passion Sunday

"Blessing of the Palms," in *Book of Worship* (New York: United Church of Christ Office for Church Life and Leadership, 1986). Used by permission.

Beth Richardson, "Passion Sunday," in *alive now!*, March/April 1992, 58. Used by permission.

Tim Rice, "Hosanna," in *Jesus Christ, Superstar* (London: Lees Music, Ltd., 1970). Lyrics by Tim Rice. Music by Andrew Lloyd Weber. © 1970 by Leeds Music Ltd., sole selling agent MCA Music Publishing, a division of MCA, Inc., for North, South, and Central America. International copyright secured. All rights reserved. Used by permission.

Holy Thursday

United Church of Christ, *Book of Worship* (New York: United Church of Christ Office for Church Life and Leadership, 1986), 194-95. Used by permission.

William Blake, *Holy Thursday*, ed. J. Bronowski (Baltimore: Penguin Books Ltd., 1958), 43.

T. S. Eliot, *Murder in the Cathedral* (New York: Harcourt, Brace and World, 1935), 20.

Good Friday

Dag Hammarskjöld, *Markings*, trans. Leif Sjöberg and W. H. Auden (New York: Alfred A. Knopf, 1966), 8, 57. Translation © 1964 by Alfred A. Knopf, Inc., and Faber & Faber Ltd. Used by permission.

Norman Cousins, *The Celebration of Life, A Dialogue on Immortality and Infinity* (New York: Harper and Row, 1974), 21. Used by permission.

Richard N. Eick, "Call to Confession," in *Flames of the Spirit: Resources for Worship*, ed. Ruth C. Duck (New York: The Pilgrim Press, 1985), 37. Used by permission.

Easter

Ivan Turgenev, *Poems in Prose in Russian and English*, trans. Constance Garnett and Roger Rees (Oxford: B. Blackwell, 1951), 103.

George Herbert, "Easter," in *The Complete English Poems* (New York: Penguin Classics, 1991).

Easter 2

Imelda Cooper, "Vessel of Wholeness," *alive now!*, March/April 1992, 11. Used by permission.

Michael Perry, lyrics; Norman Warren, music, "Heal Me, Hands of Jesus," © 1982 by Hope Publishing Co., Carol Stream, Ill. 60188. All rights reserved. Used by permission.

Ruth C. Duck, "Fourth Sunday in Eastertide (Rev. 5:12; 7:9-12)," in Ruth C. Duck and Maren C. Tirabassi, eds., *Touch Holiness: Resources for Worship* (New York: The Pilgrim Press, 1990), 77, adapted. Used by permission.

Easter 3

Review of *Babette's Feast* in *Values and Visions Film Guide* (New York: Cultural Information Service, 1989), 2.

Janet Schaffran and Pat Kozak, *More Than Words: Prayer and Ritual for Inclusive Communities*, 2d ed. (Oak Park, Ill: Meyer Stone Books, 1988), 51. Used by permission.

C. S. Lewis, *Mere Christianity* (New York: Macmillan Company, 1952), 127.

Easter 4

Huub Oosterhuis, *Your Word Is Near: Contemporary Christian Prayers*, trans. N. D. Smith (New York: Paulist Press, 1968), 23. Used by permission.

Luke, quoted by JoAnne Taylor, *Innocent Wisdom: Children as Spiritual Guides* (New York: The Pilgrim Press, 1989), 46. Used by permission.

Bobby McFerrin, "The 23rd Psalm," in the album *Medicine Music* (Woodland Hills, CA: ProNoblem Music, EMI-USA, 1990). Used by permission.

Daily Prayer: The Worship of God—Supplemental Liturgical Resource 5 (Philadelphia: Westminster Press, 1987), 213. Used by permission.

Easter 5

Walter Russell Bowie, "O Holy City, Seen of John" (lyrics), in *The New Century Hymnal* (Cleveland, Ohio: United Church Board for Homeland Ministries, 1995). © 1993 United Church Board for Homeland Ministries. Used by permission.

Amalia G., "When I Wake Up in the Morning," quoted in Stephen M. Joseph, ed., *The Me Nobody Knows: Children's Voices for the Ghetto* (New York: Discus Books/Avon, 1969), 130.

David G. Buttrick, in Cornish R. Rogers and Joseph R. Jeter, eds., *Preaching through the Apocalypse: Sermons from Revelation* (St. Louis: Chalice Press, 1992), 162. Used by permission.

Anna McKenzie, "We, Without a Future," from *Good Friday People*, ed. Sheila Cassidy (Maryknoll, NY: Orbis Books, 1991), cited in *alive now!*, March/April 1992, 46. Used by permission.

Huub Oosterhuis, *Your Word Is Near: Contemporary Christian Prayers*, trans. N. D. Smith (New York: Paulist Press, 1968), 176. Used by permission.

Easter 6

Chris Glaser, *Come Home!* (San Francisco: HarperCollins, 1990), xii.

Emily Dickinson, "Unto Me?," in *The Complete Poems of Emily Dickinson*, ed. Thomas H. Johnson. © 1929 by Martha Dickinson Bianchi; © renewed 1957 by Mary L. Hampson. Used by permission of Little, Brown and Company.

Virginia Ramey Mollenkott, *Sensuous Spirituality: Out from Fundamentalism* (New York: Crossroad, 1992), 25-26.

Easter 7

E. M. Forster, *Howard's End* (London: Edward Arnold, 1973), 334.

Beverly Wildung Harrison, *Making Connections: Essays in Feminist Social Ethics*, ed. Carol S. Robb (Boston: Beacon Press, 1985), 41.

William Shakespeare, *All's Well That Ends Well*, in *Shakespeare The Complete Works*, ed. G. B. Harrison (New York: Harcourt, Brace, and World, 1948), 1045.

Pentecost

Garth House, *Litanies for All Occasions* (Valley Forge: Judson Press, 1989), 49. Used by permission.

John Carden, ed., *With All God's People: The New Ecumenical Prayer Cycle* (Geneva: WCC Publications, 1989), 15.

Trinity Sunday—Pentecost 1

Elton Fox, *Seventeen Black Artists* (New York: Dodd, Mead and Company, 1971), 282; cited in Regina Perry, *Free Within Ourselves: African-American Artists in the Collection of the National Museum of American Art* (Washington, D.C.: National Museum of American Art, Smithsonian Institution, 1992), 39.

Pentecost 2

Shusake Endo, *A Life of Jesus*, trans. Richard A. Schuckert (New York: Paulist Press, 1973), 49-50.

Elizabeth J. Canham, "The Anointing," selections, *alive now!*, March/April 1992, 49. Used by permission.

Masao Takenaka and Ron O'Grady, eds., *The Bible Through Asian Eyes* (Auckland, New Zealand: Pace Publishing in association with The Asian Christian Art Association, 1991), 102. Used by permission.

Miriam Therese Winter, "Alabaster Jar," commissioned, © 1994 Medical Mission Sisters. Used by permission.

J. Barrie Shepherd, "Anointing," *alive now!*, March/April 1993, 12. Used by permission.

Pentecost 3

Carl P. Daw, Jr., "Like the Murmur of the Dove's Song" (lyrics), © 1982 by Hope Publishing Co., Carol Stream, Ill. 60188. All rights reserved. Used by permission.

The First Presbyterian and Trinity Church, South Orange, New Jersey, *More Light Statement*, quoted in *Open Hands* 8, no. 3 (Winter 1993), 18.

Pentecost 4

Dag Hammarskjöld, *Markings*, trans. Leif Sjorberg and W. H. Auden (New York: Alfred A. Knopf, 1981), 14. Used by permission.

Jonathan Brown, William B. Jordan, Richard L. Kagan, and Alfonso E. Pérez Sánchez, *El Greco of Toledo* (Boston: Little, Brown and Company, 1982), 241.

David B. Noss and John B. Noss, *Man's Religions*, 7th ed. (New York: Macmillan, 1984), 427.

Karl Barth, cited in Kenneth Leech, *True Prayer: An Invitation to Christian Spirituality* (San Francisco: Harper and Row, 1980), 68; reprinted in *Weavings*, March/April, 1990, 41.

Pentecost 5

Miriam Therese Winter, "Mother and God," hymn in *WomanPrayer, WomanSong* (Oak Park, Ill: Meyer-Stone Books, 1987), 207. © 1987 by The Medical Mission Sisters. Used by permission of the Crossroad Publishing Company.

Ron Zorn, "Compassion, Patience and the Womb of God," in *Ministers' Bulletin: A Stewardship Newsletter of the Christian Church (Disciples of Christ)*, January-February 1993.

David Heller, *The Children's God* (Chicago: University of Chicago Press, 1986), 74.

Brian Wren, "Bring Many Names," verse 2, in *Bring Many Names* (Carol Stream, Ill: Hope Publishing Co., 1989). Words © 1989 by Hope Publishing Co., Carol Stream, Ill. 60188. All rights reserved. Used by permission.

Pentecost 6

Dorothee Soelle, "Thou Shalt Have No Other Jeans Before Me (Levi's Advertisement, Early Seventies): The Need for Liberation in a Consumerist Society," in Brian Mahan and L. Dale Richesin, eds., *The Challenge of Liberation Theology: A First World Response* (Maryknoll: Orbis Books, 1981), 5. Used by permission.

Book of Worship: United Church of Christ (New York: United Church of Christ Office for Church Life and Leadership, 1986), 532-33. Used by permission.

Wheadon United Methodist Church, from *Flames of the Spirit: Resources for Worship*, ed. Ruth C. Duck (Cleveland: The Pilgrim Press, 1985), 73. Used by permission.

Pentecost 7

James M. Efird, *The Old Testament Prophets Then and Now* (Valley Forge, Pa.: Judson Press, 1982), 43-44. Used by permission.

Philip Guamán Poma de Ayala, quoted in *Way of the Cross: The Passion of Christ in the Americas*, ed. Virgil Elizondo, trans. John Drury (Maryknoll: Orbis Books, 1992), 3.

José Oscar Beozzo, "Jesus Is Crucified," in *Way of the Cross: The Passion of Christ in the Americas*, ed. Virgil Elizondo, trans. John Drury (Maryknoll: Orbis Books, 1992), 77-78.

Cesar Chavez, quoted in *A Lent Sourcebook: The Forty Days, Book Two*, ed. J. Robert Baker, Evelyn Koeller, and Peter Mazar (Chicago: Liturgy Training Publications, 1990), 136.

Pentecost 8

Neil Douglas-Klotz, "Armaic Lord's Prayer," in *Prayers of the Cosmos: Meditations on the Aramaic Words of Jesus* (San Francisco: Harper and Row, 1990), 41. Used by permission.

Leonardo Boff, *The Lord's Prayer: The Prayer of Integral Liberation*, trans. Theodore Morris. (Maryknoll: Orbis Books, 1985), 122. Edited for inclusive language.

Pentecost 9

Julian of Norwich, *Showings*, trans. Edmund Colledge and James Walsh (New York: Paulist Press, 1978), 299.

Gustaf Aulén, *The Faith of the Christian Church*, trans. Eric H. Wahlstrom (Philadelphia: The Muhlenberg Press, 1960), 148, 149.

Brian Wren, "Bring Many Names," in *Bring Many Names* (Carol Stream, Ill.: Hope Publishing, 1989), verses 2 and 3. Words © 1989 by Hope Publishing Co., Carol Stream, Ill. 60188. All rights reserved. Used by permission.

Frederick Buechner, *Wishful Thinking: A Theological ABC* (New York: Harper and Row, 1973), 48. © 1988 by Frederick Buechner. Used by permission of HarperCollins Publishers, Inc.

Pentecost 10

Roger Sizemore, *Keeping in Touch* (St. Louis: Christian Board of Publication, 1973), 71.

Frederick Buechner, *Wishful Thinking: A Theological ABC* (New York: Harper and Row, 1973), 25. © 1988 by Frederick Buechner. Used by permission of HarperCollins Publishers, Inc.

Pentecost 11

Margaret Walker, "Lineage," in *This Is My Century: New and Collected Poems* (Athens: University of Georgia Press, 1989). Used by permission.

Miriam Therese Winter, *WomanPrayer, WomanSong* (Oak Park, Ill.: Meyer-Stone Books, 1987), 154, 156. © 1987 by The Medical Mission Sisters. Edited to replace the word "liberated" with the word "faithful." Used by permission of The Crossroad Publishing Company.

Dhyani Ywahoo, *Voices of Our Ancestors: Cherokee Teachings from the Wisdom Fire*, ed. Barbara Du Bois (Boston: Shambala Publications, 1987), 163. Used by permission.

Paul Hammer, "The Background Word," in *Word Among Us: A Worship-centered, Lectionary-based Curriculum for the Whole Congregation* Leader's Guides (Cleveland, Ohio: United Church Press, 1994), Pentecost 11. Used by permission.

Pentecost 12

Helen Keller, "Three Days to See," *Atlantic Monthly* 151:35-42 (January 1933): 36.

Alla Renée Bozarth, "Blessing of the Stew Pot," from *Water Women* (audiocassette) (43222 SE Tapp Road, Sandy, Ore. 97055: Wisdom House, 1990). All rights reserved. Used by permission.

Aminah Robinson, "Praises to God," in *The Teachings: Drawn from African-American Spirituals* (Orlando: Harcourt Brace Jovanovich, 1992), 62. © 1992 by Aminah Brenda Lynn Robinson. Used by permission of Harcourt, Brace and Co.

Illustration Sources

Arts: Imaging the Faith

Käthe Kollwitz, *Seed Corn Must Not Be Ground*, © 1993 ARS, New York/VG Bild-Kunst, Bonn, Germany. Used by permission.

Valentin de Boulogne, *The Taking of Christ*, oil on canvas, Juliana Cheney Edwards Collection, Museum of Fine Arts, Boston. © 1994. All rights reserved. Used by permission.

Wu Yuen-kwei, *Her Sins Are Forgiven*, as reproduced in Masao Takenaka and Ron O'Grady, *The Bible Through Asian Eyes* (Auckland, New Zealand: Pace Publishing in association with The Asian Christian Art Association, 1991), 103. Used by permission of The Asian Christian Art Association.

Imagine That: An Introduction for the Young

Jacopo (da Ponte) Bassano, *The Good Samaritan*, c. 1563, National Gallery of Art, London. Used by permission.

Vincent Van Gogh, *The Good Samaritan*, c. 1890, Rijksmuseum Kröller-Müller Stichting, Otterlo, The Netherlands. Used by permission.

Seasonal Divider for Pentecost (Cycle B)

Emil Nolde, *Christ Among the Children*, painting, 1910, gift of Dr. W. R. Valentiner, The Museum of Modern Art, New York. Used by permission.

Pentecost 15

German manuscript illumination, *Christ Healing the Deaf and Mute Man*, 12th century, Munich, Staatsbibliotheque (Foto Marburg/Art Resource, N.Y.). Used by permission.

Duccio di Buoninsegna, *Jesus Opens Eyes of Man Born Blind*, c. 1310, National Gallery of Art, London. Used by permission.

Silence = Death and Pink Triangle, Donnelly/Colt Customstickers, ACT UP/L.A., 1989. Used by permission.

Pentecost 16

Jesus Among the Teachers, Vie de Jesus Mafa, 24 rue du Marechal, Joffre, 78000 Versailles, France. All rights reserved. Used by permission.

Robert Lentz, *Madre de Los Desaparecidos*, Bridge Building Images Catalogue 1990-1991, Item #PMD, 12. Used by permission.

Pentecost 17

Emil Nolde, *Christ Among the Children*, 1910, gift of Dr. W. R. Valentiner, The Museum of Modern Art, New York. Used by permission.

Rohn Engh, *Young Girl Carrying Washtub*, Pine Lake Farm, Osceola, Wisconsin. Used by permission.

Pentecost 18

Man Stopping Tank, Beijing, June 1989, color slide photographed from video, Capital Cities/ABC, Inc., New York, N.Y. © 1989 Capital Cities/ABC, Inc. Used by permission.

Brian Lanker, *Rosa Parks*, photograph reprinted in Barbara Shummers, ed., *I Dream a World: Portraits of Black Women Who Changed America* (New York: Stewart, Tabori & Chang, 1989), 17. Used by permission.

Jann Cather Weaver, *Homeless Hands*, private collection of photographer, photographed at St. Mary's Community Center, Oakland, California, 1993. Used by permission.

Pentecost 19

Jess, *No-Traveller's Borne*, detail, 1965, Philadelphia Museum of Art, Philadelphia (purchased Edith H. Bell Fund). Used by permission.

Aaron Douglas, *The Creation*, 1935, Howard University Gallery of Art, Permanent Collection, Washington, D.C. Used by permission.

Michelangelo Buonarotti, *The Creation of Adam*, detail, 1511, Sistine Chapel, Vatican City (Alinari/Art Resource, N.Y.). Used by permission.

Pentecost 20

Emil Nolde, *Prophet*, 1912, woodcut, printed in black, block, 12 5/8 x 8 3/4", The Museum of Modern Art, New York. Given anonymously (by exchange). Used by permission.

Hale Woodruff, *The Amistad Slaves on Trial at New Haven, Connecticut, 1840*, 1939, panel two of triptych, Amistad Research Center, New Orleans, Louisiana. Used by permission.

Claude Lorrain (Claude Gelée), *Landscape with Rest on the Flight to Egypt*, detail, 1600s, Hermitage, St. Petersburg, Russia (Scala/Art Resource, N.Y). Used by permission.

Pentecost 21

Giovanni Bellini, *St. Francis in Ecstasy*, c. 1485, The Frick Collection, New York. Used by permission.

Eric Risberg, *Mother Teresa*, 1986, © AP/Wide World Photos. Used by permission.

Pentecost 22

Hyemeyohsts Storm, *Untitled (Medicine Wheel)*, color plate reproduced in Hyemeyohsts Storm, *Seven Arrows* (New York: Harper & Row, 1972), 220-21. Used by permission.

Michael Pavlovsky, *Movement to Overcome*, detail, cast bronze, 1990, National Civil Rights Museum, Memphis, Tennessee. Photo by Mitzi N. Eilts. Used by permission.

Nikhil Halder, *The Kingdom Comes*, as reproduced in Masao Takenaka and Ron O'Grady, *The Bible Through Asian Eyes* (Auckland, New Zealand: Pace Publishing in association with The Asian Christian Art Association, 1991), 99. Used by permission of The Asian Christian Art Association.

Pentecost 23

Dorothea Lange, *Migrant Mother,* 1936, Nipomo, California (Library of Congress). Used by permission.

All Saints' Day

Sebastiano del Piombo, *The Raising of Lazarus,* National Gallery of Art, London, England. Used by permission.

Marcus Leatherdale, *Silent Scream,* artist's collection, New York, N.Y. © Marcus Leatherdale. Used by permission.

Pentecost 24

Paula Modersohn-Becker, *Old Peasant Woman,* 1906, gift of Robert H. Tannahill, © The Detroit Institute of Arts. Used by permission.

The Widow's Mite, Vie de Jesus Mafa, 24 rue du Marechal Joffre, 78000 Versailles, France. All rights reserved. Used by permission.

Pentecost 25

Jack Beal, *Hope, Faith, Charity,* 1977-78, Frumkin/Adams Gallery, New York, N.Y. Used by permission.

Carissa Etheridge, *Boy in Shelter,* Community of Hope, Washington, D.C., 1989, as reproduced in *Shooting Back: A Photographic View of Life by Homeless Children* (San Francisco: Chronicle Books, 1991), 28. Used by permission.

Gertrude Myrrh Reagan, *Angel de mi Guarda,* as reproduced in *Woman of Power: Art as Activism* 6 (Spring 1987): 20. © 1986 by Gertrude Myrrh Reagan.

Pentecost 26

Pietro Lorenzetti, *Christ Before Pilate,* 1335, Pinacoteca Vaticana, Città del Vaticano, Italy (Scala/Art Resource, N.Y.). Used by permission.

Seasonal Divider for Advent

Franz Pourbus the Elder, *Sermon of St. John the Baptist,* Musée des Beaux-Arts, Valenciennes, France (Giraudon/Art Resource, New York). Used by permission.

Advent 1

Paul Chesley, *Forked Lightning Reflected in Lake,* Tony Stone Worldwide. Used by permission.

David Austen, *Forest Fire at Night,* Tony Stone Worldwide. Used by permission.

Dennis Oda, *Kilanea Volcano Erupting,* Tony Stone Worldwide. Used by permission.

Naul Ojeda, *Untitled,* engraving, as reproduced in Helder Camara, *It's Midnight, Lord,* trans. Joseph Gallagher, Thomas Fuller, and Tom Contry (Washington, D.C.: Pastoral Press, 1984), cover plate. Used by permission.

Advent 2

Franz Pourbus the Elder, *Sermon of St. John the Baptist,* Musée des Beaux-Arts, Valenciennes, France (Photographie Giraudon/Art Resource, N.Y.). Used by permission.

Advent 3

Hildegard of Bingen, *Lucifer's Fall,* illumination, 12th century, Otto Müller Verlag, Salzburg, Austria. Used by permission.

Jacob Lawrence, *Harriet Tubman Series No. 4,* Hampton University Museum, Hampton, Virginia. Used by permission.

Advent 4

Giotto di Bondone, *The Meeting of the Virgin and Elizabeth,* fresco, after 1306, la capella degli Scrovegni (Arena Chapel), Padua, Italy (Alinari/Art Resource, N.Y.). Used by permission.

Käthe Kollwitz, *Maria and Elizabeth,* 1928, © 1993 ARS, New York/VG Bild-Kunst, Bonn, Germany. Used by permission.

Seasonal Divider for Christmas

Domenico Ghirlandaio, *Adoration of the Shepherds,* 1485, panel, Sassetti Chapel, Church of Santa Trinità, Florence, Italy (Scala/Art Resource, N.Y.). Used by permission.

Christmas/Nativity

Domenico Ghirlandaio, *Adoration of the Shepherds,* 1485, panel, Sassetti Chapel, Church of Santa Trinità, Florence, Italy (Scala/Art Resource, N.Y.). Used by permission.

Christmas

Henry Ossawa Tanner, *Angels Appearing Before the Shepherds,* 1910, gift of Mr. and Mrs. Norman B. Robbins, National Museum of American Art, Smithsonian Institution, Washington, D.C. (Art Resource, N.Y.). Used by permission.

Our Lady of Vladimir, 12th century, Dormition Cathedral, Moscow.

Christmas 1

Duccio di Buoninsegna, *Dispute with the Doctors,* 1308-1311, Siena Museo dell'Opera Metropolitana (Scala/Art Resource, N.Y.). Used by permission.

Hughie Lee-Smith, *Boy on the Roof,* as reproduced in Louise E. Jefferson, *Contemporary Art by Afro-Americans.* Used by permission.

Seasonal Divider for Epiphany and the Sundays after Epiphany

Byzantine mosaic, *The Transfiguration,* c. 1100, Monastery of Daphni (near Athens), Greece (Erich Lessing/Art Resource, N.Y.). Used by permission.

Epiphany

Peter Paul Rubens, *The Adoration of the Magi,* Musées Royaux des Beaux Arts, Antwerp, Belgium (Scala/Art Resource, N.Y.). Used by permission.

Baptism of Jesus/Epiphany 1

Baptism of Christ, Orthodox Baptistery (Neonian) cupola mosaic, 5th century, Ravenna, Italy (Scala/Art Resource, N.Y.). Used by permission.

Pheoris West, *The Baptism of Jesus Christ*, artist's collection, Columbus, Ohio. Used by permission.

Epiphany 2

At Cana Jesus Turns Water into Wine, Vie de Jesus Mafa, 24 rue du Marechal Joffre, 78000 Versailles, France. All rights reserved. Used by permission.

Esperanza Guevara, *Untitled (The Wedding at Cana)*, as reproduced in Philip and Sally Scharper, eds., *The Gospel in Art by the Peasants of Solentiname* (Maryknoll, N.Y.: Orbis Books). Used by permission of Peter Hammer Verlag, Germany.

Epiphany 3

Rembrandt van Rijn, *Christ Preaching*, 1656, bequest of Mrs. H. O. Havemeyer, 1929, the H. O. Havemeyer Collection (29.107.18), The Metropolitan Museum of Art, New York. All rights reserved. Used by permission.

Epiphany 4

Henry Ossawa Tanner, *The Saviour*, c. 1900-1905, gift of Mr. and Mrs. Norman B. Robbins, National Museum of American Art, Smithsonian Institution, Washington, D.C. (Art Resource, N.Y.). Used by permission.

Georges Rouault, *Ecce Homo*, Vatican Museums, Vatican State (Scala/Art Resource, N.Y.). Used by permission of ADAGP/Artists Rights Society, N.Y.

Epiphany 5

Raphael (Raffaello Sanzio), *Miracle of the Fishes*, tapestry, The Tapestry Gallery, Vatican Pinacoteca (Scala/Art Resource, N.Y.). Used by permission.

Tony Festa, *Caring Hands*, © 1994 Tony Festa Photography. Used by permission.

Epiphany 6

Marina Silva, *The Beatitudes*, 1981, as reproduced in Philip and Sally Scharper, eds., *The Gospel in Art by the Peasants of Solentiname* (Maryknoll, N.Y.: Orbis Books). Used by permission of Peter Hammer Verlag, Germany.

Epiphany 7

Marc Chagall, *Joseph Recognized by His Brothers*, c. 1931, Gaby and Curtis Herald in memory of Dr. and Mrs. W. Reichmann, Jewish Museum, N.Y. (Art Resource, N.Y.). © 1993 ARS, New York/ADAGP, Paris. Used by permission.

Bob Galbraith, *L.A. Gang Summit*, 1992 (AP/Wide World Photos, N.Y.). Used by permission.

Transfiguration Sunday

Ivan Kudriashev, *Luminescence*, 1926, The George Costaskis Collection, as reproduced in Edward Weisberger, ed., and Maurice Tuchman, comp., *The Spiritual in Art: Abstract Painting 1890–1955* (New York: Abbeville Press and Los Angeles County Museum of Art, 1986), 175. © 1981 by George Costakis

Byzantine mosaic, *The Transfiguration*, c. 1100, Monastery of Daphni (near Athens), Greece (Erich Lessing/Art Resource, N.Y.). Used by permission.

Ash Wednesday

Aminah Brenda Lynn Robinson, *Give Me Jesus*, as published in *The Teachings: Drawn from African-American Spirituals* (Orlando: Harcourt Brace Jovanovich, 1992). © 1992 by Aminah Brenda Lynn Robinson. Used by permission of Harcourt, Brace and Co.

Ann Marie Rousseau, *A Day in the Life of Darian Moore*, in *Shopping Bag Ladies: Homeless Women Speak About Their Lives* (New York: The Pilgrim Press, 1981). © 1981 by Ann Marie Rousseau. Used by permission.

Seasonal Divider for Lent

Rembrandt van Rijn, *The Return of the Prodigal Son*, 1636, The Hermitage Museum, St. Petersburg, Russia (Scala/Art Resource, N.Y.). Used by permission.

Lent 1

Master LCZ (Lorenz Katzheimer), *Temptation of Christ*, c. 1500/1505, Rosenwald Collection, National Gallery of Art, Washington, D.C. © 1993 National Gallery of Art, Washington, D.C. Used by permission.

An Dong-Sook, *Temptation of Christ*, 1990, as reproduced in Masao Takenaka and Ron O'Grady, eds., *The Bible Through Asian Eyes* (Auckland, New Zealand: Pace Publishing in association with The Asian Christian Art Association, 1991), 91. Used by permission of The Asian Christian Art Association.

Charles Burchfield, *Sun and Rocks*, 1918-50, Albright-Knox Art Gallery, Room of Contemporary Art Fund, Buffalo, New York. Used by permission.

Lent 2

Käthe Kollwitz, *Seed Corn Must Not Be Ground*, © 1993 ARS, New York/VG Bild-Kunst, Bonn, Germany. Used by permission.

Morris Graves, *Hold Fast to What You Have Already and I Will Give You the Morning Star*, 1943, Permanent Collection, University of Oregon Museum of Art, Eugene. Used by permission.

Lent 3

Judith Oelfke Smith, *Jesus Freeing Crippled Woman*, 1993, commissioned. Used by permission.

Jean Antoine Houdon, *St. John the Baptist*, 1767-68, Rome, Galleria Borghese (Ken Lawrence). Used by permission.

Colton Waugh, *Swing Low Sweet Chariot*, c. 1936, Syracuse University Art Collection. Used by permission.

Lent 4

Rob Roth, *Leaving Home*, Carol Bancroft and Friends, Ridgefield, Conn. Used by permission.

Rembrandt van Rijn, *The Return of the Prodigal Son*, 1636, The Hermitage Museum, St. Petersburg, Russia (Scala/Art Resource, N.Y.). Used by permission.

Lent 5

Jacopo and Francesco Bassano, *Christ in the House of Mary, Martha, and Lazarus*, c. 1577, Sarah Campbell Blaffer Foundation, Houston (inv. 79.13). Used by permission.

Jimilu Mason, *The Servant Christ*, Christ House, Washington, D.C. Used by permission.

Palm/Passion Sunday

Christ's Entry into Jerusalem, c. 1150-55, Royal Portal, Chartres Cathedral, France (Foto Marburg/Art Resource, N.Y.). Used by permission.

James Ensor, *Christ Entering Brussels in 1889*, 1888, oil on canvas, 102 1/2" x 169 1/2 ", collection of the J. Paul Getty Museum, Malibu, California (87.PA.96). Used by permission.

Holy Thursday

Tintoretto (Jacopo Robusti), *Last Supper*, Church of San Georgio Maggiore, Venice, Italy (Scala/Art Resource, N.Y.). Used by permission.

Pietro Annigone, *Jesus in the Garden of Gethsemene*, fresco, Santuario di Maria Santissima del Buon Consiglio, Ponte Buggianese (Pistoia), Italy. Used by permission of Edit. Giusti di S. Becocci, Firenze, Italy.

Good Friday

Valentin de Boulogne, *The Taking of Christ*, Juliana Cheney Edwards Collection, Museum of Fine Arts, Boston. © 1994. All rights reserved. Used by permission.

Seasonal Divider for Easter

Paul T. Granlund, *Resurrection II*, cast bronze, 1973, as reproduced in *ARTS Advocate* (UCC Fellowship in the Arts) 12, no. 1 (Winter 1990), cover. Used by permission.

Easter

Paul T. Granlund, *Resurrection II*, cast bronze, 1973, as reproduced in *ARTS Advocate* (UCC Fellowship in the Arts) 12, no. 1 (Winter 1990), cover. Used by permission.

Albert P. Ryder, *Christ Appearing to Mary*, gift of John Gellatly, National Museum of American Art, Smithsonian Institution, Washington, D.C. (Art Resource, N.Y.). Used by permission.

AIDS Memorial Quilt, NAMES Project Foundation, San Francisco, California. Used by permission.

Piero della Francesca, *Resurrection*, late 1450s, Town Hall, Sansepolcro (Scala/Art Resource, N.Y.). Used by permission.

Easter 2

Michael Smither, *Doubting Thomas*, mural, St. Joseph's Church, New Plymouth, New Zealand, as reproduced in Masao Takenaka and Ron O'Grady, *The Bible Through Asian Eyes* (Auckland, New Zealand: Pace Publishing in association with The Asian Christian Art Association, 1991), 91. Used by permission of The Asian Christian Art Association.

Michelangelo Merisi da Caravaggio, *The Incredulity of St. Thomas*, old copy of the original, Uffizi Gallery, Florence (Scala/Art Resource, N.Y.). Used by permission.

Easter 3

Babette's Feast, written and directed by Gabriel Axel, distributed in the U.S. by Orion Pictures Corporation. Photo courtesy of Photofest, New York, N.Y.

Easter 4

The Good Shepherd, c. 250 C.E., in Cubiculum Velatio, Catacomb of Priscilla, Rome (Erich Lessing/Art Resource, N.Y.). Used by permission of Commissione Pontificiale per Archeologia Sacra, Città Vaticano, Italy.

Luke, *Smiling Shepherd*, in JoAnne Taylor, *Innocent Wisdom: Children as Spiritual Guides* (New York: The Pilgrim Press, 1989), illustration #6. Used by permission.

Thomas Hart Benton, *The Lord Is My Shepherd*, 1926, tempera on canvas, 33 1/4" x 27 3/8", collection of the Whitney Museum of American Art, New York. Acq. #31.100. Used by permission.

Easter 5

Choi Hyun-Joo, *Jerusalem*, 1976, in *Children of the World Paint Jerusalem* (New York: Bantam Book, published by arrangement with Keter Publishing House Jerusalem Ltd., 1978). © The Israel Museum, Jerusalem. Used by permission.

Lucas Cranach, *New Jerusalem*, 1522, John Work Garrett Library, The Johns Hopkins University, Baltimore. Used by permission.

Easter 6

Meinrad Craighead, *Lydia*, as reproduced in Miriam Therese Winter, *Woman Word: A Feminist Lectionary and Psalter* (New York: Crossroad, 1992), 200. © 1990 by Medical Mission Sisters. Used by permission.

Abraham Welcoming the Three Visitors, mosaic, c. 547 C.E., Church of San Vitale, Ravenna, Italy (Scala/Art Resource, N.Y.). Used by permission.

Easter 7

Susan McCord, *Random*, quilt, Henry Ford Museum and Greenfield Village, Dearborn, Michigan. Used by permission.

Masaccio, *The Tribute Money*, c. 1427, fresco, Brancacci Chapel, Santa Maria del Carmine, Florence (Scala/Art Resource, N.Y.). Used by permission.

Seasonal Divider for Pentecost (Cycle C)

Jonathan Green, *The Congregation*, 1991, Jonathan Green Studios, Inc., Naples, Fla. Used by permission.

Pentecost

Emil Nolde, *The Pentecost*, 1909, Stiftung Seebüll Ada und Emil Nolde, Neukirchen, Germany. Used by permission.

Unknown artist, *Pentecost*, World Council of Churches, Indonesian Room, Geneva (World Council of Churches Photography). Used by permission.

Trinity Sunday—Pentecost 1

John Biggers, *Shotgun, Third Ward #1*, National Museum of American Art, The Smithsonian Institution, Washington, D.C. (Art Resource, N.Y.). Used by permission.

Pentecost 2

Wu Yuen-kwei, *Her Sins Are Forgiven*, as reproduced in Masao Takenaka and Ron O'Grady, *The Bible Through Asian Eyes* (Auckland, New Zealand: Pace Publishing in association with The Asian Christian Art Association, 1991), 103. Used by permission of The Asian Christian Art Association.

Pentecost 3

Norman Rockwell, *The Golden Rule*, 1961, The Norman Rockwell Museum of Stockbridge, Massachusetts. © The Curtis Publishing Company. Used by permission.

Soumya Mohanty, *No More*, 1992, as reproduced in Hope S. Antone and Yong Ting Jin, eds., *Our Stories, Our Faith* (Hong Kong: World Student Christian Federation, Asia-Pacific Region, 1992), 125. Used by permission.

Pentecost 4

El Greco (Domenikos Theotokopoulos), *St. Martin and the Beggar*, c. 1597-1599, Widener Collection, National Gallery of Art, Washington, D.C. Used by permission.

Jacob Lawrence, *Men Exist for the Sake of One Another. Teach Them Then or Bear with Them*, 1958, National Museum of American Art, Smithsonian Institution, Washington, D.C. (Art Resource, N.Y.). Used by permission.

Pentecost 5

Mary Cassatt, *Margot Embracing Her Mother (Mother and Child)*, 1902, gift of Ms. Aimee Lamb in memory of Mr. and Mrs. Horatio A. Lamb, Museum of Fine Arts, Boston. © 1993 Museum of Fine Arts, Boston. All rights reserved. Used by permission.

S. K. Dutt, *A Frail Baby Enfolded in the Arms of Mother Teresa*, in Malcolm Muggeridge, *Something Beautiful for God: Mother Teresa of Calcutta* (San Francisco: Harper & Row, 1986), 64. Used by permission of Camera Press, London.

Pentecost 6

Jacopo (da Ponte) Bassano, *The Good Samaritan*, c. 1563, National Gallery of Art, London. Used by permission.

Vincent Van Gogh, *The Good Samaritan*, c. 1890, Rijksmuseum Kröller-Müller Stichting, Otterlo, The Netherlands. Used by permission.

Pentecost 7

Pinturicchio, *Amos and the European Sibyl*, detail, Appartamento Borgia, Vatican (Scala/Art Resource, N.Y.). Used by permission.

Jesus of Montreal, written and directed by Denys Arcand, distributed in the U.S. by Orion Pictures Corporation. Photo courtesy of Photofest, New York, N.Y.

Pentecost 8

Orante, fresco, c. 250-300 C.E. Cubiculum Velatio, Catacomb of Priscilla, Rome (Scala/Art Resource, N.Y.). Used by permission.

Albrecht Dürer, *Study of Hands in Adoration*, c. 1509, The Albertina, Vienna (Bridgeman/Art Resource, N.Y.). Used by permission.

Pentecost 9

Still from *Family Filmstrips*, reproduced in Roger Sizemore, *Keeping in Touch* (St. Louis: Christian Board of Publication, 1973), 65. Used by permission.

William Taylor, *Mother and Child*, 1962, artist's collection, as reproduced in David C. Driskell, *Two Centuries of Black American Art* (New York: Los Angeles County Museum of Art/Alfred A. Knopf, 1976), 204.

Pentecost 10

George Segal, *Abraham's Farewell to Ishmael*, sculpture, 1987, Sidney Janis Gallery, New York. © 1994 by George Segal/VAGA, N.Y. Photo courtesy Sidney Janis Gallery. Used by permission.

Pentecost 11

David Roberts, *The Departure of the Israelites*, 1850, Birmingham City Art Gallery, Birmingham, England.

Henry Ossawa Tanner, *The Three Marys*, 1910, Carl Van Vechten Gallery of Fine Arts, Fisk University, Nashville. Used by permission.

Pentecost 12

Phil Borges, *Young Girl with Lily*. Tony Stone Worldwide. Used by permission.

Luca della Robbia, *Singing Boys*, detail, end panel on the *Cantoria*, 1431-1438, marble relief sculpture, Museo dell'Opera del Duomo, Florence, Italy (Erich Lessing/Art Resource, N.Y.). Used by permission.

Jonathan Green, *The Congregation*, detail, 1991, Jonathan Green Studios, Inc., Naples, Fla. Used by permission.

Index of Focus Scriptures

yesterday's
perfume

yesterday's perfume

an intimate memoir of
Paul Bowles

by
Cherie Nutting
with
Paul Bowles

Clarkson Potter/Publishers
New York

Book design by Elizabeth Paul Avedon
with Laura White

Published by Clarkson Potter/Publishers, New York, New York.
Member of the Crown Publishing Group.

Random House, Inc. New York, Toronto, London, Sydney, Auckland
www.randomhouse.com

Clarkson N. Potter is a trademark and Potter and colophon are
registered trademarks of Random House, Inc.

Printed in Japan

Library of Congress Cataloging-in-Publication Data
Nutting, Cherie.
Yesterday's perfume : an intimate memoir of Paul Bowles/by Cherie
Nutting with Paul Bowles.—1st ed.
1. Bowles, Paul, 1910– 2. Authors, American—20th century—
Biography. 3. Composers—United States—Biography.
4. Morocco—Social life and customs. 5. Americans—Morocco—
Biography. I. Bowles, Paul, 1910– II. Title.
PS3552.O874 Z76 2000
813'.54—dc21
[B]   00-042789

ISBN 0-609-60573-9

10 9 8 7 6 5 4 3 2 1

First Edition

for Susan Hannah, whose hand was always in mine

Because we don't know when we will die we get to think of life as an inexhaustible well. Yet everything happens only a certain number of times, and a very small number really. How many more times will you remember a certain afternoon of your childhood? Some afternoon that is so deeply a part of your being that you can't even conceive of your life without it. Perhaps four or five times more, perhaps not even that. How many more times will you watch the new moon rise, perhaps twenty and yet it all seems limitless.

Paul Bowles
The Sheltering Sky

Contents

The Time of friendship

only child

The False Desert   October 1960

My love affair with Morocco dates back to a childhood visit with my mother, a brief excursion on our way to a new life in Spain. The S.S. *Constitution* had docked for a day in Casablanca and the captain encouraged us to see the sights in Rabat. The idea intrigued me—for days I had watched the dark continent making its mighty mark in the featureless space of the Atlantic. At first it was a dim apparition in the nothingness—a trace of what was to come. But in a short time the faint outline took on more definite proportions—the mirage became a real entity, setting fresh boundaries in a world that had once made no distinction between the sky and the glassy sea.

We were accompanied on our tour by a German count who was interested in my mother. I can still smell the spiced aroma of *harira* in the air and remember how all eyes were on my mother's blonde hair as she walked through the Kasbah arm in arm with the count.

On the bus ride back to the ship, looking out of the window through the lens of my Brownie camera, the rusty terrain raced past us and I snapped the shutter. Thinking I had photographed the Sahara Desert I made a vow to return one day when I was grown. I wanted to touch the red earth and feel the barren land on my own.

Long after, I realized that the Sahara was far from the place where I had been at age ten, but I continued to cherish the picture of the false desert that I had snapped. It became one of my most prized possessions—in that mistaken image I felt a new destiny had been born and that my future was somehow contained in that tiny Kodak picture.

The Shell   1970

Ten years later I fulfilled my vow when I returned to Morocco with my friend Stacey Rocklin. In our bell-bottomed jeans we crossed the Strait of Gibraltar reaching Tangier shortly before sunset.

The day before Thanksgiving we were sitting on the beach where I picked up this shell. Stacey had the idea to marry soon but wanted

Passing through the Strait of Gibraltar in 1960, on the deck of the S.S. Constitution. *Below, the false desert.*

to go on to Israel first. I tried to persuade her never to marry and to stay in Morocco and travel with me instead. I felt there was something here for me.

The next day in Marrakech, I met an American and fell in love, and the following day I knew we would be married.

My husband and I returned to Morocco many times. Before our last trip he handed me a book with a message inside: "This book was written for you." It was *The Sheltering Sky,* and he had been right. The book meant everything to me and it accompanied me on all my future journeys—through the eleven years of our marriage and its subsequent end.

I carried the shell, too, until 1987 when I gave it to Paul. I always felt that in some strange way this shell was the beginning of all my future affiliations with Morocco.

Mom and me on the deck of the S.S. Constitution, en route to a new life. Meko, my first husband, and me in our Moroccan Store in Provincetown, Massachusetts, 1970.

artificial flowers

The earth, the wind, and the artificial flowers.

In New York I was bombarded by a series of dream images of birds, knives, fish, and flowers, which came to serve as leitmotifs in my life. In one, an enormous dark bird with smooth black wings and a huge yellow beak came crashing into my left eye.

By this time Paul had become my only hero and in some crazy way these recurring dreams served as an inspiration to write to him about my life and why I felt it was in my destiny that we should meet.

Then one day, the letter came: Paul invited me to visit him in Tangier.

In the fall, Al Dilauro, an artist and close personal friend, suddenly died. The *artificial daffodil* was an emblem throughout his collage work. With this death the frequency and intensity of my dreams increased, prompting me to hurry my plans for my journey to Tangier.

At the funeral his protégé, Charnick, handed me a small silk daffodil and instructed me to place it on Jane Bowles's grave.

"This trip is blessed," he said.

Jane's Grave   Málaga, 1986

I didn't want to meet Paul without first paying tribute to Jane, so I asked for directions to the cemetery in Spain where she was buried. On February 24, 1986, I boarded a plane in search of Jane Bowles's unmarked grave in the Cementerio San Miguel, Málaga. In my hand I carried the artificial daffodil from Al's grave, for Paul a recording by Allen Ginsberg and a tiny crumpled note from Gregory Corso printed in the penciled letters of a child—"Hi Pauley" was all it said. I also brought a photograph of the grave reproduced from the biography of Jane by Millicent Dillon in order to be able to recognize the exact plot.

Finding the plot wasn't easy as the surrounding trees had changed over the years, but I decided it could be in one of two possible locations. On the first site I felt nothing and so made my way toward the other. A wind blew out of nowhere—the earth trembled—my head

Bird dreams beckon me to Morocco.

began to swim, and in "another kind of silence" Jane talked to me and I felt her power. When I finally opened my eyes, returning to the windswept grave, I looked at the ground and noticed a bouquet of white plastic forget-me-nots.

Mechanically placing the artificial daffodil on the ground I picked up the new bouquet and a handful of earth, which I put in a film canister, to bring as gifts to Paul.

The search for Jane's unmarked grave. Below, the City of the Dead.

In "another kind of silence," Jane talked to me and I felt her power.

The Hotel Las Vegas: The Miracle of the Rose

Late that night
I couldn't get the image of the flowers on Jane's earth from my head.

Relaxing in semi-slumber
the daffodil
......dissolved.......

and it was replaced by

the vision of a rose.

fresh meat and roses

Ibn Battitou, the Ferry to Tangier

The Ibn Battitou was just about to depart as I arrived, so I bought a ticket and raced through customs just in time. As the ferry cleaved the deep water a thrill passed through me as Gibraltar slid by in the chilly breeze. It made me think of the first time I sailed these waters in 1960 with my mom.

Soon the Moroccan coast appeared along with Tangier's minaret.

A friend had told me to go to the Hotel Continental. I checked into Room 104, which had a balcony and a perfect view of the port.

That night I dreamed of birds and knives.

Itesa

That night at the Hotel Continental I dreamed of birds and knives. Below and opposite are photos made on the road to Paul's.

In Tangier, finding Paul's home, Immueble Itesa, wasn't easy either, as Paul had given me the old name of his street, Calle Campoamor. I searched and searched but no one knew where the Street of Lovers could be. It was colder now and the sun had slipped behind some clouds. I'd let the taxi go and was getting worried because I had been walking around in circles and had no idea where I was or how to get back to the hotel. As darkness approached drops of rain touched my cheeks and I started to cry. I was sure that I wasn't going to find him. Then just as I was wiping the tears from my eyes I heard a very loud bark. It made me jump. I turned around. Beside a prehistoric old mutt stood Paul Bowles's golden Mustang and I knew I had found the building.

Taking the elevator to a pitch-dark fourth floor I felt my way along the walls to his doorway. I knocked. I waited and knocked again and then finally I heard slow creaking movements from behind the door. It opened on a chain catch and pink light spilled into the hallway. There was an aroma of kif and coriander in the air and the two blue eyes were like kaleidoscopes in the gloom.

"I'm Cherie Nutting."

"Oh," he said. The door slammed shut, which made me a little

The aroma of kif and coriander filled the air and a pink light spilled into the hallway.

worried, but immediately I heard the sound of the chain disengaging and by the time he had unlatched and opened the door again I knew I'd fallen in love.

The moment that I stepped inside the foyer half-filled with old battered suitcases and slipped through the white woolen curtain that led to the salon I felt an extraordinary presence in the room, which struck me with great force. Within these few short moments I knew also that I was changed, and there would be no turning back.

There was a warm fire crackling in the grate. Paul was wearing a red tie with beige brown slacks and sweater. He told me that a French schoolteacher called Robert Briatte was due to arrive for an interview shortly and that he was disappointed that he had to deal with journalists on our first meeting. I told him it didn't matter and that I was just happy to be there. Briatte and his crew soon arrived and the conversation turned to French. I could tell that Paul was exceptionally professional in his dealings with the media, because he immediately appeared to be happy to give the interview, whereas before he had told me that the reason he answered my letter and invited me to visit was precisely because I was neither a journalist nor an assigned photographer. He's had enough of interviews—always being asked the same questions.

I curled up like a cat in front of the fire and took a few photos while Paul imitated Truman Capote and told his life story. It was all new to me as I watched in disbelief—was I really here?

Robert left, making a date to continue in a few days. Paul made me Earl Grey tea with lemon and showed me photographs of Taghit in Algeria, the place where he wrote *The Sheltering Sky*. He lent me his copy of the novel as I thought I'd like to reread it now that I was here. We made a date to meet the following day.

First Date   March 1, 1986

I arrived as arranged at 3:30 P.M. Walking into Itesa I saw an extremely handsome Moroccan carrying an armful of wood. We didn't speak but there was something about him that made him special. I took the elevator to the fourth floor, and as I entered Paul's flat, he followed me. He dumped the wood by the fire. He shook

Abdelouahid holding "the gift."

my hand and then placed his on his heart. I soon found out that this was Paul's driver and most trusted companion, Abdelouahid, whose name means "Slave of Allah" or "Slave of the Unique."

Paul put on his overcoat and sunglasses and we set off to see a building that had collapsed during the night. Standing in front of the ruin he said, "Things gone and things still here."

Mohammed Mrabet

Mrabet was sitting by the *taifor—sebsi* in hand—listening to the *fútbol* game when we walked in. The instant that our eyes met I knew his contained a formidable power. Dark and intense, they concentrated on their subject unblinking and somehow mesmeric. I'd never read his books but the moment he started to perform for me I felt he was like a brother of mine in some former life. He jumped and moved about as he spoke—I liked him because he made me laugh.

"Quién es esta chica delgada morena?"

"Dámela por la noche y tú puedes tenerla por la mañana."

When he finished reciting poetry to me he went out of the room and returned wearing a striped djellaba, and without another word placed a live snail in my hand and left.

Knives   March 6, 1986

After a trip to the market Mrabet came in bringing a bird in a cage, which he put in the study. Before he left he talked of blood and butter . . . slaughtering a sheep and drinking its blood . . . then he invited me to dinner. Paul said I should be honored, for he rarely makes dinner for anyone. So I accepted the invitation for Sunday afternoon at Itesa.

Paul and I spent the evening together, smoking kif and listening to recordings of his Latin American compositions. He showed me books by various photographer friends that he thought I might like. He had autographed books from his friends Cartier-Bresson, Mary Ellen Mark, and numerous others. When I told him of my idea for a photo book on his daily life he took down a volume saying:

"I think this is right up your alley."

It was Peter Beard's *Longing for Darkness.*

Overleaf, Peter Beard made this collage for the book, in memory of Paul.

Driftwood Cove, MONTAUK POINT —
+ a pile of time-capsule-collaged diaries
that burned in my windmill —   P.B.

Peter Beard
Driftwood Cove
Box 603 MONTAUK POINT
Long Island, NY 11954

airmail

To

Mr. Paul J.
2117 Tanger Soc
TANGIER
MORROCCO
north Africa

AIR M

Driftwood Cove, MONTAUK POINT
+ a pile of time-capsule-collaged diaries
that burned in my windmill

SHOUTING ANGRILY, THE W
SURGE OFF IN ALL DIRECT
EACH EAGER TO BE THE F
TO FIND THE RASH INTRU

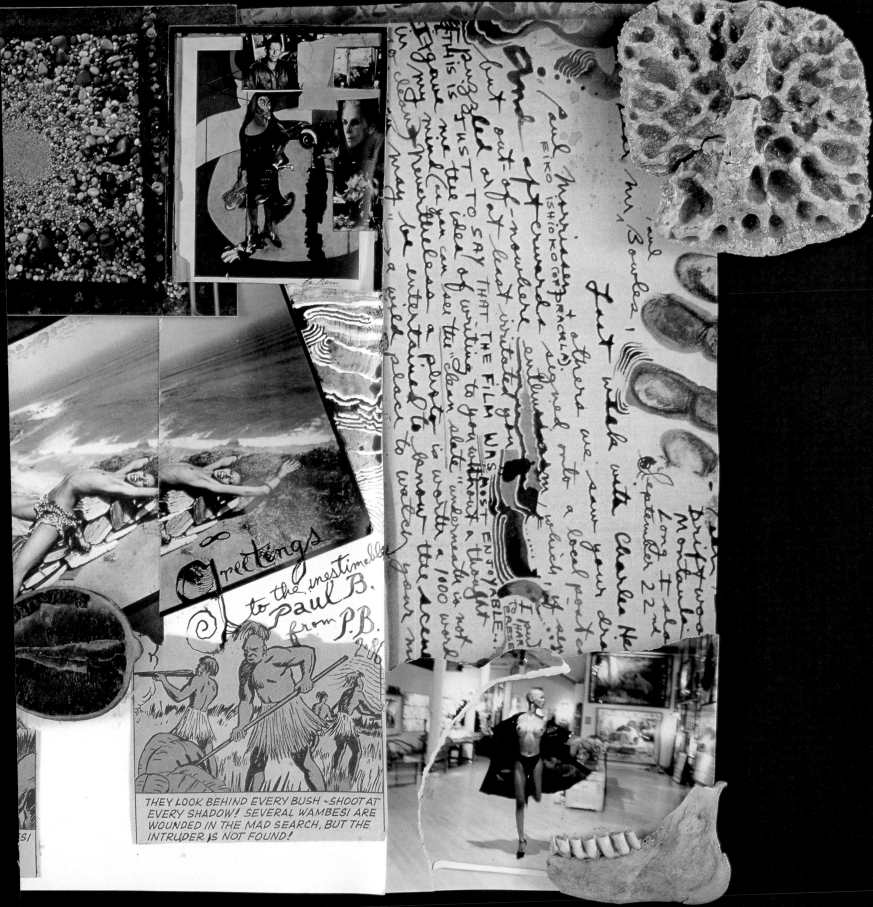

THEY LOOK BEHIND EVERY BUSH - SHOOT AT EVERY SHADOW! SEVERAL WAMBESI ARE WOUNDED IN THE MAD SEARCH, BUT THE INTRUDER IS NOT FOUND!

Greetings to the inestimable paul B. from P.B.

left: from Joe McPhillips
middle: from my mother
right: bought from Ahmed Yacoubi

I asked Paul about the three rings that he wore. One had diamonds and blue stones, which he said was his mother's, and another was three interlocking wedding bands with the inscription "To Libby from Bill Ballard."

"Did Libby really propose to you?" I asked.

"Yes, but I told her I already had a wife."

"Libby was fascinated by daffodils," he reminisced, showing me her silk scarf.

Scarf that once was Libby's.

"What are your favorite possessions?"
He pulled out two very old knives . . . and I remembered my dreams.
One was from the Congo and the other from the Rif Mountains.

HOTEL CONTINENTAL

The Hotel Continental is the oldest hotel in Tangier. It was in a bad way when I lived there for about a month in the early 1950's. There was only one bathroom per floor and there were probably fifteen rooms on each floor, so it was not very comfortable. On the second floor there was no privacy whatsoever because the rooms all gave on to a long balcony. One could walk the length of the terrace looking into every bedroom as one went by.

The Continental had an acceptable dining room on the ground floor where the food wasn't bad. Some of the waiters from that time are now working at the Hotel Minzah, so when I go there they remember me and we reminisce briefly about the old Continental.

Paul Bowles

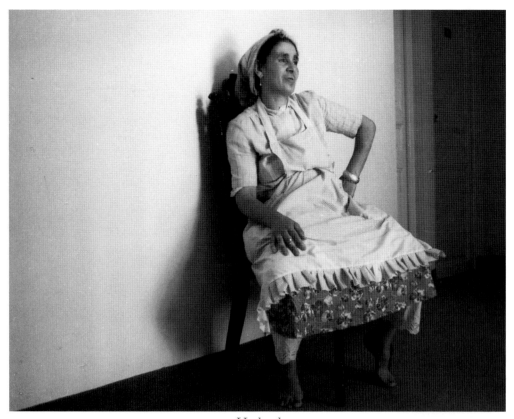

Hadoosh

Jimmy

Tifo

THE HOTEL CONTINENTAL *opened in 1888 when, as a study of the retaining structures from the terrace shows, the sea came right up to the base of the walls. Since its heyday as the town's premier hotel it has also been used by smugglers attracted by such convenience. Presently being renovated to its former glory it still retains an air of raffish charm, which makes it for me the most agreeable of all Tangier's hotels. Paul lived here for a while and it was one of the locations used by Bertolucci for* The Sheltering Sky. *Managed by Abdeslam and his brother, Tifo Chatt, the owners and employees treat each guest as if they were cherished family.*

The Owners

JIMMY'S
WORLD FAMOUS
PERFUMERIE

PATRONISED BY
FILM STARS AND
THE INTERNATIONAL
JET SET

Old Photo of Mohamed V

Abdeslam

Paul seemed always to be tapping his fingers and whistling a secret tune.

Jane's parrot died and she had asked Cherífa to bury it here.
We didn't find the grave and Paul thinks that Cherífa threw it in the garbage.

Every day in the afternoon, we'd go to the market of Fès.

"I hope I don't remind you of a dead chicken," he said, and then he told me he loved roses.
So I bought him a blood-red bouquet.

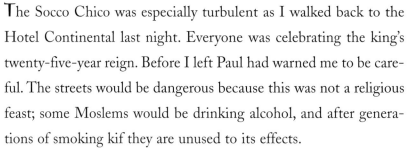

The Socco Chico was especially turbulent as I walked back to the Hotel Continental last night. Everyone was celebrating the king's twenty-five-year reign. Before I left Paul had warned me to be careful. The streets would be dangerous because this was not a religious feast; some Moslems would be drinking alcohol, and after generations of smoking kif they are unused to its effects.

The next day Robert Briatte was to return with his crew to finish the interview at Cap Spartel where Paul was first inspired to write *Let It Come Down.* I arrived at 4 P.M. and Paul's eyes still twinkled when he answered the door elegantly dressed in a tweed jacket, sweater vest, and tie, each in differing shades of gray. He realized that he still had on funky Moroccan red slippers so he changed them for a pair of chic black pointed Moroccan shoes.

"It's hard to find subtle and well-made Moroccan slippers anymore," he said, "because Moroccans are sadly switching to Western clothing and the tourists all want gaudy styles. The young are wearing blue jeans instead of traditional dress. Proletarian attire," he sniffed.

He had a bad back today. At the last moment I'd bought a packet of cigarettes.

"How did you know that I'd had no time to pick up cigarettes today?"

Briatte and his crew arrived and after the trip to Cap Spartel the interview resumed in the apartment. Paul didn't smoke kif today as he usually does at about this time. Instead he waited until the four-hour interview was over. I watched his face, his movements, and every inflection through the lens of my Nikon. It wasn't what he was saying that held my attention as much as the complete charm of his general demeanor. We all moved toward the doorway. Paul said goodnight to the crew and then he took my arm and pulled me aside.

"When shall I see you again?" he said.

"Whenever you wish."

"Good, then come tomorrow at three for tea. And before the hippies come we'll go to the Old Mountain."

KODAK TX 5063   KODAK TX 5063

▷27A   28   ▷28A   29   ▷29A

It wasn't what Paul said that
captured my attention so much as
the complete charm of his demeanor.

45

The Secret Closet of Smells

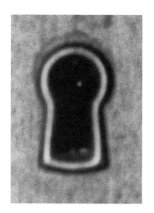

Had an appointment to meet Paul at 3:30 today so I could take pictures of him in his study. But first we sat in the salon for a while, with Paul in his usual high-back cushioned chair. I asked him if he had anything that had belonged to Jane and he showed me a beautiful scarf from Paris, black but shot through with golden flecks. I took it and held it to my face.

"Why does this scarf smell so good?" I asked.

"I don't know," he replied.

I asked him how it was when Jane was so ill, and his eyes became dim and distant. He told me in a quiet voice that her sixteen years of illness had made him ill too and that sometimes he wanted to take his own life. He didn't because he realized that this would hurt her more and so went on living for her. I'd always wanted to ask him if he'd lived for Jane—now I realized I didn't have to.

There was a moment's silence and then he added that some people seem to have the false impression that Jane was crazy.

"She wasn't crazy. She was simply very ill and couldn't write, so of course she was depressed—but she wasn't crazy."

She was so ill for so long and could only rise above it in the increasingly infrequent periods of remission. He also suspected that Cherífa was slipping something into Jane's food in order to control her mind and get her money.

Without notice he got up from his seat and left the room, returning with a bundle of old keys. He opened a cabinet set into the wall of the room, which turned out to be a secret closet full of smells—perfumes that he'd collected from all around the world. There was one aroma which I really loved that came from Thailand, and even a perfume for embalming the dead. (I'd often wondered where the elusive perfumed scent in the room had come from.) He told me that he and Jane didn't connect right away because initially she wasn't very nice to him. He added that she was one of those people who picked you up and took you somewhere, and if you didn't like it—then you didn't like her. It wasn't her prettiness that attracted him, he said, rather her alertness.

First Kiss

Then we went into the study. He picked up a mask which he lifted to his face. I snapped away with my camera, and when he removed the mask we kissed.

Afterward he showed me more of his favorite things.

Just before I left he gave me perfume from Bangkok and he sat with his back toward me while I took a snip of his hair.

The kif after it has been cut.

Fresh kif from the mountains.

This Place of Fire

During the days that followed Paul and I spent most afternoons and evenings together. Each day we drove by the now-familiar route to the post office and the Fès market and then back to Itesa for cookies and tea. We had fireside chats with his Casa Sports cigarettes lined up on the hearth, all emptied and refilled with kif *msouss*, which means "kif with little or no tobacco," or as the Moroccans would say, "with no spice." We talked about everything, from mothers and fathers and only children (as we both were), to his typhoid and how the penicillin he'd been given to treat him in England had been left over from the war. This caused a temporary paralysis in one leg, and he was delirious when they brought him to the hospital. He told me about having pneumonia in Morocco and how, to reduce the fever, they placed him in excruciatingly painful tubs of ice. He played me all kinds of music and introduced me to many new composers and authors.

The box full of magic.

49

Paul's Studio Mate

Mrabet has eleven birds which he keeps on the roof of his apartment in town. He had about thirty but twenty-three died from a draft.

He says that he loves "Animals . . . plants and a good woman."

This bird came to Paul's today because he is a loner. The bird had a trauma when he was very young and was hit on the head. So now, although he will make love with a "woman bird," when she tries to build a nest he throws her out and destroys the home.

The bird sings all day long at Paul's
And Paul whistles back to him.

One afternoon we
talked about Jane

THE CHERÍFA PLANT

In the spring of 1948 I was here in Tangier with Jane. I think she was enjoying herself but there seemed to be another way of making her enjoy herself more intensely and that was to introduce her to a person that my friend Boussif had told me about. He said there was a wild girl selling grain in the market and he found her very interesting; he sometimes had lunch with her. I got Jane to meet Boussif who was not Moroccan but Algerian, and eventually he invited Jane to come to his house for lunch. He was married to a Moroccan girl and they had a formal sort of meal. Afterward he went out and left the two girls together and Jane began talking to her. "What do you do all the time? Do you go out?"

"No it's forbidden. I can't go out. My husband won't allow it." That was a common state of affairs in those days. It's only fifty years ago but still, things do change. Jane said, "But what do you do here?" and the girl said, "I sit here all day bored." Jane said, "That's a very bad thing. You mustn't do that. I think you should go out and see the world a bit. It's not good for you to sit here all by yourself all day and never see anyone else."

The girl agreed. But the next week Boussif seemed annoyed
and said he had seen his wife pack up all her things and
leave the house, not just go out, but leave him, leave
everything; and he was rather upset about that. But I don't
think he realized that it was Jane's doing. As it was she
escaped a very boring matrimonial life.

Boussif also introduced Jane to the "wild girl" whose name
was Cherífa, and Jane bought a bottle of whisky and arranged
to go and see her in her home. I remember that because I
went too and it was boring for me because I don't drink and
everyone was getting drunk fast. So I decided to leave and
go back to the hotel, but of course Jane stayed on drinking
whisky; and Cherífa was completely drunk.

Cherífa soon realized that she had Jane on a hook and she
could throw her around as though she were a fish. Jane asked
Cherífa to come and stay with her in the house that I had
bought in the medina and where I was not living, but Cherífa
wouldn't go there. It took a long time, maybe two years,
before she agreed to spend the night. Jane was getting more
and more nervous about it. And then Cherífa said she wanted
Jane to buy her a taxi, which was an absurdity. Jane asked,
"You want to be a taxista?" and Cherífa said, "Yes, yes,"

but I don't think she really understood. Anyway she didn't get a taxi.

From the beginning, I had an unfavourable impression of Cherífa. She was too much interested in the effects of alcohol. She was really a drunk, but of course being a Moslem she couldn't admit that she ever drank to anyone she knew except for her little group of friends. This group included the wife of a well known gangster who was in jail at the time for killing his brother.

Little by little I realized that she was extremely eccentric. If you saw her in the street, she looked like any other Moroccan woman, covered with a veil. But when she came inside she would take off her veil and djellaba and one saw that she wore blue jeans underneath. In the pocket of her jeans she had a switchblade knife which she loved to bring out very rapidly and show how she could use it. I thought she was rather sinister. She said, "I'm not afraid of walking about anywhere at any hour because I can deal with any man with my switchblade. I know how to use it."

Of course I had been told by Boussif that Cherífa was a wild girl, and she looked the part. She had black hair and tried to wear it up, but it wouldn't stay. So she had

tresses behind her and it made her look wilder. She wasn't
bad looking in the beginning but she soon outgrew her good
looks and became something else, what with all the alcohol.
She meant to look masculine.

There was another woman called Tetum, selling dry goods in
the same market as Cherífa. (They had little huts big enough
to sit in but not to stand. They'd sit inside while the buyer
sat outside in the street.) Tetum was very ugly, which Cherífa
wasn't—then—and she had a heavy moustache. Jane was always
attracted by fairly unlovely looking women and this one was
particularly unattractive. Jane was fascinated by her.

Cherífa was probably always hostile to me but I didn't
know it. Much later in the story, she came to live here in
Itesa as a servant, and she also hired other servants so she
commanded the whole house in apartment fifteen below. I was
living there with Jane some of the time. For me life became
impossible, there were too many of them and they were up all
night, laughing and shrieking. Whenever Cherífa wanted something she would clap her hands and say, "Bring me a bottle
of whisky or vodka." So I moved up here to apartment twenty.

One day Cherífa threatened to attack me. Jane and I had
bought a large climbing plant and we had it on the terrace

of number fifteen. So I went down to get the plant. It was in a huge pot and I got it as far as the kitchen. There, Cherífa stopped me and said, "You're the snake around here," and I replied, "I don't know what you're talking about. I'm going to take this plant upstairs." "No, the plant stays here," she declared. She was very firm and belligerent. Then she lunged at me with two fingers of her right hand spaced so that each would go into a different eye, and as I only had two eyes I backed up and left her there. She was guarding the plant like a mother hen with her chicks. When I came upstairs Mrabet was here. I said to him, "I can't get the plant because Cherífa won't let me and I don't want my eyes

Borght for Jane in Marrakech

gouged out or have scratches all over me because of her fingernails. Mrabet said, "I'll go down and get it." "Yes, but be careful." And he did get it, paying no attention to Cherífa. I was of course very pleased. Then he said, "We have to get another jar bigger than the one it's in and some extra earth and give it more room. The roots are coming right out of the top of the dirt." A few days later he got a large terracotta jar. He dug around the edge and lifted the plant out to put in the new receptacle. But along the roots at the bottom of the old jar were strange things. I couldn't really make out what they were because of the dirt. My maid was horrified. "Don't touch it," she warned, as though it were a cobra. But I did touch it because I wanted to know what it was. It turned out to be just a lot of fingernails and hair mixed up with rags. Mrabet wouldn't touch it, so I picked it up and dropped it in the toilet.

The reason Cherífa wanted to keep the plant was that she was using it as a kind of informer. She would speak to it and tell it what she wanted from Jane. She believed that when she communicated her orders through the leaves of the plant, her words went in the roots. Cherífa spent a lot of time every night on her knees beside Jane whispering into her ear when she slept, saying things like "I need 50,000 francs tomorrow morning first thing." Of course Jane would have it in her mind when she woke up and it worked every time. "Oh, I have to give Cherífa 50,000 francs," she would say. "But Jane you gave her 100,000 francs yesterday," I'd reply. "You keep out of this. It's not your business," Jane would say to me. Cherífa just glared at me. She knew she was going to have her way. When she lost the plant it was very bad for her as it weakened her power. At the time the plant was discovered, Jane was in the hospital in Málaga. Cherífa had to keep the set-up intact because she knew Jane would return in spite of her doctor, who advised me not to bring her back to Tangier. But Jane begged me to bring her back here, so I did, but then it went very badly. She had several strokes.

Jane's original trouble came while I was in Kenya, and I didn't know anything about it. I had to take a ship which went around the Cape of Good Hope, around South Africa and up on the Atlantic side. It took a long time, so I didn't hear about it until much later when I disembarked in Tenerife, in the Canary Islands. The telegram said that Jane had had a slight stroke—minimizing its importance. When I

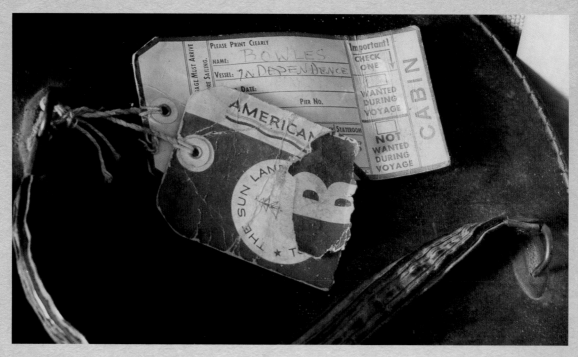

Relics from the Age of Travel

got back to Tangier, Jane was living at the Bonnet House on the edge of the cliff. She wasn't making sense. She had aphasia and she was saying up for down, hot for cold, so it was very difficult to know what she was talking about. It was very disturbing to see her that way because I didn't know if things would get better. Little by little they got a bit better but not much.

The doctor said that Jane must at all costs get away from Cherífa because she was a bad influence; and that was the only thing that Jane did not want to do. Cherífa mixed up the medicines and made her worse. I asked the doctor whether she felt that Jane's state was due to having imbibed something that Cherífa might have concocted and she said, "It's quite possible. I've been practicing medicine for eighteen years in Morocco and I've seen many analogous cases, so I don't put it beyond possibility. The important thing is to get her away from Cherífa, now." But that's what I couldn't do. Finally I had to take her, along with a psychiatrist from the mad house here in Beni Makada, over to Málaga and get her into a hospital. It was an awful job because we got to the hospital after dark and the nuns refused to open the door. Jane and I had to go to a hotel. There, she tried to jump out of the window several times and the psychiatrist had to battle with her. Jane returned to Morocco only once after that.

In 1973, Jane died in Málaga, and after that I had no more contact with Cherífa. In 1992, I believe, I had word that Cherífa had also died. But in 1996 Jennifer Burchwill, who was making a film here, looked for her and found her alive. This enabled Jennifer to make photographic sequences in which Cherífa denied accusations of sorcery with regard to Jane. She looked like herself in the film although more than two additional decades of alcoholism had taken their toll.

Jane's notebook.

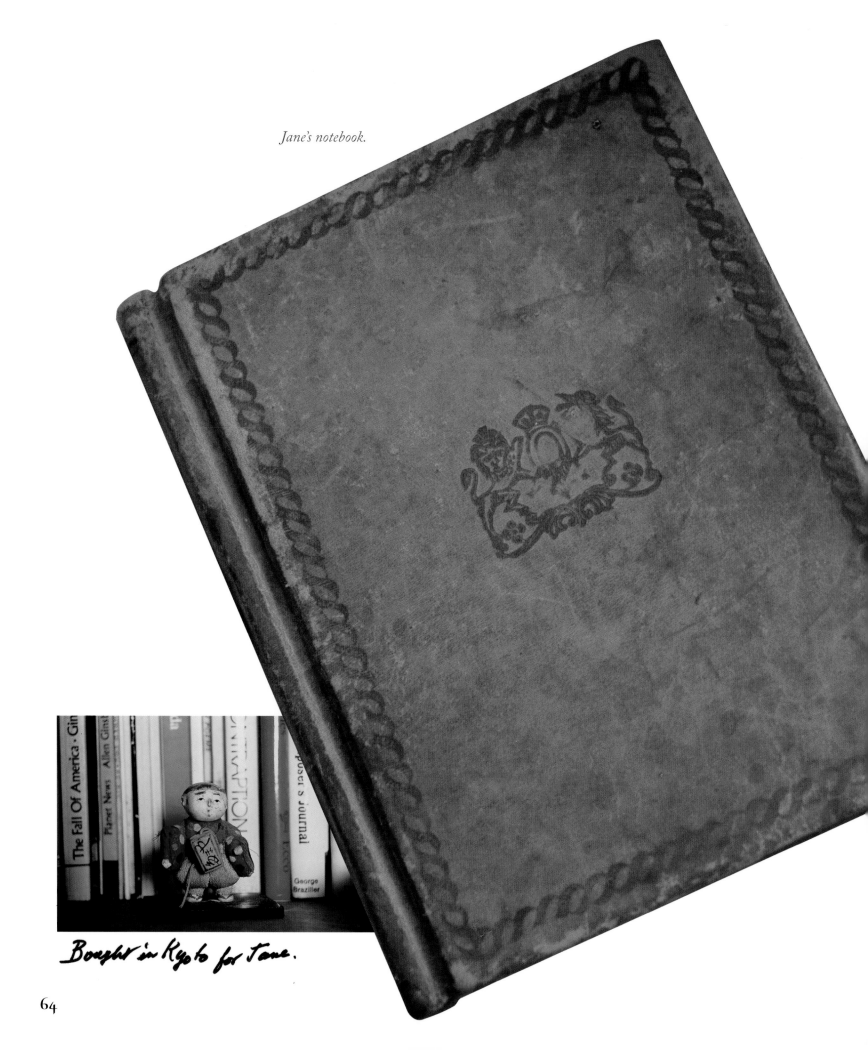

Bought in Kyoto for Jane.

He corn.

tturls and a quiet country.

Face –

Jennifer – Madeline – She
seems to move in an afternoon light –
a Brilliantly lighted cold afternoon –
Just Before sunset – the melancholy
gold gold color of hay fields from
(another) time – an earlier time but
seen in our day –: Part of our time –
the corn – But not the light – –
the double heart – Not a drama.
But Both Families – the final
Painful – experience – there
must Be no more –– Pain like
this – death – is better – than
a long murder – the murder
of a life –. the murder of a life –

Last Day

I went to Itesa to get a few last shots of Paul. He stood by the big picture window and posed with his cigarette, his face wreathed with the swirling smoke.

We took our walk, and I asked two questions. Later, he wrote his answers on the borders of the photos.

"If you were an animal what would you be"?

A cat or a macaw.

... "describe yourself in 3 words":

I am here.

sliver moon

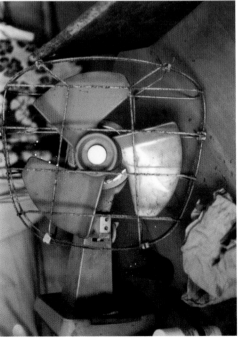

Aunt Adelaide's bonbonnière
(stolen while I was in Alabama.)

Awoke to the call of the *muezzin* and screaming cocks. Rolled over and went back to sleep. While the sun moved across the sky I had the strangest dream of interplanetary flight. When I next awoke there were bites on my neck which left dark scratches.

In the late afternoon I went to Itesa after buying my usual bouquet of roses for Paul. He was looking gorgeous in cream-colored pants, socks, and shoes and a wild print shirt from Ceylon. Paul asked me to bring him a copy of *Night Without Sleep*—he had never heard it. We sat and listened to this recording of his music, and the room seemed odd with an empty fireplace.

The next day I met Mrabet, who also had two dark scratches on his neck. He was thrilled to see me and grabbed me and without warning gave me a kiss on the forehead.

I threw an M&M into the air and caught it in my mouth. Paul and Mrabet both laughed. *"Atini busa m'neinick,"* said Mrabet and he kissed my right eye and then left.

Paul on M&M's: " I suck the first layer of candy coating then turn the chocolate and divide the nut into four pieces. I stick three in my cheek and nibble each portion one at a time. I do this without thinking."

Insomnia

Paul uses *"Quies"* earplugs and a mask to sleep. After a little kif before bedtime he locks himself in his bedroom. His bed has to face the north and he finds it

The fan Paul referred to as "fan #1."

Paul listens to the recording of Night Without Sleep *for the first time.*

necessary to sleep on his right side. The window must always be slightly ajar and covered by a thick black drape. On the table by Paul's bed I once accidentally touched a coat hanger and he almost had a heart attack. An old fan lies on its side precariously balanced in a lopsided fashion on a board that leans on a box and everyone is forbidden to touch it. The fan is attached to a hanger, which is arranged so that it oscillates at a tone and a frequency that drowns out the sound of barking dogs, which would otherwise keep him awake. It is Paul's greatest fear that the fan would be moved and this carefully arranged balance destroyed, making sleep impossible.

Desk chaos, 1986

74

THE PASSPORT

Ahmed and I were invited one afternoon by the brother of
Justin Daranayafala, who was the curator of the Dehiwala
zoo. I had expressed a great desire to see the tiger cubs.
He brought them out. Of course they were beautiful, a little
larger and heavier than full grown cats, and with enormous

paws, already capable of doing damage with their claws, which they kept politely sheathed. Indeed, their behaviour was impeccable throughout the meeting. It was hard to believe that one was holding and caressing a real Bengal tiger. Presently our host announced that he was willing to sell the couple, and for a reasonable price: $800 for the two, brother and sister. I was tempted, but quickly realized that travelling with tigers, even in their infancy, would present insurmountable problems. And when they grew up, what would one do with them? It would be worse than what Sir Michael Duff was faced with, when he purchased a young elephant and took it home to Wales. An elephant can be managed if it has a wise mahout with it always, but two adult tigers would present problems.

Perhaps the pleasure of holding and stroking these two innocuous babes helped to diminish Ahmed's instinctive sense of dread. Clearly he knew tigers were dangerous beasts, but when we got to Mysore and had the Maharaja's tiger fields to ourselves, he seemed to forget what he knew, and let what he felt direct his actions. He remembered the handfuls of soft fur, and since this had been his only tactile contact, the tiger became a friendly animal. At all events, he came per-

I had always thought it would be a great pleasure to own an island and live on it. Consequently, when I had the opportunity of ... Taprobane off the south co... immediately ... on the p... the site a year earlie... the beauty of the o... of tropical vegetation... house in its midst...

Talvande, who co... place, a botanist and ... sible for the handsome ... Peradeniya, near Kandy. T... (died) was ... place to wor...

TAPROBANE
EEN DROOM DOOR WATER VAN DE WERKELIJKHEID GESCHEIDEN

"Het gekras van kraaien in de heilige boom tegenover het eiland is de wekker die Gunadasa op doet staan om onze thee-op-bed te bereiden. Elke dag verschijnt hij vanachter het kamerscherm en roept met een gorgige stem: 'Good-morning-Master-tea-Master!' Verkwikt door twee, drie kopjes sterke Tangana-thee en een paar schijven witte ananas, doe ik mijn dagelijkse ronde om het eiland, die meestal eindigt op een stenen bank vanwaar je een prachtig uitzicht hebt over de baai van Weligama. Hoewel de zon nog maar net over de landtong in het oosten komt kijken, geeft hij al een indringende, krachtige hitte. Een vloot van vissersprauwen glijdt langs de witte lijn van het rif naar de open zee; de geheven zeilen zijn van de ruimtemes zeilen...

for Chérie:
This all took place in
Trivandrum, Galle and finally
Madrid in the autumn of 1952.
Long ago.
Paul

... the shore there wa... ... sea sounds ... ... was hot, ... high, and ... ... Weligama Bay ... sitting on a bench on the cliff, watching the sunrise. Then ... early tea was served me in bed. Breakfast came about... some...

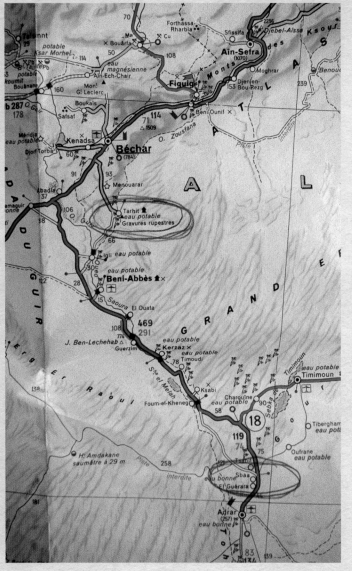

ilously close to losing his life as a result.

I believe that the Maharaja had consulted Hagenbeck in designing the topography of his zoo. The tigers had a large tract of land at their disposal, and there was no wall to enclose them. The outside was protected from the inside by a deep dry moat, into which the animals were careful not to fall. There was a low white building which served as a bridge across the ditch. It had metal rings up the side, and Ahmed was quick to climb to the top. It was a flat roof with no railing. Three tigers became aware of his presence and came rushing down the hill. I assume it was from that roof that the attendant tossed their

food down to them, for they were in a state of great excitement. They leapt and roared again and again, and their huge
claws scraped the wall. When Ahmed saw how close they came
to his feet as he stood at the edge he seemed to have
dropped into a state of hypnosis, and might have fallen
either backward or forward. I began to shout, "Don't move!"
This may have brought him back to reality, as he began to
move away from the edge. The roaring and leaping went on,
even after he climbed down to the ground. Later he was not
eager to discuss the incident.

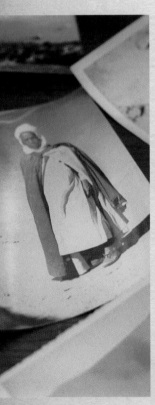

The Aid el Kebir

I kissed Paul through the crack in the door today and two cats tried to slip in with the kiss.

"Too many visitors in summers—no time to be alone with Paul," I groaned.

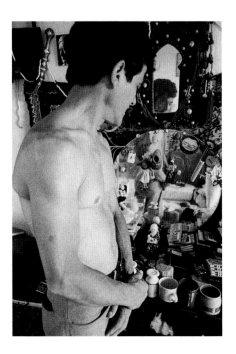

"Will you still love me . . . when?" he sang.

And then I was lucky, no one arrived and we sat listening to the romantic music of his friend Samuel Barber. Listening with eyes half shut I curled up on the floor with a pillow on the rug.

We laughed about some of the odd visitors that had come and he showed me snaps of William Burroughs posing with arrows, bows, and guns.

A dark night and the drums were beating as I finished the chapter in *The Spider's House* on the Aid el Kebir. I awoke at 2 A.M. and they seemed louder, and as I slipped back to sleep I began to dream. . . , the moon hung big and yellow in the black night. In a pure white mist two translucent dotted multicolored figures danced, their heads uniting into one. When the heads joined together I suddenly became self-conscious and woke up.

The next day I was invited with Paul to dinner at the home of his French translator, Claude-Nathalie Thomas. We were greeted by a pair of dalmatians dancing in unison round our feet.

"Watch out, or you'll wake up," said Paul.

That evening, sipping sherry, Paul named me "Jerez de la Frontera."

Sliver Moon

There's a hot dusty wind blowing through the city and the shutters of the hotel bang in the wind. An English girl screams in the night. She thinks her companion is dead, but it's just a false alarm. I eventually fall into a deep sleep and when I awake I have a big mosquito bite under my right eye.

Paul had his portrait done today by Claudio Bravo so I went to Mrabet's apartment in Ankatouit and took shots of him with his favorite things. The walls were hung with knives, several Brion Gysin paintings, and a stuffed panda from Gibraltar. When I asked what his favorite thing of all was, he picked up his collection of money from various countries and caressed the notes. He showed me his canaries and I took a photo of a newborn bird lying feebly in the nest. It had been born with a sick leg.

We went for dinner at Mrabet's with a man from the BBC. I photographed Paul and Mrabet both dressed in white. Paul's suit was the one he bought to wear to Libby Holman's performance of *Yerma*. Mrabet also has a mosquito bite under his right eye. He gave me a painting of a heart with a knife. When we left Paul and I walked down the slanting road that led to the parked Mustang.

"Where is the moon?" I asked.

And Paul found the moon for me.

The Letter

I decided not to go to Paul's for a day or so. That Sunday, taking a break from rereading *The Spider's House*, I went down to the port for food. When I returned, Abdeslam, the concierge, had a big envelope for me, which he handed over with reverence.

"A very famous man come here and he leaves this for you."

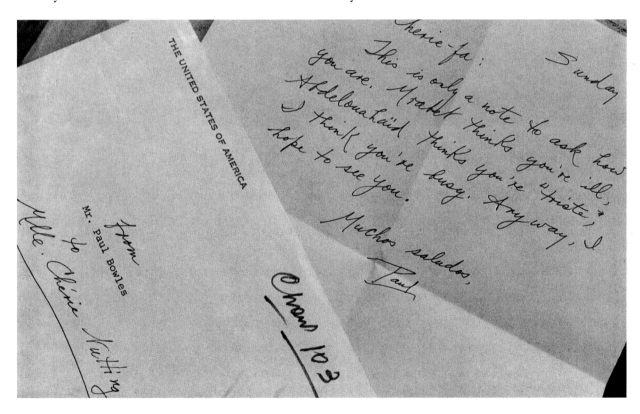

That afternoon I went to Itesa with three red roses.

Paul was listening to his music and the voice was wailing "You can't stop death," the shades were drawn and the light was dim. He looked up and said: "Mrabet said that Abdelouahid must have made you angry. Abdelouahid said that it must have been Mrabet who made you sad."

"No, I thought you might be sick of me by now so I thought I'd give you all a vacation."

"Well, I wanted to take you to Asillah on Friday, but you didn't come, so I went without you."

That night I dreamed of Paul in a fetal position on a woman's lap and he seemed ill.

Abdelouahid's Country House

August 21, 1986

Today, Paul, Abdelouahid, his son Mohammed, and I drove toward Ksar el Seghir on the Mediterranean coast. First we stopped at the post office and collected letters from Gore Vidal, Allen Ginsberg, and William Burroughs.

We took the coastal route, passing an old fortress on our way, toward Djebel Moussa, which is the Moroccan counterpart to the Rock of Gibraltar. Abdelouahid's house sat on a hill at the end of a dusty trail in Farsioua. It was surmounted by turrets and surrounded by fig trees. Kaftans hung from the whitewashed adobe walls and opaque white curtains waved gently in the breeze. Paul and I ate fresh figs and drank tea while I read him the letter from Gore Vidal lamenting Gysin's death. On the terrace overlooking the sea we smoked kif.

Looking at Paul's zany red shirt I became dizzy. "Do you hear that sound, Paul?"

"What sound?"

"That crazy ringing?"

"Oh—that sound," he said. "I often hear crazy sounds in my ears and I figured that it was just me."

So we listened to the strange music in our ears, smoked more kif, and watched the fog roll across the strait from Spain.

Feast of L'aachor

We went into the medina with Abdelouahid to see the festival of *L'aachor*, when each child is given a drum. Paul likes this fiesta because the streets are arrayed the way they were in Tangier of the 1930s when he first arrived. Row upon row of candy, food, and magic stalls. A man pushed Paul and his leg hurt. He almost fell but I grabbed him. The man was trying to pick Paul's pocket but Abdelouahid managed to prevent him.

Later, after a trip to the market by car, he let me feel a lump behind his knee. Abdelouahid says it's *nada* but it didn't seem like nothing to me.

Paul's Sick Leg

On my last day we took a trip to the Old Mountain to test Rodrigo Rey Rosa's camera, but Paul's leg hurt so we went home. I was sad all day. Mrabet said he was sick too. Paul gave me a little book of drawings by Yacoubi. "This all happened long ago," he said.

He also gave me his shirt that still preserved his scent.

Later I returned to Itesa with roses to say a last goodbye. Paul could barely walk. He looked pale and drawn. "Sorry to be ill on your last day."

Paul's leg was getting colder and colder—and I decided there and then not to fly in the morning.

I fell asleep that night in Paul's shirt. I had a wild dream where I was fishing in a boat. The fish turned into birds and one struck me in the right eye as it took off. In the morning Paul's leg was worse. He wouldn't leave Morocco and wouldn't go to the Spanish Hospital as Joe McPhillips advised. He was afraid that if he left he'd never get back in the country, or leave the Spanish Hospital alive. I felt his foot, it was cold and blue.

Eventually I decided to go to the American consulate. Paul thought that no one would be able to help but it was my only hope. Straightaway the consulate called a hospital in Slâ (Sale) and arranged for Paul to be admitted at once.

The day before Paul's leg got sick.

We packed and set off for Slâ within a few hours. Paul seemed worried but composed, meticulously dressed in his gray tweed jacket, his hair slicked back with pomade.

We checked Paul in at the Clinique Beausejour and Abdelouahid and I found a hotel.

I didn't sleep all night.

Sooner or later
one comes to this.

87

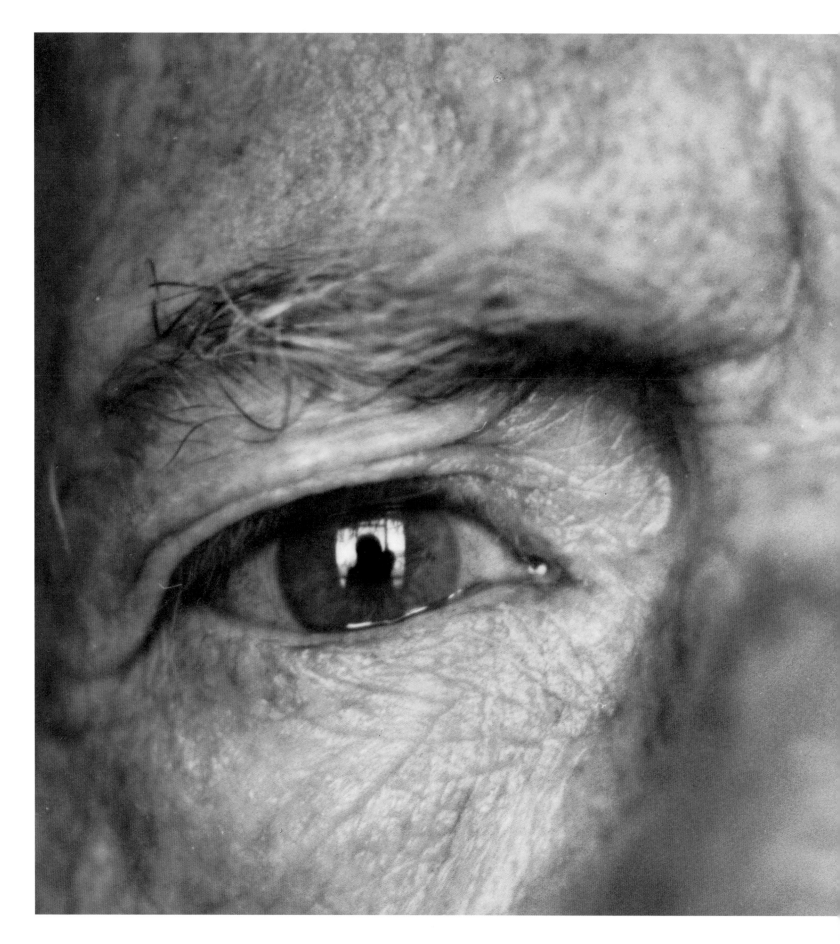

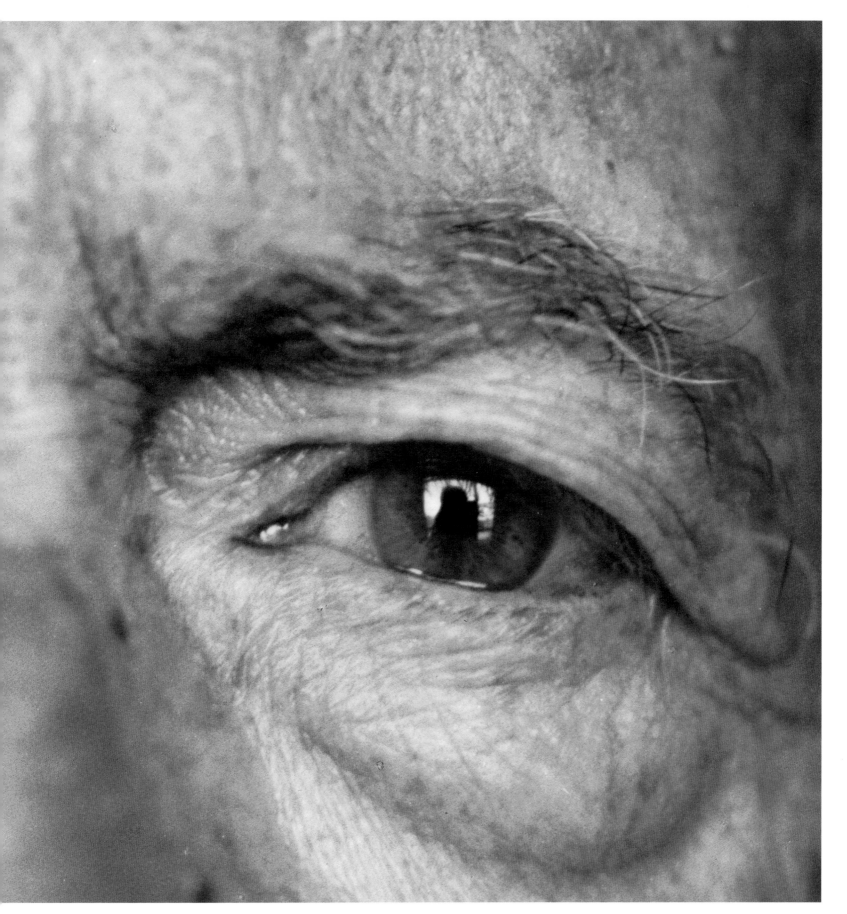

I saw myself reflected in his eyes 89

Back in Tangier I took refuge in Paul's shirt.

Under the Knife in Slâ

Alone with Abdelouahid in Paul's room I began to cry.

"Don't cry—*la vida es asi*—it's a sin to cry," he said.

Later Paul was wheeled in on a stretcher. He opened his eyes and said in Arabic "ana aaish" and then in Spanish "Estoy vivo"—I'm alive.

"I love you," I said and he closed his eyes and smiled.

The room was very dark and for eight hours Abdelouahid and I watched Paul toss and turn. He looked beautiful, like a recovering bird.

The next day Paul had a terrible headache. As I massaged his head he told me of his dream as he was coming round from the anaesthetic.

Last day

My tears fell like rose petals all over Paul's hands.

And Mrabet tickled me so I could laugh.

And I elbowed Paul's wound and he cried, "Ouch."

"You'll be back," Paul said.

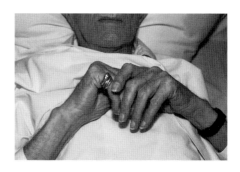

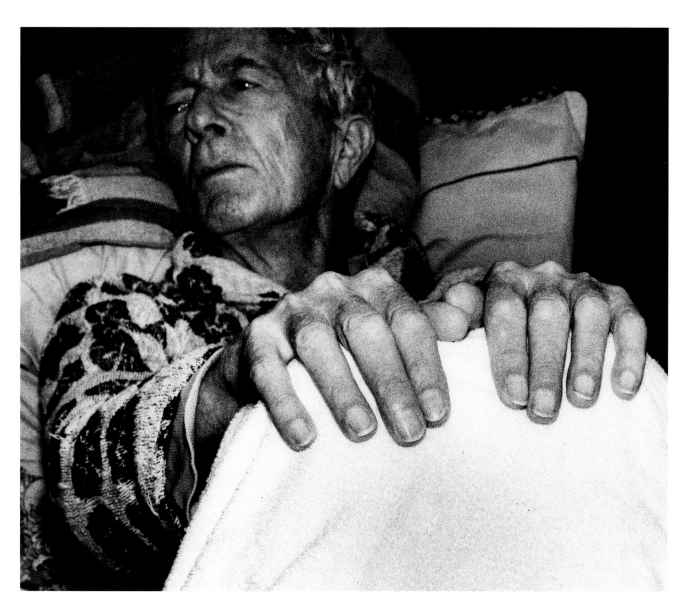

Last view.

2

Beside the Strait

charchumbo

Dust on
Her Tongue

Rodrigo Rey Rosa

TRANSLATED BY
PAUL BOWLES

EPIGRAM

Rodrigo Rey Rosa

Like all true artists, he knows the value of work. His activity is propelled by an understanding and love of the natural forces with which he is in touch. It could be said that the rain forest of Peten is for him what the Faubourg Saint-Germain was for Proust.

Paul Bowles

Return

As I boarded the Royal Air Maroc plane for Tangier there were rose petals on the floor of the entranceway.

When I arrived, it was a moonless Tangerine night and the rain came down in buckets.

The following day I went to Paul's carrying multicolored roses and wearing crazy plastic teeth, which held a mouse between them that dripped blood. Paul's face filled with horror as I tried to kiss him. I was glad to be back. That night on the hotel balcony flashes of lightening bounded across the moonless sky.

Rodrigo Rey Rosa and the Dream Flower

Rodrigo and I were walking on the Charf when we saw some flowers he recognized from Guatemala whose perfume, if placed beside the bed, induces dreams in the sleeper. I picked one but it had no smell at all so we named them the pseudo-dream flowers.

Mraierh

Mrabet knew that I was looking for an inexpensive house, so he had sent Rodrigo to tell me that he would call tomorrow to take me to see his land.

So the following day we drove to Mraierh, and then walked through rows and rows of cactus which lined the path to the plot. Mrabet said, "Cherie—the garden is planted, the well is deep, and the bricks for the house are ready. I swear to you upon Allah that you can build a house here and you can live there as long as you wish. If you ever want to leave I'll reimburse you. Think about it—we'll talk later."

Paul's Terrace

Paul was working on his plants on the terrace and his hands were all covered in soil. The kitchen was full of tools and pots, the surfaces plastered with mud.

"It looks like Beirut in here." Mrabet laughed as he tried to clear a space to make tea.

When I left, Paul was in bed with his dinner tray. I blew him a kiss and it fell into his soup, but he said it was okay because he was eating it.

Rain

Next day I found Paul in the dark and the torrential rain was seeping in from a crack in the ceiling above his bed.

"The rain is raining all around me," he said.

Mrabet laughed as he set my things to dry by the fire. He was unshaven and weary but in fine form. His eyes danced as he told me he had bought the nails for the house.

"So are you serious?" he asked. "If you are we'll start right away. I'll put up the initial money so that the workers can begin and you can pay me later." He held out his hand. I took it but felt nervous.

Later I asked Paul about wiring money from America and it struck me that Paul seemed to know nothing about the plan. In the kitchen I asked Mrabet about this.

"Paul would prefer to know later, so let's make it a surprise," he insisted.

I told Mrabet that I hated this secrecy but went along with his decision since I felt he knew Paul better than I.

Rodrigo arrived. He said he had come because he felt something was "off" with Paul.

"Something's going on and I don't know about it," he had told Rodrigo.

Mrabet was unshaven and surly, and while Paul and I were listening to a recording of his music in Amsterdam Mrabet turned on the radio.

"Shh—I'm listening to the *fútbol* game," he said in a rude tone.

"Cherie and I are listening to music, so why don't you go to the kitchen with your radio?" Paul replied. This Mrabet did but he turned the radio up to full volume.

"Someone, I know, will arrive in the middle of this music," Paul said, but the doorbell didn't ring until the last chord.

In the kitchen Mrabet began a diatribe, saying I didn't want the house, that I was the wife of the wind, that my word was no good and I wanted him dead. I began to argue but he left the kitchen, slamming the door behind him. He next began to attack Paul for being bourgeois.

"But I was born bourgeois, I can't help it," said Paul.

I stuck out my tongue at Mrabet and got up to leave. He put his hand to his dark unshaven face and grinned. "I know—ugly huh?"

I dreamed that night of bleeding fingers in the earth.

Three Words

One morning in the Zoco Chico I ate *baisar*, which is a Moroccan version of pea soup, but didn't finish the bread, which was quickly snatched up by an old man who placed it in the hood of his djellaba. A boy with a trained pigeon sat in the square. He was throwing it into the air over and over and each time the bird fluttered for a moment before returning to the boy's shoulder.

When I next saw Paul he said, "You've been gone a week." It had only been three days. I gave him a kiss on the forehead. Mrabet came in and stared at me. I stared back.

"She likes to stare at me to instill fear—but I'm not afraid—I like it," he said in Spanish.

"I have three words for you, Cherie," he continued.

"Will I cry?"

"No—you'll laugh."

"Three thousand dirhams. I need it to start building," Mrabet explained.

Suddenly a gust of wind opened a door to another room. The fire sizzled, a door slammed shut, and I looked up.

"The wind," said Mrabet. "Yes, I am a friend of the wife of the wind and that friend of mine, the little fish, has told me all her secrets. She wants to come and go as she pleases, but I don't want that. At first she was scared of the house, now she is scared of me. But that's because she doesn't really know me yet."

Rodrigo likes the times when the moon is a sliver rather than when it is full or there is none at all. We were walking down to the Boulevard Pasteur on our way to eat at Romeros. Over dinner he said that Mrabet had taken my hesitancy about the house personally.

"It's not Mrabet, Rodrigo, it's the circumstances," I said. "But tell him I trust him, I guess I'll do it."

I thought that even if the house only lasted five years it would be worth it. The next day I gave Mrabet his three words.

The Cat Who Went to College

On a beautiful but windy day Paul arrived at the Hotel Continental at 11:30. I watched him from my balcony coming up the stairs, feeling like Juliet.

We took a long walk to the port and I told him all about my plans for the house and how it had bothered me keeping this secret. He told me that he knew all the secrecy came from Mrabet, because he thought that if it were known he was getting money from me then he wouldn't be able to get any from Paul.

"Well, he's not getting it from me—it's *for* me," I replied.

We walked down Boulevard Louis Pasteur and I saw a huge python skin in a shop window.

"I had a large snake once," said Paul. "But Mrabet took it one day and never brought it back. When I asked him about it Mrabet answered, 'What snake?' and changed the subject."

Beyond the Café de Paris we turned left up Avenida de España past the Big Mosque heading back toward Itesa. By a datura tree with yellow flowers Paul was entranced by three cats. He patted one cat and we moved on. At the doorway to Itesa his favorite feline approached.

"He's the cat who went to college," he said.

Wife of the wind.

The wind at my window.

CATS

Alec Wilder first came to my attention around 1940 with a
very pretty series of jazz-inspired pieces for chamber group
featuring harpsichord. I met him briefly in Denver with
Libby Holman when we were there trying out the doomed opera
Yerma. Then I began to hear strange reports of how I had
conned Libby into giving me a large sum of money for fewer
than twenty-five pages of music. This sounded like the work
of a jealous composer. More rumours came to me, these about
the poor quality of the music. I reviewed the meeting with
Wilder in my head, and understood that he was truly enraged.
Clearly it all had to do with money, since it was common
knowledge that Libby had a great deal of that. I could only
assume that at some point Wilder had hoped to get a commis-
sion from her to write some music. His imagination had run

riot when it came to estimating the amount I had received.
Originally Libby had offered me one thousand dollars to
translate the Garcia Lorca text and set it to music. It was
Oliver Smith who persuaded her to raise the sum to twenty-
five hundred dollars, which she reluctantly agreed to do.
That was still a scant recompense for the endless work
involved. I thought no more about Alec Wilder until I read
the typescript of Jon Bradshaw's book about Libby. I had
often heard that Wilder was a heavy drinker, but now I came
face to face with what can happen when a man gives free rein
to his alcoholic fantasies. When he was interviewed by
Bradshaw he announced that Paul Bowles was a notorious
sadist, and that he had seen me pick up a cat and hurl it
with all my might against a brick wall. There was no indica-
tion of where or when this act had been perpetrated. We had
seen one another only during an intermission in the audito-
rium at Denver. I told Bradshaw immediately that he would
have to delete the account, which he agreed to do.

I thought about this for a long time afterwards. It seemed
a particularly diabolical twist of fate to have made the
victim of my cruelty a cat, the animal I love above all others. The cat is the ideal wild beast to have with one in the

house. Cats have their mental processes and emotions like other mammals, but they feel no need of expressing them; on the contrary, they often attempt to hide them. What goes on inside a cat is a private matter. The dog on the other hand, wants to exteriorize his feelings as a token of submission and loyalty. But it is not pleasant to be an object of mindless devotion, it entails a reciprocal sense of responsibility. Apart from that, dogs are dirty and noisy and do not make perfect companions for a person who leads a quiet life. There is a personality gap between the admirers of the canine and feline species. The individual whose ego is massaged by an adoring dog is going to feel contempt, and outright dislike of cats. One alluroophobe put it recently: "Snakes in furs."

I am convinced that any mammal, if treated in terms of the distinguishing characteristics peculiar to its species, will respond to overtures of friendship. It would seem less certain in the case of reptiles, although snake trainers tell me that serpents show a distinct sort of friendship, perhaps more properly called preference for certain individuals, and not for others. The reasons for this have not been studied, to my knowledge.

The Mustang pulled up and we parked at the edge of the Charchumbo trail that led to Mrabet's land. Paul mounted a donkey. There were wild iris everywhere and I picked some for Paul but the donkey ate them.

The whole hillside had been cleared and construction seemed to have begun though I'd only given three thousand dirham. Workers were chipping the stone that would be the foundation for the house. Paul, Rodrigo, and I sat on the hillside shading our eyes from the sun. Paul liked the spot.

That night at Itesa we were all exhausted. Paul and I talked about Mrabet and the house. Paul spoke as if Mrabet was building a stall for his animals and that the house was less important.

"You mean I might not get my house?" I asked.

"No, I don't mean that. I mean that it might not be the house that you envisaged, but I believe Mrabet cares for you and might not take advantage and you'll get it . . . eventually. He's like a baby with money; many Moroccans are the same. One thousand dollars is the same as a hundred thousand to him, he has no conception of its value. He's not a farmer or a contractor as he thinks he is and the house may not be as great as he dreams it will be. So be very strong with him, keep a list which will be difficult as you'll be away. I'll try to keep tabs on him if I can but Mrabet is tough to deal with. He'll hate this but you should have a notary say you invested ten thousand dollars, and do it now because you've given almost nothing and so you have the leverage."

Paul's eyes narrowed. "And isn't leverage what life's all about? At least in Morocco it is."

The terrible ride on the poor donkey.

13/viii/87

Dear Jerez:

The cat photos came and I was delighted to have them. I'm glad
you took the "good cat", white and grey, who was always outside my
door and behaved so well, because shortly afterward Paco told me
he'd found it dead behind the garage, and I was sad to lose it.
There's one black cat left, but there are so many children teasing
it and kicking it that I feel it won't be here very long. Itesa is
crowded with small children now. One can hardly get out the front
door.

Your superintendent sounds like a madman, or a Mexican! Why
would he attack anyone with a machete? Why would he have a machete?

So far I haven't received your letter about the gallery, and
wasn't aware that they'd scheduled Mrabet's show for October.

I gave Mrabet another 15,000 dirhams ($1,800) yesterday, for
windows and doors. Sometimes I wonder if there's any house at all.
I haven't been out there since we went together. He keeps saying
that he doesn't want me to see it until it's more or less finished.
One of these days I'll have to insist. Of course I don't believe
for a minute that the doors and windows are costing 15,000 dirhams.
I give him these sums to shut him up, because he keeps harping on
his inability to continue building the house without more money.
So I can scarcely claim that you owe me what I've given him. If
I had refused, I suppose he wouldn't have built the house.

Seth and Jean-Bernard came only this week. They couldn't get
passage southward from Paris, and had to wait a long time there.
They haven't been able to find a house, although they've been here
only five days. Anyway, that's the news.

love, Paul K

It not only assumes that dreams can be thera-
eutic, but ~~offers a~~ ~~viable~~ ~~method~~ technique for achieving

{ What The Wind Wants

Caught by the Cat   } Late In the Day

Once Too Often }

A ... ...dge against B. When B. is made a
... money to him, ~~six~~ seeing to it that
... of the gift. B. is reprimanded
... E. is given a pair of ...
~~Ewhich makes~~ ~~...~~ them too small
~~...~~ ... finds that
... kitten because its name was
... over the head of a stray bird
... y with it. G. eats so many
... vers his gun with the
... frighten a Jewish woman
... dients of magic on her
... ~~a witch~~
... actual. ... the Djilala. All this
~~...~~ ~~...~~ ~~Add thi.~~ ~~...~~ Combines A & B
... & H. Combine C & D with F. Combin

The cat that went to college

alien shelter

My head is my only house unless it rains.
—Don Van Vliet

Cap Spartel, the approach to Tangier.

TANGIER

When I first arrived in Tangier, although it was primarily
a port, there was no breakwater and no dock. The ferry from
Gibraltar would cast anchor in the harbour, and passengers
were rowed ashore in a dinghy. The railway station was outside the town among the sand dunes; you reached it by a
boardwalk that ran along parallel to the beach. If it were
raining, you could hire a carriage drawn by one weak horse,
which you hoped would get you to your train. The carriage
was an agreeable way of getting around the town, for the
streets of Tangier were shaded by high vegetation. The
closely packed Medina was another story, but even there a
tree was sometimes visible behind a wall, or its branches
spread across the street. There was one alley I loved to
pass through, for the odour of jasmine that emanated from a
hidden courtyard.

The Medina, a compact collection of buildings enclosed by
ramparts, never ceased to fascinate me. Like the sea, it was

always there, but always different from what it had been the moment before. The dramas played by the Moslems in its labyrinthine passageways were like the inventions of an inspired playwright. (The Spaniards, many thousands strong, presented their own dramas of a different sort, but these were intrinsically less absorbing, because they were usually fuelled by alcohol, a substance

TANGER — Une rue du Socco
A Street in the Socco

in those times Moslems did not touch.)

The town was so small and close knit that from the Grand Socco, which was its centre, I could walk in a half hour to my house on the Old Mountain and be completely in the country, where the only sounds were the crickets in the fields and the wind in the trees.

The only Moslems to be seen on the beach in those years were peasants riding their donkeys, come to town for the market. The Tangerines considered the sun poisonous and did what they could to keep out of it. It was only later that a few young men were courageous enough to imitate the French, who had no scruples about swimming and lying on the sand in the sunlight.

And it was still later that women began to venture (fully dressed) into the waves.

In the Medina the only sounds were those made by human voices. The radio with its distorting amplifier had not yet arrived. For those who wanted music there were ancient wind-up gramophones to be rented by the hour; small boys delivered them, wearing the flaring horns over their heads like huge morning-glories and thus often unable to see where they were going. The Socco Chico, in the centre of the Medina, surrounded by cafes on all sides, presented a symphony of hundreds of conversations. In the early 1930's the clientele thinned out after midnight, but after the war, in the 1940's, when Tangier was packed with tourists and foreign residents, the cafes were busy until dawn; exhausted party-goers arrived to take black coffee before retiring.

Those were the liveliest years for the town. Dollars and pounds fetched more than twice as many francs or pesetas in the International Zone as they did in Paris or Madrid (or Casablanca for that matter). With a dollar account here one could live in Paris on francs changed in one's Tangier bank, at the rate of 550 francs per dollar instead of 220. There were money changers throughout the town, displaying blackboards on which the latest rates were marked in chalk. A few people rushed from one changer to another all day, buying and selling currencies, and managing thus to eke out a living; I never understood exactly how. The only legal tender accepted by the canny peasant women who sold fruit, vegetables and eggs under the trees in the Grand Socco was silver. One had to change one's European money for silver Hassani coins before marketing.

I knew a man who came and got a cobbler to make him a pair of shoes with elevated heels. Into each heel he put a half kilo of gold bullion, so that he was able to leave

Tangier with an entire kilo, in order to sell it elsewhere at a good profit, or so he claimed. I found it difficult to believe that the difference in price would have made it worth his while. But some people seemed to attribute magical powers to the International Zone. It excited them to feel that they were in no country, that the Zone was a kind of no-man's land where everyone did as they pleased, and with no interference by the law. And it is true that the town had an aura of general permissiveness, and this to an extraordinary degree, the like of which I had not seen before, nor have seen since.

The old Tangier I had known in 1931 did not last. When I returned after the war, in 1947, it was scarcely recognizable. Apartment houses had gone up, trees had been done away with, streets had been cut through the outlying countryside; and in the Medina new facades had been given to the houses, in every case destroying the moorish arch over the entrance door, thus depriving the streets of visual charm. But most Moroccans are entirely indifferent to such details. They admire that which is new, regardless of its appearance. Apart from a few ancient buildings in the Casbah, the only place I can think of which has not undergone modernizing alterations is a small cafe on the Marshan, at the edge of a high cliff above the sea. In the thirties I used to go there during Ramadan and play lotto, and it was there that I learned to count in Arabic. This little establishment, bearing a sign identifying it as La Guinguette Fleurie. What is astonishing is that after nearly sixty years it should still look the same, should still be its delightful self, with its series of terraces leading down to the edge of the cliff. Seagulls sail, and turn in the wind, and occasionally a tanker moves slowly through the water, on its way to or from the Strait of Gibraltar. Now the place belongs to Moroccans and has no sign out, but everyone knows it as the Cafe Hafa, or Cliff Cafe. If you were not certain of where it is, you would never find it.

In the years since I first came to Tangier and was captured by its charm, the town of sixty thousand inhabitants has become a city of ten times that number and judging by the widespread construction going on now, it will continue to expand as long as the present surge of prosperity lasts.

Compared to most cities, this is still a pleasant place to live, even though today one must accept a great deal of ugliness which was not originally here. The ugliness, of course,

is an inevitable concomitant of present day construction in
third world countries. Walls are built quickly out of cement
blocks, and there is none of the careful attention to detail,
which can be realized only by the human hand.

Recalling that usually one writes best where one feels the
most intensely, I tell myself that I'm justified in speaking
of a Tangier which now exists only in memory but which, in
spite of having been left behind by the passage of time, is
in this case no less valid.

I had planned to return to Tangier in under three months, but it was six before I could get back.

As I approached Tangier a thrill of anticipation came over me—watching the squadrons of gulls diving for fish, their reflections caught in the dappled sea. As the boat pushed closer and closer to my new home I held on to the shell I had found in 1970.

Later on the balcony of the Hotel Continental I looked out at the American ships that had pulled into port. I saw the beads of light wrapped around the superstructure as strings of hope under a cloudy night moon.

First Days

After a long dreamless sleep at the Hotel Continental, I skipped through the streets of the medina greeted by everyone and happy to be back. I bought a large bouquet of red roses and made my way up from the Socco Chico toward Itesa. I couldn't wait to see my new house. Paul gave me a big kiss, and overly excited I almost lifted him off the floor, laughing as we danced round the room nearly falling over the *taifor*. But my heart sank when I saw Mrabet lying kiffed and stone-faced on the couch. He looked thin and gray and cold. When he left to go into the kitchen I asked Paul what was the matter. Paul said that for some months he had worked enthusiastically to complete the house, but that suddenly his spirit seemed to crack and he started saying, "Cherie doesn't want this house— for her it was just caprice." The money seemed to have run out so Paul had given Mrabet another $7,000 to allow the work to continue.

"What happened—what's wrong?" I finally asked Mrabet.

"It's my liver," he said and left.

"Mrabet doesn't want you there or he'd have taken you himself," said Abdelouahid.

"Well, she's going to be there whether he likes it or not," said Paul. And we went.

Paul grabbed our arms and shoulders as he walked over the rocks through the spiny cactus-rimmed path. Just around the next bend and over the second hill I could see the top of the unfinished house peeking through the trees and thorns. The earth at our feet was a dusty yellow. A skinny dog, tied to a small concrete house, was barking madly. The cows lowed in the finished stable beneath the dwelling place proper and above was the skeleton of my house. Paul thought it would be quite charming when complete. I looked out of the window and saw the tightly chained dog straining at the leash. But in the distance I also saw the beautiful horizon and a strip of blue sea and I felt there was still hope for Charchumbo.

Mrabet was waiting back at Itesa. "So you saw the house," he said.

"Yes—there's work left to do, but I like what I see. How long will it take?"

Mrabet quickly became agitated and began hurling insult after insult. Then he left.

"This is a novel," Paul said.

"You should write it."

"Will he hate me forever?" I asked Paul.

"No, he'll switch back. Sometimes he's terrible with me too and he won't even speak to me."

He looked up at the ceiling and said, "Go on with the house, I'll fund it."

Then looking into my eyes he suggested, "Make it a summer house."

"**Y**our Christmas stocking is not on the wall," said Paul when I arrived. Mrabet had snatched it in a rage and thrown it across the room. Paul had retrieved it and pinned it to the drape that covered the window by the bed.

"Don't worry, it's safe. Mrabet seems to think it's magic and that you want power."

Some days later I was having breakfast at the Café de Paris. While sipping my *kawa b halib* (cafe au lait) I saw Paul in the street and went out to greet him. I grabbed him from behind and kissed him on the back of the neck. He turned around smiling and we stood, hands on hips, in our sunglasses and talked.

"You'll never believe what happened today. Mrabet drew the drapes and found the stocking. In a rage he seized it and raced to the kitchen. When he came back I asked what he'd done. 'I threw it out of the window,' he said. 'But there was a gift inside,' I told him. He went out again and soon came back with only the little gift, a silver box which he had wrapped in paper and tape saying, 'If she wants to go crazy she should go back to New York and do it there.'"

"I've got to have it out with Mrabet," I said.

"It'll do no good, because Mrabet is the one who's crazy," he sighed.

Christmas Times

Mrabet has stopped smoking so much kif, but he still looked sick and gray today. He sat on the big chest in the salon—Paul's Moroccan *sandook*—with folded arms. He handed me a package, which I opened. Inside was a gold pendant with the engraving "Shirly Bowles." Did I want to buy it so he could buy five cows? I refused.

Later I told Paul, and how Mrabet had said he had taken it from Carole Ardman, an old friend of Paul's from the 70s.

"That's impossible," said Paul. "He probably stole it from my jewelry box thinking it was gold."

Paul cupped his hands around my face. His eyes twinkled. He rubbed his nose with mine Eskimo-style.

On Christmas Eve after another session of insults from Mrabet I followed him through the big white curtain that led to the kitchen. He was cutting strawberries and lining them up in a row on the sink.

"Why are we enemies?" I asked.

He answered with double talk.

"But you gave me Allah's word that you would do right by me. You shook my hand and placed it on your heart and promised."

This seemed to send a spasm through his mind. For a moment he froze, but quickly regaining his composure he answered:

"Allah? Who cares about Allah? The face you see is the face you will see to the end. Good night."

The many colored lights that usually decorate the Boulevard Pasteur in honor of King Hassan were off tonight so no one could mistake them for Christmas decorations. I had bought Paul his Christmas present. New argyle socks from Gibraltar.

He handed me a package saying, "This gift might be too bright for you, but I bought it in Gibraltar twenty-five years ago and I thought it might keep you warm."

It was a beautiful pink woolen scarf.

"Though my future seems dark, my present is pink," I said and gave him a big hug.

New Year

December thirtieth is Paul's birthday. Wearing my pink scarf and carrying pink roses I arrived for Paul's party. Abdelwahab el Abdellaoui and Mustapha Ouaffi were there and also Gavin Lambert.

"How's your house?" asked Gavin.

"Don't ask," I groaned.

Paul cut the cake and said, "A memorable birthday with too much cake."

On New Year's Day my mom calls. She is on her way to live here, arriving in mid-March. I'm trying to rent a house for the two of us on Dar Baroud.

Jamal is at top. Above right are Mustapha Ouaffi and Abdelwahab Abdellaoui at Paul's birthday party. Below, Mom, Rachid Bousellam, Jamal, another guest, and me at the house on Dar Baroud.

White Marble

Dreamed all night of Paul's one blue eye. This is what happened the night before I dreamed: I'd gone to Itesa carrying twenty-four red roses for Paul. I'd seen them in the flower stall and, since they were exceptionally beautiful that day, I bought the whole two dozen that Mohammed the florist had.

Mrabet answered the door and slid into the kitchen. Two American students from New York were visiting Paul. When he tried to take the roses from me I told him I'd take care of them.

"Do the roses have thorns? I hate roses with thorns," one of the two girls said.

"Of course they have thorns—what's a rose without a thorn?" I snapped back.

Whisking the roses away to the kitchen I knocked on the door.

"*Puedo entrar.* May I come in?"

I went in even though I heard no reply. The sound of the *fútbol* crowd filled the air. Mrabet sat at his table intent on the game with a head full of kif, his scoreboard, and a glass of Lipton tea in his hands. *"Hola,"* I said but made no other attempt at conversation. I placed the two dozen roses on the far side of the sink's white marble counter. The big Moroccan vase stood empty on the other side of the sink. I opened the drawer and took out a sharp silver knife and began to cut the stems of each crimson rose. One by one I cut each rose and placed it in the blue mosaic vase. In the thick silence I felt nervous but I took a few long breaths and soon got absorbed by the rhythm of the ceremonial cut and placement of each flower.

I fell into a trance.

—Cut

—Cut

Mrabet was stealing looks at me though I pretended not to notice, and soon he seemed to be in a trancelike state as well.

—Slice

—Slice

—Snip

—Snip

In a quick glance between trances I noticed the embroidery of two crossed knives on the arm of his olive-green sweater.

—Knife

—Life

—Slice

—Slice

Each rose cut one at a time—each rose.

One rose petal dropped to the floor by our feet . . . or was it a drop of fresh blood?

—Slice

—Slice

I picked up the blood drop from the cold tiles and left it on the marble next to the vase.

One by one.

—each rose

—twenty-four cuts

—Cut—Cut—Snip—Slice

On the twelfth stem Mrabet turned off the radio and in the silence I felt his eyes on me, both of us falling into the rhythm of silver steel on marble. When the bouquet was complete I was gentle with the silver knife that slid between my fingers back and forth in the running water. When it was clean I placed the knife on the marble and I broke the silence. *"Te gusta?"* I asked. *"Si,"* he smiled and nodded in approval. Oh, a smile at last! I smiled back and picked up the vase to bring to the salon where Paul was sitting in his usual place. I left the one rose petal behind—one blood drop on the cold floor for Mrabet.

Mrabet brought me tea by the fire, holding the cup close to my face. Then just as close he held out the bowl of sugar. I tried to take it from him and put it on the table, but he wouldn't let the bowl go. "No, no, take it from me," he said, so I dipped my silver spoon into the bowl as he held it in his hands smiling down at me. The American girls were discussing life and love but Mrabet broke in: "Mejoud, it's time for bed." Paul went to change into his pyjamas and I followed him to the bathroom door and, lifting my jacket over my face, I kissed him from behind the black leather. Mrabet walked me to the door and I was followed by Paul's guests. He held it open and it remained so for a long while, but when I finally glanced back the door gently shut.

Back in my room, I sat on the balcony and looked at the cool blue light of the sky and thanked Allah two or three times for the miracle of the roses. In the middle of the night I awoke in terrible pain. There was a thorn deeply embedded in my thumb. I didn't feel it go in. How did it get there?

I kissed Paul and started practicing my new Arabic words. "By spring you'll know enough Moghrebi to speak to your neighbors in Charchumbo," said Paul. "And I gave Mrabet the rest of the money. The house will be ready by May."

I was thrilled.

Paul introduced me to Bachir Attar from Jajouka. Later, when Paul went to get ready for bed, Bachir and I talked. He told me about Jajouka and the music that comes from there. Bachir was young and handsome, gentle and sweet. There was an air of innocence and uniqueness about him that was attractive and I liked him right away.

On the radio in the kitchen, the Egyptian singer Abdelwahab was singing "Love is a rose," a song about how he must love the rose despite the thorns.

The Falcons

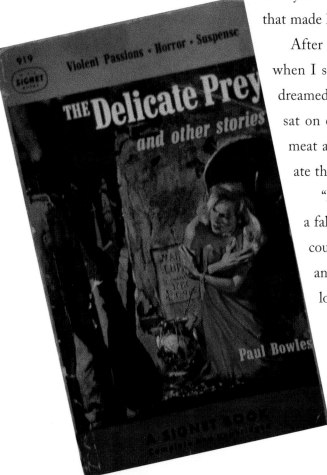

"Mrabet will never change," said Paul.

"Why? I thought the house problem had been settled."

"He expects anger from you since he's treated you badly and feels guilty. Since you don't get angry he's waiting for you to attack. It was the money that made him hate you—he became greedy."

After dinner I was having a final cigarette before going to sleep when I saw a falcon insignia on the book of matches I'd bought. I dreamed all that night about falcons. One flew into my eye. Another sat on eggs in a nest. They were feeding other young falcons red meat and then a falcon larger than the rest flew over the nest and ate the eggs.

"Mrabet hates falcons," Paul warned Rodrigo when he brought a falcon to Itesa the next day. The bird had a damaged wing and couldn't fly so Rodrigo hid it. I gave Rodrigo the match cover and told him about my dream. Even Paul seemed interested and looked at the matches, perplexed.

A week or so later Paul and Rodrigo went to the mountain to release the falcon. Mrabet had found out about it and wanted to keep it for hunting so was annoyed when it was released. Rodrigo hoped it wouldn't hurt their friendship.

"Today I feel magic," I thought as I dressed quickly so I could get to Paul's on time. Abdelouahid was late, but Paul answered the door and he seemed in good spirits too. I sat in the back seat behind Paul as we drove, with my hands on his shoulders.

Charchumbo looked different as we approached. The trees had been all cut back and a bulldozer had been at work at the bottom of the trail where we pulled in. Abdelouahid walked ahead, and I walked with Paul over the rocks toward the house. His leg began to hurt. We had to sit on a rock and rest and I massaged the leg. The lump from the pre-Slâ days was still there but smaller. Two Berber girls came by and stared at us because I was massaging a man's leg. Embarrassed, Paul suddenly said the leg was completely better so we got up and continued.

"Good water," said Abdelouahid as we passed the *ain* (spring), but it seemed to me there was only a little water in the spring.

We looked up and there it was—the house. My house—all painted white with blue shutters. Clothes hung from the roof—someone must be there.

"Well, there it is—let's go," said Paul and he turned around to go back to the car.

"Can't we go inside?" I asked.

"Of course," said Abdelouahid, so Paul turned around and we went to the door. A young boy let us into the main room. Mrabet had placed a large photo of himself taken by Paul in the middle

My house at Charchumbo, and Paul in the mud outside. I took the picture of Paul from the roof of my house.

of the room and the rest of his things were scattered everywhere. Paul peered at the bookcase as Mrabet couldn't read.

"All my books, he just took them without asking, doubles and triples of the same ones," he said.

On the roof some of Mrabet's things were lying out to dry. "That's mine," said Paul, pointing to a velvet and wool opera cape from Spain. It was soaked through and was drying dirtily in the sun. Abdelouahid had been searching the grounds and he came back with a baby donkey which Paul promptly patted.

It was time to go. The story finished. Paul struggled with his bad leg down the spiny path, while Abdelouahid went ahead to start the car. A locust flew by and perched on a cactus. I stopped and engraved "Jerez" into the flesh of the prickly plant. Something was wrong with the Mustang as we pulled away. Paul's leg was terrible.

"That's my last trip to that house," he said.

The Denouement   May 1, 1988

The last day before I leave for New York for a month. As I always do before I leave I brought Paul roses. When I arrived the blue vase was already full. Mrabet had known I'd be bringing some and had decided to beat me to it. Paul went to the kitchen at once and removed Mrabet's bouquet, placing it in a green ice bucket to make room for mine.

"Oh, we're going to get into trouble," I said, but Paul's eyes just twinkled with his elfin grin. He put Mrabet's on the *taifor* by his usual spot and mine next to his seat.

I was on the floor with my back to the room facing Paul. Abdelouahid and Abdelwahab were seated next to Paul facing me. We spoke about what new videos I should bring from New York when suddenly the key rattled in the lock and I remembered the roses. "Oh no," I whispered and we looked at one another and continued our conversation nervously. My back was to Mrabet when he entered the room but I was told he looked at his roses and then mine and started to make faces. Then he picked up a log of firewood and made gestures to hit me with it. Next I heard a loud noise and turned around to see Mrabet violently grab both bouquets and disappear behind the curtain. There were rose petals on the floor making a trail toward the kitchen. He came back almost at once carrying the good vase that now contained his roses. Mine were nowhere in sight. I got up and followed the petal trail to the kitchen and saw my roses thrown in the waste bucket. Quietly I returned to my previous seat by Paul's feet and Mrabet sat close to me on the couch.

"I'm sorry," I said, "but I'm leaving tomorrow and you know it was my time to bring roses."

"Din din muk," he kept saying in a voice that came from hell.

"What does *'din din muk'* mean?" I asked him, and with that he threw a pillow at me. I slung it back with equal force, and with that he swung his arm and cracked me across the face with his hand. My cheek stung and felt hot and I leapt up raising my fists and said, "Mrabet, I'm sick of this—a man doesn't hit a woman—you stole my money and what have I done to you? Nothing—okay, so you want to fight—let's fight—*safi*—I've had enough."

Mrabet just shrank in his seat looking scared and very small.

Paul went into the bedroom and I followed in tears. I put my face in his lap and wept while Paul

timidly patted my head.

"I'm sorry," he said. "I gave him the money for you."

"Will Mrabet and I ever be friends again?"

"No never."

"Will he kill me?"

"No he won't kill you. Go back to New York and I'll see you

when you return."

Mrabet was in the kitchen when I slammed the door on my way out.

"If she comes back I'll kill her," he yelled, but luckily I didn't

hear him. I didn't know what to do. My mother had arrived and knew nothing about the trouble. I went back home and at the door of our house on Dar Baroud someone had dropped a bunch of roses and they had been squashed by a car or a cart. Petals lay scattered all over the street by the front door.

the sky

The Rose Attar

"I am the lion of Jajouka and I've come to save the deer."

Bachir had heard of my recent trials and tribulations.

"I have mercy in my heart for you because I too have had many problems with people as I dedicate my life to save my father's music."

We walked hand in hand back to Dar Baroud from Paul's. A small blackbird on its first flight from the nest fell between us, landing on my left shoulder then falling on the ground beneath our feet. Before we could intervene, it flapped its wings and struggled into the air.

Later that same evening a princess gave Bachir a rosebud, which he promptly handed to me. It had the fragrance of fresh morning dew. We kissed. It was then that I knew that our union was more than just an association of chance. We had something worthwhile to do together that would make history for Jajouka, Bachir's band.

Bachir brought me to Jajouka and late into the night the music would get wilder and wilder, and on some trancelike nights a scent, both sweet and yet primordially ancient, would permeate the air while the jackals in the mountains barked at the starry sky. We decided that I should manage the band and be its photographer.

With a recommendation from Paul, Bachir got a visa and we left for America. We held hands and closed our eyes as the plane took off. For eight years we spent our time between New York and Morocco, struggling and penniless. Paul helped, sending money from time to time.

During our first visit to New York Bachir dreamed of Mick Jagger, and one day when walking down Houston Street a paper flew in front of him and got caught between his legs. It was a clipping of Jagger on one side looking like Christ and on the other wrapped up like a Moslem woman. "My best friends aren't famous," he was quoted as saying.

Bachir encouraged me to write to the Rolling Stones that night. We composed the letter together. Within a month we received a reply, which eventually brought the Rolling Stones to Tangier to record "Steel Wheels" for their album *Continental Drift*.

Paul with Bachir Attar and the Master Musicians of Jajouka on the road at Medieuna.

Bachir Attar and Mick Jagger, June 1989.

Bachir Attar and some of the Master Musicians of Jajouka off-set during filming of The Sheltering Sky.

*Above, Ron Wood. At left, Mick Jagger, Mom, and Paul
watch the Master Musicians of Jajouka.*

THE INTERVIEW

This is in the nature of an exemplary essay whose message is that to discuss oneself is to invite disaster. The reason for this is not immediately apparent, although it is clear that a conversation in which even one participant insists upon talking about himself soon becomes static and dies out. Not for nothing is it considered bad manners to discuss oneself.

But I'm thinking of the kind of conversation in which one is urged to speak, to tell more about himself than it would ever occur to him to tell. I refer, of course, to the interview.

It is a quiet morning. I sit alone in my little flat, reading or writing, perhaps hearing the muezzin call from the nearby minaret, enjoying being alone, enjoying the quiet. Suddenly there is a knock at the door. Several people stand outside. One of them announces: "We are from Zurich" (or Paris, or Madrid, or wherever they are from). "We wish to make an interview with you." They come in and explain

that they tried to telephone, but could not find the number.
I don't tell them I had the instrument taken out thirty
years ago.

The interview begins. Often these people arrive armed with
a list of questions, most of which I can guess before they
ask them. "Why did you decide to live in Morocco?" "What is
it that attracts you to Tangier?" "Are you a Moroccan citi-
zen?" "Have you become a Moslem?" "Is this a good place to
work?"

In the beginning I would try and answer seriously,
explaining that Morocco sixty years ago was a tranquil pastoral land where the course of urbanization had not yet
arrived, and that Tangier, profiting by its international
status, offered a surprisingly favourable exchange rate - up
to two or three hundred percent more than in the rest of
Morocco.

Often they let me see that this was not the kind of
answer they had been hoping for; they wanted a personal,
emotional reply, and they would go out of their way in their
attempts to get one. As the years went by, I found myself
nurturing a growing hostility to this kind of absurdity.
Finally I began to announce flatly that I did not give

interviews, foolishly adding that I was prepared to enter into normal conversation. This provided a respite from the list of previously prepared questions, but it was not the ideal solution. The ideal solution would have been simply to say: "Goodbye."

But after all the queries and responses are over, the interview remains at the mercy of the journalist, who is likely to misrepresent his subject in one way or another. There will probably be small factual errors, and if the subject is not misquoted or tendentiously quoted out of context he is fortunate. Generally there are passages whose meaning is deformed thanks to caprice, carelessness, spite or simple stupidity. It is to be expected that he who considers himself maligned will claim (and probably with reason) that he has been misinterpreted or misquoted, but no proof is possible.

Often, on reading the published article, I find myself thinking: "If only I had kept my mouth shut! If only I'd told them: 'No interview, and no conversation either.'"

In spite of all the negative aspects of the game, one continues to play it in the hope that next time he'll get an intelligent partner. (They do exist, and I think there are

more of them now than there were two or three decades ago.
Nevertheless, they are in the minority.)

If speaking about oneself makes for trouble, the person
who agrees to write about himself has to be partially
insane. I recall my initial reaction when I was asked to
write an autobiography. I was totally against the idea.
Without knowing the possible results, I suspected that if I
were to write it I should regret having done so. I refused

for a year, and then accepted, aware that I was now laying myself open not only to the stings of literary journalists, but also to the fiery breath of the arch-ogres called literary critics. These creatures can claim to have copied your text from The Book word for word and to be quoting it exactly; they can present you as having said quite the opposite of what you did say. After all, they have The Book behind them, and no one is going to check on their accuracy.

The most fearsome of these enemies of writing is a species of critic who believes he has not appraised a work until he has appended his own bit of fiction to it. These little inventions generally betray an intense preoccupation with Freudian theory; the writer is subjected to a lay analysis whose conclusions are often purely ludicrous.

Thus in considering an early poem of mine, one of these psychiatric destroyers quoted six lines (which I too must quote in order to be convincing).

 A complete silence wafts down across the wet terraces and moist petals
  Wrinkle and fall the little diamond lights by the sea in a long

Curving line glimmer twinkle shiver on the brink of
a grey eternity

The pool is still with warm dark water the masses of
froth do not move

A dark form impenetrable silent in the fast twilight
hugs the hot earth

Close to its face

His comment is as follows: "There is, to be sure, little
tension in the Bowles poem, where the relaxed sensuality of
the experience, hinting at oral sex, descends with marvel-
lous control, linguistic and spatial, into the image of a
disappearing face."

I assume that it did not occur to the critic, who had
remarked that the poem had been written when I was fifteen
years old, that it could scarcely have been "hinting at oral
sex." A child of fifteen is not likely to have heard of such
a thing, and is even less likely to write about it. But the
critic's little invention had to figure in his review, no
doubt because he thought it threw light on other aspects of
his piece.

Another equally ridiculous example of the Freudian

approach to literary criticism is the case of a woman who insisted on believing that when I was seven my father punished me for suspected masturbation, even though the text makes it clear that he was angry because I had locked the door of my room in order to draw houses, which was forbidden before breakfast. That was not dramatic enough for this woman; besides it didn't fit any case history she had read. After all, everyone knows that writers write only what they are compelled by their conditioning to write; they invent nothing. According to this point of view, all writers are equals, even if distinguishable one from the other, just as there are no superior or inferior schizophrenics one from the other, they merely present varying symptoms.

When the ogre finishes with you, you are not a writer at all; your works all combine to form one amorphous case history. And it is one which cannot even be used as therapy, since you are stubborn and refuse to be cured.

So do not talk about yourself, never give an interview, never under any conditions write the story of your life. (And it would be better not to write poetry either. Even fiction can incriminate you.) The safest procedure, it goes without saying, is to write nothing at all.

Interrogations

Bernardo Bertolucci wanted Bachir to return to Morocco to take part in his filming of *The Sheltering Sky* in the desert. So in the fall of 1989 we returned.

Paul has interviews today, so I went to sit in the studio to read about Ouarzazate where I will go with the Jajouka musicians in a couple of days to do our part for the film. The house is silent and through the walls scraps of conversation drift by. . . .

"What changes did Bertolucci make to the novel?" asks the interviewer.

Paul is tired and he answers sharply: "Putting *me* in it. . . .

"And the love scene—where they actually have sex— unheard of. . . .

"I don't understand it," he concludes.

Again I hear Paul's voice:

"I don't like America and I never want to see it again. . . ."

My mind turns back to the books and the pictures of the far south and again his voice cuts into my reverie:

"Here you don't announce plans or entertain them. *Inchallah* is what one says. . . ."

"I don't believe in God," he says in reply to a question I didn't catch. "But I believe in Allah."

"So you are sympathetic to Islam?" says the interviewer.

"Yes."

"Do you find it attractive?"

"No religion is attractive."

The words become less and less audible so I return to the books, slipping in and out of a desert dream. The disembodied voices rise and fall and then I hear in his tone that he is worn out and wants the interview to end.

Bernardo Bertolucci testing the lighting on set for the next scene in The Sheltering Sky.

*I snapped the back of Paul's head on the road to see Bruce Weber and continued to
take pictures while Bruce photographed Paul.*

for Cheri — Paul remembering — on a rooftop — a story — Bruce Weber

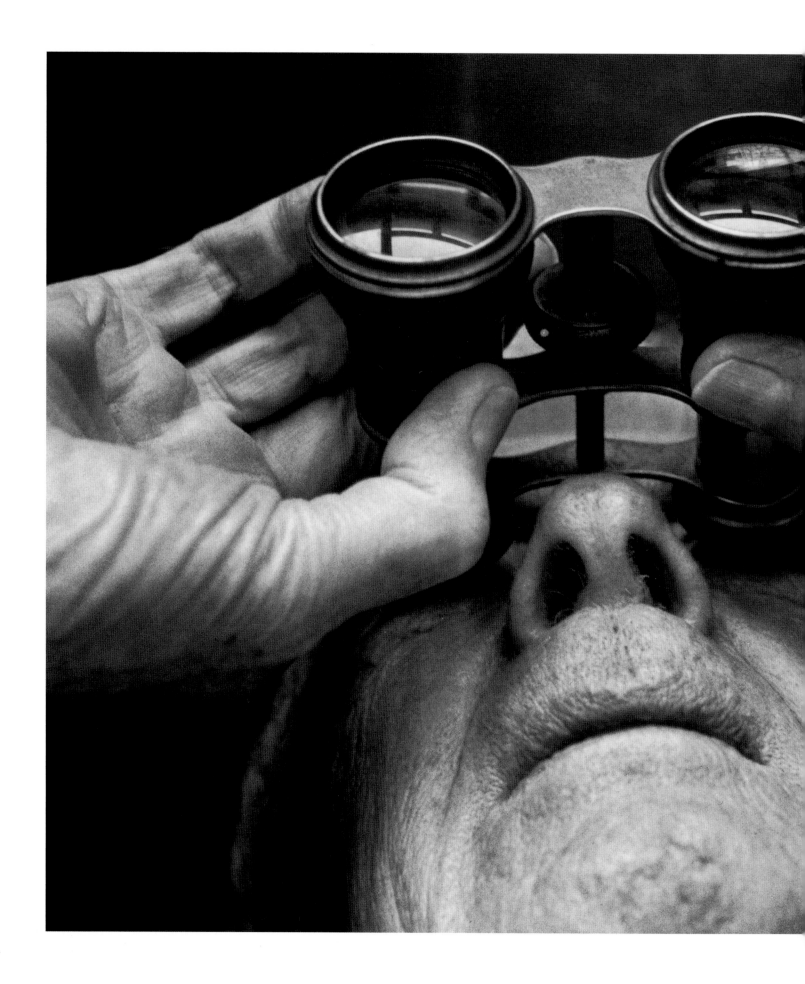

Walk After Filming

Paul and I walked arm in arm down the long familiar road that led to our old spot "The Stork's Nest," but this time the nest was empty.

"Birds fly north," said Paul as I laid my head on his shoulder thinking of my flight back to New York.

"Shooma . . ." Paul whispered as people gave us the eye. "It's shameful for men and women to show affection here." But I kept my head resting there. A little further on we stopped to relax on an old stone wall that encircled sloping grass hills that looked out on white houses glistening in the Tangerine sun.

"Paul, what did you dream last night?"

"It's funny you should ask because I had a strange one. I was in Paris and I called Gertrude Stein on the phone. Alice B. Toklas answered and then I spoke to Gertrude who asked, 'Oh, are you here to study war?'

"I wasn't, but she made me feel it was my duty to do so.

"Then there was static on the line and Gertrude asked: 'Won't you come to dinner Thursday night? We'll have Chicken a la Cologne. Let's not say goodbye,' she said. Then the dogs started to bark and the static increased and I woke up."

desert storm

Someone asked Genet "Is there God?"
and he just said "God knows."
—Paul Bowles

Paul's 80th Birthday

I was completely broke in New York and wanted to get back to Tangier to be able to celebrate Paul's forthcoming eightieth birthday. Fortunately a friend repaid the money he owed me and I was able to get my flight sponsored by Royal Air Maroc in return for photographs of the country that they could use for their publicity. I was also able to stay in Buffie Johnson's flat in Itesa, number fifteen, which was Jane Bowles's old apartment directly below Paul. In return I had to do three things for her. Change the locks, bring an enormous trunk and a large framed painting back to New York, and fire the maid who was suspected of stealing. I readily agreed.

Unfortunately, I discovered that Mrabet was hosting Paul's birthday party, but to my surprise he invited me.

"Should I go?" I asked Paul.

His face dropped and he looked surprised, but said, "Of course— why not? You see, he can't remember why you are annoyed with him. He thinks *he's* forgiven *you*. So you should come. Mrabet thinks you're a dangerous woman ever since you put that Christmas stocking over my bed a couple of years ago. He's convinced that you're a sorceress and fool with magic."

"Then he should be good to me," I replied.

"Unheard of," said Paul. "One never deals nicely with a sorceress."

The Jilala *musicians were led by Zane Adjani, in the white djellaba.*

At Paul's party the *Jilala* musicians played and as the music reached new heights Paul nudged me: "This is the *real* hot jazz," he whispered.

A few days later I was standing by the fire warming my hands as I did in the days before Charchumbo when Mrabet arrived. He looked me in the eyes and smiled. We shook hands gently and softly touched our hearts. I remained skeptical yet felt glad that we could arrange some momentary cease-fire.

During this time I traveled to Fès and Marrakech to photograph for Royal Air Maroc. The tension in the Gulf was beginning to make itself felt and landing at night in Fès with the whole city under curfew felt like entering the twilight zone.

War with Saddam

We began to feel that the threat of war was vanishing. The light was orange as I set out with Bachir for Jajouka and a party for peace on New Year's Day. When we got to the bottom of the Jajouka trail the sun had already slipped behind the foothills making the low Rif appear as black paper cutouts against a smear of pastel sky. The next day we went down the hill to Ksar-el-Kebir. On an old TV hooked up to a car battery we saw Hassan II appear to address his Moslem nation. His face was composed but his hands betrayed an inner tension. Though he was backing the U.S., the hearts of his people were with Saddam. Hassan announced that he had telephoned Saddam asking for a peaceful solution and he added: "If anyone is not sad about this war then he is not a Moslem."

We took the midnight train to Tangier. In the time it took for us to arrive Bush had declared war.

We watched Hassan II address the nation on television.

الاقتصاد. الدكتور الفنجري يقدم اجوبة

الكويتية والعراقية

Printed in Paris

طبعة باريس

AL-HAYAT WEDNESDAY, 8 AUGUST, 1990 ISSUE NO 10051 — بنت الحياة عقيدة وجهاد — الاربعاء ٨ آب (اغسطس) ١٩٩٠ الموافق ١٧ محرم ١٤١١هـ/ العدد ١٠٠٥١

الاساطيل تحاصر الخليج والعراق يباشر "ضم" الكويت

اعلان "جمهورية الكويت" وتوحيد الدينارين
وزير عراقي في دمشق والشيخ سعد في الاسكندرية
مجلس التعاون الخليجي يقرر تحركا دوليا

تسارعت امس التطورات في منطقة الخليج مع مرور اسبوع على اجتياح القوات العراقية للكويت. ففي حين بدأ الغرب يفرض حصارا محكما على العراق لارغام العراق على سحب قواته من الكويت، ظهرت اشارات جديدة الى احتمال حصول صدام عسكري في المنطقة. فاضافة الى الحشود البحرية، باشرت قاذفات قنابل اميركية من طراز «ف – ١١١»، مماثلة لتلك التي استخدمت في الاغارة على ليبيا عام ١٩٨٦ تدريبات في تركيا على بعد ساعة طيران من العراق.

وصرح مصدر باسم السفارة الاميركية في انقرة ان الطائرات موجودة في البلاد منذ يوم ٢٠ حزيران (يونيو) الماضي قبل ان تفجر ازمة الخليج.

لكن ناطقا باسم القوات الاميركية الموجودة في بريطانيا اوضح ان قاذفات من طراز «ف – ١١١» ارسلت الى تركيا واسبانيا في ١٩ تموز (يوليو) الماضي.

وفي كلمة تلاها مذيع في التلفزيون العراقي مساء اكد الرئيس صدام حسين ان الاجتياح العراقي للكويت «يضع حدا لتقسيم استعماري، وضع «الثروة مع الاقلية، وترك «الغالبية» من دون ثروة»، واشاد بـ «صانعي التغيير الثاني من آب (اغسطس)» في الكويت في تلميح الى «الحكومة الكويتية المؤقتة». واعتبر كلام الرئيس العراقي بمثابة تأكيد جديد للنية العراق ضم الكويت.

ورافق بدء تدريبات القاذفات الاميركية في تركيا اعلان الدولة التركي لشؤون النفط محمد جبروت ان بلاده قررت امس حظر شحن النفط العراقي عبر ...

العراق

ومع استمرار الاتصالات العربية الهادفة الى احتواء الازمة والتي تمثلت خصوصا في الزيارة التي قام بها للاسكندرية مبعوث الرئيس صدام حسين هو السيد عزة ابراهيم الدوري نائب رئيس مجلس قيادة الثورة حاملا رسالة من الرئيس العراقي الى الرئيس مبارك، تابع العراق تحركه الهادف الى الخلق واقع جديد في الكويت، فقد اعلنت «حكومة الكويت الحرة المؤقتة» التي شكل اثر الاجتياح برئاسة العقيد علاء حسين علي قيام جمهورية في الكويت.

ونبأ رسمياً في بغداد ان «الحكومة الكويتية المؤقتة» قررت اعتبار الدينار الكويتي في مستوى الدينار العراقي. (راجع ص ...).

واعلنت «وكالة الانباء العراقية» الرسمية ان الرئيس صدام حسين استقبل امس في بغداد رئيس «حكومة الكويت الحرة المؤقتة» الذي شكر للعراق والجيش العراقي «دعمهم لانتفاضة الشعب الكويتي».

وفي اللقاء اشاد الرئيس العراقي باعضاء الحكومة الكويتية الجديدة «الشجعان» الذين «اعادوا الكويت الى حقيقتها الوطنية والقومية الصافية».

ويذكر ان اللقاء الاول الذي يعلن عنه رسمياً بين صدام حسين والعقيد علاء حسين علي بعد الاجتياح.

وذكرت الوكالة العراقية ان نائب رئيس مجلس قيادة الثورة العراقي السيد عزة ابراهيم الدوري ووزير الخارجية السيد طارق عزيز ووزير الصناعة والتصنيع العسكري اللواء حسن كامل حسن حضروا اللقاء الذي حصل قبل ان يتوجه الدوري الى الاسكندرية.

وكتب سلامة نعمات «الحياة» نقلا من مصادر دبلوماسية في العاصمة الاردنية امس عندما وصل امس الى دمشق وزير النفط العراقي السيد عصام الجلبي في خطوة تشير الى احتمال تحسن العلاقات العراقية - السورية.

وكتب مراسلو «الحياة» في جدة والرياض ان مدينة جدة شهدت امس نشاطا دبلوماسيا مكثفا «في اتجاه انهاء الاحتلال العراقي للكويت واعادة الشرعية الكويتية ممارسة مهماتها ممثلة ببقية الشيخ جابر الاحمد الصباح. وعقد وزراء خارجية الدول مجلس التعاون الخليجي اجتماعا حضره وزراء خارجية الدول الست الاعضاء بمن فيهم الشيخ صباح الاحمد الصباح نائب رئيس مجلس الوزراء وزير الخارجية الكويتي.

واستمع الوزراء الى تقرير مفصل من الشيخ صباح الاحمد الصباح، الذي ابدى ...

جدة

ووصل الى الاسكندرية فجأة امس الشيخ سعدالعبدالله ولي العهد رئيس الوزراء الكويتي لاجراء محادثات مع الرئيس حسني مبارك.

... تفاصيل عدة ... وعرض وزير الخارجية السعودي الامير سعود الفيصل الجهود السعودية.

حرب .. سلام .. حرب .. سلام .. حرب .. سلام ..
حرب .. سلام .. حرب .. سلام .. حرب ..
سلام .. حرب .. سلام ..

نهاية عصر "السلاح الذري"

A cold and cloudy February. B52's fly from America to England. I'm trying to send Buffie's twenty-seven-kilo trunk and deal with my mother's packing as she has definitely decided to return to America.

It's still tough on the streets and there are no happy faces to photograph for Royal Air Maroc. Buffie calls just before the ground war begins to say that Paul and I should leave immediately.

"There are no planes," I said.

Paul has received the soundtrack for *The Sheltering Sky* and hates it. We sit and talk about the war, about the seven-billion-dollar U.S. aid for Morocco and we laugh at the scaremongers calling for all U.S. citizens to flee the country.

Flights finally resume on Jane's birthday. On my last morning, before my mother and I left, I went upstairs as usual to find that Paul had already gone out. I was annoyed as it was my last morning, but I found him seated on a bench watching the birds.

"Paul, you're being aloof—I hate that," I said. He just hugged me and we went to look at the storks. After lunch, sitting on his bed, I laid my head on his shoulder, feeling sad about leaving.

"Now don't find a new girl when I'm gone—you're too old, Pablo," I told him.

He laughed. "There is no one else."

Then he sang me an old forties song . . .

Why does it get so late so early
When I'm so in love with you?
We never dance enough
Don't get the chance enough
Why Honey, we don't even get to romance enough.
Just think of all those hugs and kisses
That we never will get through.
Why does it get so late so early, Honey,
When I'm so in love with you?

In the middle of the tune the bell rang and my mother burst in all excited about not missing the 'plane. Paul dressed and came downstairs and my last view of him was through the car window.

In the days before the war, Moroccans wait and pray.

things gone and things still here

Itesa Winter

Fan #2 surrounded by other medicines

After a poverty-stricken eight months in New York, attempting to find work for Jajouka, Bachir and I managed to return to Tangier. Through David Silver and Judy Nylon, we connected with Bill Laswell and secured a record deal for *Apocalypse Across the Sky*, the first Jajouka album since 1972. Burroughs agreed to write the liner notes. Paul had enabled us to survive in New York, with a large check.

Paul was in good spirits when I arrived though he was upset that the red cat from the market wouldn't talk to him anymore. He was dressed in orange socks, tan shoes and pants, and an orange suede coat, and I commented on how perfectly he'd match the cat should we meet him at the market. On the way to the chicken counter I noticed the stiff corpse of a cat being swept into the trash. I didn't tell Paul who was busy talking to the parrots in the pet shop.

At night in number fifteen, wrapped in Paul's djellaba, I read Norman Lewis while the wind whistled through the windows, shutters rattled, and doors slammed. I could hear Paul listening to *Music for a Farce* from above. When the music stopped I next heard the hum of the antinoise device and knew he was ready for bed. My bedroom was directly below his. I'd knock on the wall and he'd knock back good night before he slept.

One night, I knocked on the door and Paul answered, peering through the chain with his glasses askew, a cookie between his teeth, and a Patricia Highsmith novel in his hand. The maid hadn't come, the chicken was uncooked, so under Paul's severe supervision I prepared the chicken and brussels sprouts.

"Do you like to cook?" he queried afterward.

Chicken, Soup, and Other Small Disasters

"Well . . . did you like the soup?"
Both Rodrigo and Paul winced.

During the next days I made a few more soups, only a couple of which passed the test. One was labeled "Consommé Printenee," another "Potáge a la Plantana." Rodrigo decided to help me in preparing Paul's food. It was around this time Paul noticed that the portrait of him done by Claudio Bravo was missing. Mrabet apparently told him it must have fallen behind the bookcase. However, a day or so later, Paul took a photographer who was looking for Mrabet out to his house. When they got there Paul found not only Claudio's painting hanging on the wall but several others, including some by Brion Gysin. He wanted them back.

I threw away Paul's more than half-eaten avocado.

"You don't know me very well," he snapped.

There were two sips left in his Heineken.

"Glad you didn't throw this out too."

Christmas Eve, 1991. We listened to Aaron Copland's Music for the Theatre . . . *and while we were sipping sweet Chambord the music flooded the room . . . and Paul's red slippers tapped on the old Moroccan carpet. . . .*

I am retracing my steps, returning to Tangier to continue work with Paul Bowles, this time editing his letters. I am long delayed, manuscript mislaid through complexities more than Byzantine, Tangerine, beyond my control, and thus, perforce, I must wait on others: It is Africa where waiting attends all endeavors, patience the requisite virtue, and too, as a wit observed, "Time passes on slippered feet in Tangier."

I work with Paul in the late mornings, we are interrupted each day by visitors from the four corners of the planet, without appointments, come to pay their respects: Paul is gracious, generous, but cuts such *entretiens* short, pleading the necessity of completing work. He shifts from language to language with dazzling facility: English, French, Spanish, Moghrebi Arabic, a bit of Portuguese, Italian, and treats all with patrician courtliness, deft, humorous courtesy. In private asides Paul still exhibits the most uncanny ability for mimicry.

—Jeffrey Miller

Jeffrey Miller took this portrait of Paul and me in a children's park near Immueble Itesa.

Walking to Abdeslam's

The Book of Letters

The Hotel de France has been sold to an Iraqi consortium who plan to tear it down. For once all Tangier is up in arms and the people who work in the hotel are in tears. The room where Matisse painted is the main concern, and there is an attempt to save the structure for use as apartments. Jeffrey Miller is staying there the last months before it closes waiting for a diplomatic pouch of Paul's letters, which he and Paul will then edit into a collection.

Debra Winger is one of many who were asked to provide letters. She replied to Jeffrey that she can only give three because the rest are too personal.

"But I only sent three," said Paul, and wondered what he had written that was so intimate.

Words and Music

Another cold sunny day. The mosques are full with people praying for rain.

The diplomatic pouch with Paul's letters finally arrived. The letters were piled in a box by his feet when I went upstairs. Rodrigo mentioned how the earlier letters were more revealing.

"Ah, but when you're young, you feel the need to express yourself more," said Paul. "But when you grow older you see that your ideas are neither so important nor original and you feel less need. You don't want to."

Rodrigo went to the kitchen to cook the chicken while Paul and I smoked a *grifa* (joint) and listened to Poulenc, whose music Paul especially admires.

"What kind of music did Jane like?" I asked.

"Jane liked consonant music and hated dissonance."

"Well, what kind of music is this?"

"This music is romantic, not dissonant; it's consonant."

He got up to warm himself by the fire and as we spoke I began to smell something burning. It was Paul's bathrobe and Rodrigo and I had to extinguish him.

Abdeslam the acrobat, Paul's friend.

173

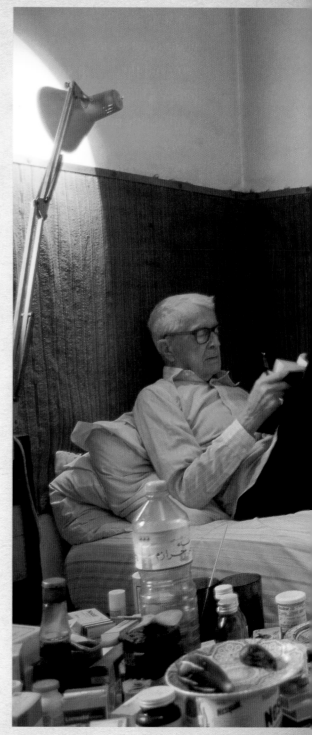

EPIGRAM

Joseph A. McPhillips III

Joe cannot conceive of the existence of a power which might prevent things from being the way he would like them to be, no matter how absurd.

Sober, he submits to the inevitable with good grace.

Otherwise, all hell.

Paul Bowles

Ramadan

The Ramadan cannons sound across the city. Jeffrey has left having finished his work with Paul on the book of letters. I'll miss him. Paul was a little grouchy when I went upstairs. Abdelouahid was rushing off to break his fast and Rodrigo hadn't arrived. "You never know who's coming these days," he grumbled.

Paul had decided he didn't like how the new maid made the bed: no tucked-in sheet corners and the quilt not centered. He asked me to instruct her the next day. Upstairs from my window the sky is dark, but I focus on one silver star that glimmers faintly. A lamppost illuminates the street and I see a man walking alone. The lamp casts a soft black shadow. He's faceless in his djellaba hood and the shadow. I look at the star again and a comet falls over Merkala.

"Well, what's new?" I asked Paul one afternoon later in the month.

"I told you . . . I took a walk to the park and as I sat there a tortoise walked by. I was afraid that it might be hit by a car or that the boys would stone it."

"Did you pick him up and move him then?" I asked.

"No, I left him to go his own way just the same."

The American School is to perform *Hippolytos.* Claudio Bravo will do the sets, Yves St. Laurent the costumes, and Paul is to write the music. Joe McPhillips arranged for a synthesizer to be sent and it arrived today. Paul's desk has been cleared and the machine now sits there looking far too modern in this setting. Paul hasn't been able to work out how to operate it. The instructions look "Greek" to him.

As I was lying dreamily by the fire upstairs that night Paul came up behind me. I heard the strike of a match and looked up to see Paul's face with the cigarette holder in his mouth.

"I looked up and there you were," I said.

"A good title for a song," he replied.

THE AMERICAN SCHOOL OF TANGIER PRESENTS
EURIPIDES'

HIPPOLYTOS

IN ARABIC AT THE PALAIS DU MARSHAN AT 20:00 H ON JUNE 15, 16, 17, 18, 1992
TICKETS ON SALE AT THE «LIBRAIRIE DES COLONNES»

Le Rouge et le Noir

Early in May we set fire to all of Rodrigo's diaries and manuscripts in the woods of the Charf. The burning pages opened like a rose and a spider crawled through my hair as the pages burned. The white pages turned black in the fire and the typing turned red.

We returned to Itesa and showed Paul the remnants.

Stravinsky was playing and Paul said, *"Le rouge et le noir."*

I took a specimen of the conflagration.

EPIGRAM
Phillip Ramey

He has the forbearance of a mud wasp, but tempers such as his are easily lost and found. His core is of stainless steel.

Paul Bowles

EPIGRAM
Kenneth (Krazy Kat) Lisenbee

Kenneth is pathologically nervous. Goaded to exasperation, he is capable of exploding in a burst of sheer hypocrisy, claiming that he is "sorry." He is aware, however, that this is never mistaken for regret.

Paul Bowles

The Perpetrator

Phillip and Krazy Kat arrived and we all ate dinner with Paul.

"So you have a synthesizer?" said Phillip.

"An electric copulator?" asked Paul.

"No." We all broke into laughter.

"An electric percolator?" Paul tried again.

"No—the synthesizer."

"Oh—the perpetrator." Which was what the synthesizer would be called in the future.

Paul continues to have trouble with the "perpetrator." Power cuts affect Itesa frequently, and when this happens he loses all of his current work.

I was now living in an apartment at Val Fleuri. I went to Spain to get my visa renewed. When I returned to Itesa, Paul opened the door and smiled. "You knocked the moment I finished the piece. Want to hear it?"

How I got sciatica.

We went to the studio to listen, but it seemed that the perpetrator had somehow erased the work. Paul was a wreck but he tried to stay calm even though he felt the piece had been lost. He kept on pressing keys but it did no good. The next day he told me he dreamed all night about the machine but that something in the dream told him the music was safe. As indeed it was.

Ornette Coleman called wanting Jajouka to perform with him in Munich.

Endless Summer

Front seats at the American School play with Paul. Hamburgers after at Phillip's. We made howling dog sounds under Paul's bedroom and the neighbors complained.

A cockroach walked across Paul's silver breakfast tray and the maid "slaughtered it with her thumb." Paul was disgusted.

"You know Charchumbo has been sold," said Mrabet. "Zohra has just come back from Mecca—she's a *hadja* now." Money from the sale had presumably financed her saintly expedition.

I helped Paul tidy the mass of papers lying around his bed. He told me that his aunt took him to a fortune-teller when he was born who predicted that when he was old he'd be surrounded by many papers.

The long stints at the "perpetrator" have greatly exacerbated Paul's sciatica. "Kif is the only thing that takes the pain away," he says.

Paul told the press today that he didn't believe in love. "Love is from the waist down," he quoted Jane. "Obsession is in the head." He went on to say that sexual love is all there is unless it's a case of one person wanting something from the other. I disagreed. "Why did you stay with Jane so long when she was sick?" I asked.

Went for a walk in Bubana, which is fast becoming a suburb. Just past the pet cemetery is Barbara Hutton's old estate where Jane and Paul used to picnic under the jasmine. Abdelouahid has quit his job as chauffeur at the American School so Paul can have full-time help. He's very happy and his mood has lifted considerably.

Tea on the mountain and a jack-o'-lantern moon walk with Paul and Abdelouahid.

Practising to be Krazy Kat.

EPIGRAM

Claude-Nathalie Thomas

Chic et sans chi-chis.

Paul Bowles

What goes on in Claude's garden?

The Selfish Cat

I was just in time to throw a party for Paul's birthday when I returned from New York, but I had to leave almost immediately for a Jajouka performance in Paris. When I got back, Paul shocked me by saying he was going to Meknes to have a hernia operation.

The white cat with the black spots, pregnant this year, was begging for food by the doorway. Paul was about to go to the kitchen to get some milk when the cat slipped through his legs and into the apartment. He gave her the milk, and after the cat had licked the saucer clean she went about the apartment looking for a soft warm spot to have her kittens. Paul became alarmed and decided it was time to get her out but the cat had other plans and slunk and darted round the apartment, under chairs, into the studio, behind boxes, with Paul all the while trying to keep pace and catch her. He finally gave up and went to bed but couldn't sleep. Later, peering into the salon he saw the cat rolled up in a ball with her tail round her legs, asleep in his cushioned chair. He let her be and went back to bed.

The Meknes Incident

This is not a good time.

Paul and I had a fight. I don't think the hernia operation in Meknes is a good idea. In any event I wanted to go but he wouldn't let me. I continued to argue.

"I see you're accustomed to getting what you want," he snapped.

"Do you prefer I live in New York?"

"If you were in New York, I'd be in Tangier, so no I wouldn't prefer you to be in New York unless I was in New York too."

"Well why can't I go? I'll be worried," I said. "Would Jane get to go?"

"No."

I sat on the bed and told him I loved him.

"I don't think anyone loves me," he said.

"I do," I answered.

"I'm not talking about you."

"There's no such thing as love?"

"I don't know if I can love. I don't know what love is."

"Well, you said the feeling was mutual and the other day you wrote in my book 'I have great love for you.'"

"I hate people seeing me in pain—I can see you don't know me very well," he said. "My mind is very exact and I see things clearly."

I wasn't sure what he meant by that. Upset, but also half joking, I said, "Wait till I tell Phillip about this."

"Why would he care?"

"Because he thinks you love me."

"This is dialogue for a novel." He laughed.

Abdelouahid came in.

"You just want to take pictures," he said to me.

"No, I won't even bring a camera."

"No. Because you won't be there," said Paul.

Paul's constant companions.

We watched a video of *Black Narcissus* together even though I was still upset. I tried to kiss him good night but he was tight-lipped so I gave him an Eskimo kiss.

"My nose hurts," he complained. "It's been hurting for a few days now."

"Did you tell the doctor?"

"You can't tell doctors everything."

Next day, I got to Paul's early and put water on for coffee. I went to the bedroom. Paul's head was drooped over his knees, his shoulders slumped, and his mind seemed confused.

"I'm very depressed and couldn't sleep," he said feebly.

The maid was helping him pack and had all sorts of things out on the bed. Paul couldn't seem to make up his mind, looking at each item as if he'd never seen it before. He'd touch them saying: "Funny material" or "Very mysterious." Finally I packed for him, just tossing things into the suitcase. After lunch he was more alert and insisted that he needed a white shirt. He dressed and went to the bathroom to fix his tie. He just sat there, disheveled and distraught with the tie half round his shoulders.

Even Abdelouahid was worried. "*La vida es dura*—life is so hard. How can Paul have this operation? He's so weak."

As he and Paul prepared to leave in the Mustang, I said, petulantly, "You hate me!"

"You're so dumb" were the last words Paul said as they drove away. He waved back to me. I could see his little round head with the ears protruding from the big collar of his overcoat.

This is not a good time.

A week later Paul returned. I didn't want to bother him so I sent a note. A day later the maid was at the door.

The salon at Itesa.

"He wants your mashed potatoes," she said.

I went upstairs and we made peace.

"Abdelouahid said you wanted to be there and see me die."

I said of course I wanted to be there, but I didn't want him dead. I told him with tears in my eyes how much he meant to me and I noticed his eyes were tearful too. But he looked at me and said:

"I want no one there when I die."

"Isn't it okay to love you?"

"Yes—but don't *show* it."

By the time Rodrigo arrived Paul was feeling better.

"Let's have lasagna tonight—I feel like it," said Paul.

So Rodrigo and I walked to the Casa Italia and brought it back. The three of us watched an Almodovar film.

The masseur brought an exercise bike to help Paul's leg. That evening Paul came downstairs to eat *tagine* with us. It was his first time out of the apartment since the operation. Afterward I walked him upstairs, very slowly and carefully. I took his keys and opened the door and lit the gas heater. We sat awhile on the couch. He held my hands and as I got ready to leave I kissed him on the left cheek. As I moved toward the right cheek, he stopped me and kissed me softly on the lips.

I was glad the Meknes incident was completely over.

EPIGRAM
Karim Debbagh

It takes courage to be a free spirit in a place where the mere concept of individuality can be construed as tantamount to apostasy.

Let us hope that at a later date he will not suffer for having let his courage and intelligence show now.

Paul Bowles

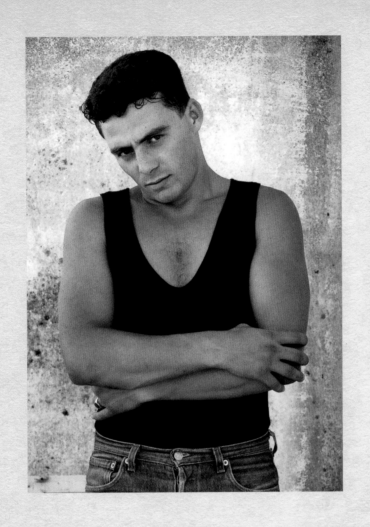

EPIGRAM

Karim Jihad Achouatte

An exquisite creature, sculpted, polished and made superb
by arrant indiscipline.

Paul Bowles

Souad, Paul's housekeeper.

Each morning Souad tells me: "The city is like an oven. There's not a breath of air stirring." This is at nine, but at twelve when I go out the east wind is blowing in violent gusts. Sometimes I can hear the needle of a cicada, but not often or for long. Behind the walls where I sit there is a rubber tree. The large flat leaves curl when they fall and dry, and they scud along the ground in the sudden blasts of wind. The tops of the trees wave and make a sound like the sea in the distance. The only nearby sounds are the stiff rubber leaves scraping the ground. One would think it was footsteps crunching gravel in the road.

Paul Bowles

Drips and Sparks

Paul has given up the exercise bike. Now, listening to classical music, he walks eight laps around the apartment. I can hear the slow thumping of his cane from above as he walks. "I walk best to Stravinsky," he says.

Donovan—the famous pop singer from the 60s and 70s—and his wife, Linda Lawrence, arrive with their son Julian, whose father was Brian Jones. They want to go to Jajouka and they also want to meet Paul for tea. It began to rain at last. We went for lunch in the Socco Chico and we watched the sparks fly like insects round the little kitchen as they cooked our fish. At 4:30 we went to Paul's. In every room the sky was caving in and Paul was seated in his little bed letting it all come down in buckets all around him.

An electrician who looked as if he'd never seen an electric light in his life was attempting to fix the wiring.

"In Ireland electricians are called 'sparks,'" Donovan said.

"Then what's a plumber?" said Paul.

"A 'drip.'"

Sparks filled the room later as we cooked lamb cutlets on the open fire.

Donovan, Julian, and Linda.

An American Hero

Paul is preparing to go to Madrid for a performance of his music.

The day Paul was due to leave I went to make him lunch. He answered the door all covered in shaving cream and we both laughed.

"I love the back of your head," I said to him running my fingers through his hair as he sat at lunch.

He grabbed my hands and said, "You love the side of me I can't see."

On the way to the airport Paul told us he had dreamed that he was in the Astor Place subway in New York looking for the S.S. *Independence* rather than taking the Lexington Avenue train. Three storks promptly took to the air as Paul, Phillip, and Abdelouahid's plane taxied down the runway and rose into the sky. Phillip had to give Paul a Valium—travel by plane makes him nervous.

Premonition in green. Dreaming of flying I saw a vision in the form of a green rectangular shape. When Paul came back, he'd brought me a few gifts including mints wrapped in squares of iridescent green foil.

"How does it feel to be treated like a hero, given bouquets of roses and cheered by the crowds?"

"It made me feel sad," he replied.

"Sad? But why?"

"Because they all think I'm so good and I'm not that good," he said.

194

In January 1995, the young conductor Jonathan Sheffer visited Phillip Ramey in New York with a proposal: he wanted to present a festival of Paul's orchestral music with Paul in attendance. Phillip was enthusiastic and contacted Paul in Tangier and strongly advised him to agree. As Paul was eager to hear his old music and trusted Phillip's judgment, the answer was yes. So it was that Paul, Phillip, and Abdelouahid arrived at JFK from Morocco the evening of September 16, to be met by Sheffer's limousine.

Paul had not been in New York since 1969, and the press considered his visit an important occasion. Unusual also was the fact that Paul was being celebrated as a composer rather than as a writer. Sheffer's festival consisted of several events, and though I was extremely busy at the time preparing for the Jajouka musicians' grand tour of America, I was able to attend—without camera—some of them.

There were two concerts at Alice Tully Hall, Lincoln Center, in which seven works by Paul were performed, including the ballet suite *Pastorella*, the *Suite for Small Orchestra*, the *Concerto for Two Pianos and Orchestra*, and the zarzuela (operetta) *The Wind Remains*. On the day between the two concerts Phillip threw a party for Paul at his penthouse; among the friends invited were Ned Rorem, Gavin Lambert, Claude Thomas,

Paul and Ned Rorem in New York.

Rodrigo Rey Rosa, and Joe McPhillips. That evening, there was a Paul Bowles symposium at the New School during which Paul and Phillip engaged in public conversation, the high point being when Paul, a natural comedian, described the drudgery of his daily life in Tangier.

Friday afternoon, Paul had lunch with his old cronies William Burroughs and Allen Ginsberg, the last time he would see them for they both died not long after. Saturday, he attended recording sessions of his music. The next day, Paul, Phillip, and Abdelouahid flew back to Tangier, and, seated happily in his first-class seat enjoying a butterscotch sundae ("I haven't had one of these since I was a kid," he told Phillip), Paul admitted that he had been pleased by hearing his music again and gratified by the enthusiastic response of the public. "A nice ego massage," he said.

If all artists are the sum of their contradictions, then Paul Bowles is an extreme example of that definition. Throughout his nearly nine decades he practiced two parallel careers, which seemingly never overlapped. In 1949, with the publication of his very successful novel *The Sheltering Sky*, Paul became the author-who-also-writes-music, after having long been the composer-who-also-writes-words. He was the only significant fiction-writing composer since Richard Wagner, but if history remembers him it will be for his musical gifts.

Paul's music is nostalgic and witty, evoking the times and places of its conception—Paris, New York, and Morocco during the twenties, thirties, and forties—through languorous triple meters, hot jazz, and Arabic sonorities. Like most nostalgic and witty music that works, Paul's is all in short forms, vocal settings, or instrumental suites. The intent of his music, which can be downright chummy, is to please, and to please through light colors and gentle textures and amusing rhythms, unusual for the time and quite lean, like their maker.

Paul was the first professional composer I had ever encountered. He introduced me to the music of Aaron Copland and Virgil Thomson, and especially himself. The main soprano aria from his zarzuela, *The Wind Remains*, with its recurring drop of a minor third, so bewitched me that to this day it has become the single most telling influence in my several hundred hours of music.

—Ned Rorem

Fragments and Dreams

In October 1993 I returned to America. During this period I was completely engaged with record contracts and touring plans for Jajouka. In January 1994 Paul sent an exorbitant check, more money even than Mrabet had stolen, "for your darkroom so you can print all your photographs of Morocco." But instead, because we were broke, we used it to pay debts and to survive the winter while looking for work.

After an eight-year struggle we finally secured the promise to re-release *The Pipes of Pan* from the Rolling Stones. Bachir and I were able to return to Morocco but not before Phillip and I journeyed to Atlanta

Paul in Atlanta with Virginia Spencer-Carr.

where Paul had gone for leg surgery and where Paul's biographer, Virginia Spencer Carr, threw a party for him.

That fall we all returned to Itesa, and I spent the winter on the telephone arranging for the Jajouka tour of Europe and the United States.

Leaving Itesa   March 23, 1995

Last night I had a dream that startled me from my sleep. It was one of those bird dreams with a message that was both ominous yet also seeming to presage good fortune . . .

I was in Jane Bowles's old flat but the window where my bed was had somehow changed into the shape of my altar in New York. At the apex of the window hung a few strands of ivy. Suddenly a black bird hit the pane with his beak and then flew upward and away. There was a good feeling about the crash and I thought how nice it was to see birds outside my window. If this apartment were mine, I thought, I would place food up there so more birds would come and sing.

I looked out of the window to the usual view of Marchan, the Old Mountain, and Merkala Beach. Heavy clouds hung over Merkala forecasting rain. Because there was a drought in Tangier it made me happy to see that.

But when I awoke the sun shone over Merkala and only the *cherqi* blew.

Buried Treasure

For Bachir and me the culmination of our years of struggle to save the music of Jajouka came when we obtained the rights from the Rolling Stones to re-release, on Point Music, Bachir's father's recording of *The Pipes of Pan*. In 1995, with Eric Sanzen, we embarked on a twenty-six-city tour of the United States to promote that record and a new album, recorded at Peter Gabriel's Real World Studios.

In our time together we realized there were many obstacles in our path, the result of the differences in age, culture, and background, but because we loved each other and because of the importance of our work together, I decided to take a chance that our shared dreams were bigger than our differences. Above all I found Bachir to be pure and honest, dedicated to his work; and in my mind he was a hero whose destiny was to become known and respected by the Western world.

But eventually these differences became insurmountable, which led irrevocably to a parting of the ways. I shall always feel pain and regret over this loss and will forever miss his sparkling smile.

Because of Bachir's selfless dedication, the music will survive. Both William Burroughs and Paul Bowles have agreed, in writing, that Bachir is the true heir to the mantle of Jajouka music.

Wherever the path of flowers has led me and wherever it takes me in the future, Bachir Attar, the savior of this music, will always have a special place buried deep in my heart.

Bachir's guimbri.

Bachir Attar.

3

After the flood

child in time

Sins are finished.
—Paul Bowles, *Let It Come Down*

The Return Trip (De Vuelta)

*Les sons rentreront dans l'orgue et l'avenir s'invaginera
dans le passé comme il a toujours fait.—H.M.*

Imagine a situation involving a man with two lives moving in opposite directions simultaneously, one of which goes toward the future in usual fashion (from today to tomorrow, from childhood to maturity and on to old age), while the other life goes toward the past. Thus, inside the child born in 1910 there lived an old man in his eighties. This would explain how in 1930 Gertrude Stein, after exchanging letters, was convinced that her correspondent [Paul Bowles] was a gentleman of at least seventy. So that today we have an octogenarian in whom is imprisoned a child traveling into the past. And this explains how one forgets that he is old, and how being in his company provides a delight similar to that provoked, as if through contagion, by the presence of small children. More than half a century ago those attempting to educate him considered him a stubborn youth; they warned him that unless he studied music as tradition demanded he would never succeed in being a composer. But they were unaware that this student needed no other teacher than himself, because in spite of his youthful appearance he had already made the return trip.   —Rodrigo Rey Rosa

Dream flowers . . . Rodrigo at work . . . Paul photographed with Basket by Gertrude Stein in 1931 at the terrace at Bilignin.

Distant Childhood

DISTANT CHILDHOOD

Among the photographs on my Aunt Mary's desk there was one in a silver frame of a young man with large black eyes. My father once asked her who the man was, and she replied:

"Prince Mozundar, and he's a hundred and thirty-eight years old."

"Oh, come, Aunt Mary. You don't believe that, do you?"

"I don't care. He is. He told me so."

"But Aunt Mary. Be reasonable. That man's not even thirty-eight, much less a hundred and thirty-eight. Look at his face. Who is he anyway?"

"He lives in India, and he's in touch with the occult. That keeps him young. I know you don't believe it, but it is so."

"Oh, Aunt Mary, don't be absurd. He's just another one of those fancy charlatans you let pull the wool over your eyes. You know he's lying. You know it's impossible."

"Remember that those in touch with the occult are not bound by physical laws."

My father was growing impatient.

"Oh, have it your own way. Have it your own way."

"I'm sorry you haven't an open mind," she said.

Paul Bowles

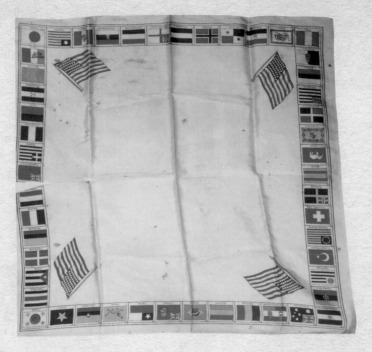

Given by Grandmother in 1915

My mother's mother-in-law, that is to say my paternal grandmother, gave her some interesting information about my father as a small child. She would get him all dressed and ready for a walk. Then he would begin to pee, soaking his clothes so that she had to dress him again. When she remonstrated with him, he shrugged and answered: "I just hasta." Yet she knew that he had been waiting to empty his bladder when it would cause the most trouble. Apparently, he was motivated by hostility from the beginning, and unfortunately for him and those around him, he never outgrew it.

Paul Bowles

Childhood Friends

Paul showed me a letter, written when he was only four, to an eccentric friend of his mother's.

"Who taught you to write so young?" I asked.

"I had wooden blocks with letters on them. No one encouraged me," he replied.

He paused and continued. "When my father saw this he'd tell me to go out into the yard. His dentist's office was on the first and second floors. My mother was on the third. I had to stay out in the yard for an hour. It was a long hour. I'd walk in circles around the wall of the yard and if I ran or sang or hummed the secretary would rap on the window. My father didn't want me to make noise, so I'd walk again. A long, long hour."

"You didn't see another child until you were five? How did you feel?"

"Terrified."

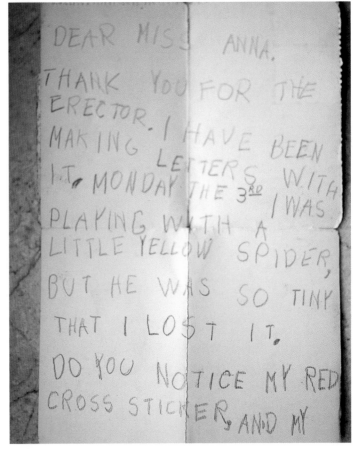

He paused again before continuing. "The first child I saw on the street was a dirty ragamuffin. I'd seen children in books so I knew they existed. In school I didn't play with other children, I didn't know how. At recess we had to play volleyball. I wasn't very good. I had no sense of competition. I didn't see the sense of it. Volleyball, I mean."

"Who was your first friend?"

"It must have been in high school—yes—a boy named Colombo and I couldn't bring him home. Nor could I bring my second friend home. He was a Jew and he wouldn't have been accepted either. It was the same with another friend. She was a girl who had had polio and wore a brace on her leg. My parents called her 'the cripple.'"

Every evening right after supper, while Mrs. Van was still
trimming the lampwicks and pol-
ishing the chimneys, I would take
the aluminium milk canister and
climb up the two-story ladder to
the top of the cliff. Immediately
I would be in the thick of the
woods, where the ground was soft
as a mattress with the millions
of hemlock needles fallen over

the years and the air was vibrant with the calls of the
katydids on all sides. It was dark up here and I needed my
flashlight. In all the years of being here I had never met
another person in these woods. I took it for granted that no
one would ever pass through, although there was no hindrance
at any point. Anyone could have come by, but no one did.

The first stream had a wooden bridge across it. I walked
as noisily as I could, shining the flashlight to left and
right, but particularly straight ahead into the even deeper
woods through which I had to go. Soon there was a steep hill
to run down. This was pleasanter. At the bottom another

stream had to be crossed, this one by fording it, using boulders. There was no more forest on the far side of the stream, it was open pasture land. Behind me the unchanging insect choir sounded in the dark woods, but out here there were only crickets. The canister I swung creaked a bit as I walked, so that I felt accompanied. Some nights there was a moon, so that each clump of bushes in the pasture stood out as I climbed. Then it was downhill again to the Peche house on the dirt road, where the other canister, this one with two quarts of milk in it, sat on the rock where Mrs. Peche always left it. Now I set out on my return journey, through the pasture, across the stream and into the woods. I could not swing this pail as I had the empty one. It merely made a slight creak as I walked. I had to be careful not to stumble and fall. Carrying the milk was a physical task which I was performing, and this lessened the energy of my imagination as I passed through the dark woods, so that in a way having the milk was a consolation, absurd though it may sound, because I was participating in the life of the household. Once I had negotiated the long ladder leading down to the house I knew my work was completed.

Paul Bowles

the bed

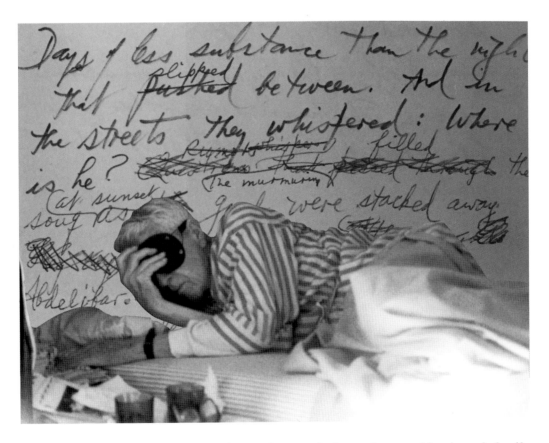

Since early childhood it has always been a fantasy of mine to dream a thing in such detail
that it would be possible to bring it across the frontier intact.

—Paul Bowles

Dream Before Arrival   Winter 1997

I am sitting as a passenger in the front seat of a car. The window is open and I look out onto a place, which is the Djema el Fna only there are white marble steps that lead up to the square where all the snake charmers are.

Behind the car there is a European bar where Martinis and Scotch are being served to two old grotesque French women dressed in short mink jackets over disco clothing, wearing too much gold and heavy makeup. Two tiny Pekinese dogs on each arm yap furiously. There's a small dance floor in the bar and I see Paul in the white suit that he wore for Libby Holman's Denver debut of Lorca's *Yerma*. A tall, attractive, and obviously rich French woman in a long mink coat is being obnoxious and she grabs Paul, insisting that they dance. They look like Ginger Rogers and Fred Astaire. They dance round and round. And although the woman is offensive and drunk Paul continues to ignore me and dance with her.

Okay—fine—have fun . . .

I shrug my shoulders and go to wait for him in the car. As we are driving home we pass Charchumbo and there is a grave on a hill.

"Don't look," Paul says as we pass by.

The Glaucoma Times

Last August, when I left Tangier, Paul had agreed to continue writing pieces for my book. However, a few days after my departure he lost his eyesight, experiencing a great deal of pain and depression. Glaucoma was diagnosed but fortunately with proper medication a limited amount of vision returned. Worried that he would be alone in winter and virtually sightless I very much wanted to be with him and hoped, too, that we could continue our work on tape during my visit. I made plans to arrive in Tangier for his eighty-seventh birthday.

Landing in Tangier on the thirtieth of December, a fingernail moon hangs low on the eerie horizon heralding the advent of

Paul in his white suit.

Ramadan, which begins the next day at dawn. I worry I won't get to the party on time, the holiday season and full planes meant I had to take a late flight. Finally arriving at Itesa I find a note telling me that the party is being held at a house on the Old Mountain. The taxi dropped me off by the old Spanish wrought-iron gates at the entrance to the estate. I groped my way down the unlit hill following the lights of the distant house and the sounds of the *Jilala* musicians carried on the night air. I glanced into the window before knocking on the front door. Paul was seated in a large chair by the fire and the people around him were all dancing to the swirling music. I opened the heavy wooden door and went into the room. Paul was just about to place a forkful of beets to his mouth when I came up behind him and wrapped my arms around his shoulders, kissing him on the cheek. He looked up both happy and surprised. He thought I wasn't going to make it in time. The party went on around us—Abdelouahid danced a bravura solo and I jumped up to dance with him then jokingly fell to my knees as I took his photograph.

Later the guests gathered round Paul, listening to his stories and hanging on every word. While Abdelouahid went to fetch the car Paul and I sat on a couch in the foyer, and looking up at the ceiling he said: "That would make a good picture."

The car was sick, and with myself and half the *Jilala* musicians in the back seat we couldn't make it up the hill. Finally we all got out and after three or four more attempts Abdelouahid managed to

Paul's dream, January 19, 1998.

achieve enough momentum. It was two in the morning, and Paul was tired. In three hours Ramadan would begin so I was lucky to find a taxi by the big mosque, leaving Paul to get to bed and Abdelouahid to a long day of fasting and no sleep.

Paul's Dream   January 19, 1998

"Well . . ." (tap, tap, tapping of fingers on the dinner tray as Paul relates his dream while sitting in bed) ". . . I was way down beyond the Anti-Atlas Mountains in a part of the desert which was several days away from any city . . . which didn't bother me because I've often been in places like that, but this time I was with— I think it was a girl—I didn't know who it was . . . and she dropped dead . . . and I knew it was my duty to send her body somewhere it could be taken care of . . . I couldn't do anything with it . . . so I . . ." (tap, tap, tapping of fingers) ". . . so I saw a row of houses rather like in the suburbs of New York or any other big city . . . all in a row . . . what they were doing there I don't know, but there they were. There was one of them that had a stairway leading from the yard down to the cellar and the woman of the house said: 'May I help you?' and I said, 'Yes . . . I need to get rid of a body,' and she said, 'Just a minute,' and she began calling to her husband nicely. He didn't answer—then suddenly she said sharply, 'Come out here' and he appeared. He was the kind of husband that needed to be treated like a dog . . . and . . . he came out and she explained to him that they would have to give me a suitcase or something . . . a trunk . . . to put the remains of the girl in . . ." (tap, tap) "Then the husband brought out one thing from the cellar and she said, 'Give him the big new one.' That meant that she would ask more from me because I was going to have to pay for the service, naturally, and I mean you can't go around getting rid of bodies normally . . . though I didn't feel guilty—I was just getting rid of something. . . . So they brought out a big suitcase . . . huge, really big enough to hold everything and ah . . . I . . ." (tap, tap) "they took care of all that. They put the remains of the dead person into the suitcase and they put burlap around it and rope and I used a marker and I addressed it to the American embassy in Rabat. I couldn't think of anywhere to place it except to the American embassy in Rabat and ah . . ." (tap tap, tap tap) ". . . I wondered if it would get there . . . it was very slow moving, you know, getting anywhere from down there, and I was worried they'd discover it on the bus and throw it out because it would smell . . ." (tap tap . . . tap tap . . . tap tap tap) ". . . Then this suitcase was kind of a mattress and I was standing on the end of the pier at Glenora Point. So I let the mattress fall into the water and it floated" (tap tap)—"so the old man didn't have much trouble pushing it ahead as he swam with one hand toward the land and I thought, 'How am I going to pay him? I haven't paid anybody yet. This is terrible,' and the mattress I had to re-address to the American embassy and I thought, 'This is never going to get there . . . this is ridiculous . . . but I'm doing my duty . . . it's all I can do.'" (tap tap) "This old man pushed it to the land and carried it away with him and I was very grateful to him because I hadn't paid him a penny . . ." (tap, tap, tap) ". . . and I noticed that there were octopi swimming around in the water and that's impossible in a freshwater lake, they only have them in salt water . . ." (tap, tap, tap) ". . . I thought there was something fishy about that."

JEREZ: "So you were in Glenora?"

PAUL: "Yes, I was at the end of the pier of a place called 'The Point,' which stuck out at the end to the lake and that's why I dropped the mattress over into the water and then I half woke up—and I asked myself what I would do for myself if it were I who was down there and died? How would I take care of sending my remains to the embassy? No one would do it for me . . . they can't . . . they wouldn't know how . . . and then I thought the main thing is not to die when I am down there . . ." (tap tap tap . . . tap tap . . . tap tap).

Another Dream   January 27, 1998

"Well, it was longer but I forgot the beginning. It was about a parrot I had . . . It wanted to stay down on the ground floor of the house and I had to, for some reason"—(tap, tap)—"take it upstairs—and I didn't want to offend it and it seemed very unhappy and I looked down at it, of course. It was an old-fashioned telephone"—(tap tap)—"an old-fashioned upright telephone and I thought, 'That poor bird.' I felt very sorry for it and began to pet it a little and it didn't answer or anything. It was just a telephone but I knew it was a parrot . . . and I, ah . . . woke up before I was able to lift it . . ." (tap tap) ". . . and take it upstairs."

JEREZ: "So you were going to take it upstairs anyway?"

PAUL: "I had to . . . but it didn't know it; it thought I wanted to take it upstairs . . . that it was just my idea, but it wasn't. I was saying, 'Poor thing . . . poor bird,' and the telephone knew."

PARROT JOKE

Well, a man had a parrot. But the parrot was a very dis-
gruntled, disagreeable person—bird. The man would say, "Good
morning Polly" and the bird would say, "Ya fuckin' son of a
bitch" and always replied in "termes grossiers"—ah, in bad
language—and the man couldn't do anything with the bird, it
would not pay any attention to his argument. And so he said,
"Well I'm going to fix that parrot" and he took it and he
put it into the freezer of his fridge and left it there, but
not too long, only about five minutes. He didn't want to
kill it. He only wanted to teach it a lesson, imagining that
he could. Well as a matter of fact he did. The parrot came
out very chastened and sad and shivering and said to the
man, "I'll never be...mean again...I'll never be nasty. I'll
never use a 'terme grossier.' I'll be a good bird."

And the man was happy...delighted. But the next day the
parrot had been thinking about it, because in the fridge, in
the cold part was a chicken ready to be cooked with all his
feathers, all...you know...pulled out and its head cut off.
And the parrot was thinking very hard and it finally said:
"Tell me...tell me something."

And the man said, "Yes."

And the parrot said, "What did that chicken do?"

There are no roses in Tangier today. But finally I managed to find three, straggly, almost weedlike; they were half dead but at least they smelled like roses.

Later at Itesa we were speaking of love.

"What is it? I don't know what it is," said Paul.

Jane's Birthday

JEREZ: "Pablo?"

PAUL: (waking from an afternoon snooze) "Yablo?"

JEREZ: "So, did you have any dreams last night? A few weeks ago you told me a dream about you and William Burroughs. You were on your way to Mexico but you had to cash travelers' checks. Bill said if you tried to cash them in Mexico there would be men with guns who would open fire on them if you tried, so you decided to go to Arkansas instead and you woke up."

PAUL: "No, I don't, but I remember another dream last night . . . more or less about cashing travelers' checks and trying to get to Mexico.

"I was with either Ahmed Yacoubi or Mrabet . . . I don't know which, and we were in a deluxe train that had no lights and it was all pitch dark and it was very silent and long and ah . . . low, and we went on and we came to where we were going, which was a station near the water where we would get our ship, but it was still pitch dark and we couldn't get any light and we couldn't see anything and we tried a lighter but the lighter didn't work. I only found a man up the flight of steps with the door shut but I could hear him talking and then I saw a slight ray of light where he was and I asked him, 'What are we supposed to do? There's no light here, we can't see anything.' And he said, 'Well, that's the way it is.' And ah . . . there was a—not sure who it was, as I say it may have been Mrabet . . . it may have been Yacoubi . . . and he had all of the papers but he had lost them and so we didn't have any identification at all . . . so we went up to the desk and there was a man there who said, 'Well, what's the point in going . . . you have no money . . . you have nothing . . . we have a guarantee that you've paid your fare and you are going somewhere . . . Teheran . . . or somewhere . . . what good is it? What are you going to do there?' And I thought, 'Well, that's all right . . . don't worry . . . I guess I'll get hold of some money somehow when we're on the way and we'll have some sent . . . some travelers' checks or something.' The clerk was very pleased to see that an American didn't have any money. I said, 'Well, we did when we started out.' He said, 'Well, have you got it now?' And I got hold of the man who had escorted us to the desk and he spoke only Spanish and ah . . . I said, 'Are we far from the water here?' And he said, 'Zig-a-zig . . . zig-a-zig,' which

On the hood of the Mustang before it died.

doesn't mean anything, and I thought, 'Oh, they're going to be difficult,' but I didn't say anything, so I thought we would get into the boat, but that wasn't so easy. I never did because I woke up before I got there."

The Clockwork Toy

Awakened from a scary dream. . . . A party in some small room with a white fireplace. I was dancing cheek to cheek with Pablo and over my shoulder to my left and slightly behind us I could see Rodrigo dancing with Melanie. We caught each other's eye and he smiled

A portrait of Ahmed Yacoubi, taken by Paul Bowles, in Paul's study.

and winked approvingly as we sailed across the dance floor. There was a large chair near the fireplace and I found myself holding Paul in my arms as he sat in the chair. I watched him suddenly slow down like a wind-up toy that had lost its vigor as he fell asleep. I kissed his cheek and was shocked to find it was stiff and cold like a rock.

"So this is what it feels like to lose him?" I said to myself.

I didn't cry. Slowly I got up and drew away from him looking at the slumped body, keeping my composure but feeling an immobilizing terror. Then suddenly the wind-up toy came to life and I felt an intense relief. . . .

March 1998

Claude-Nathalie has gone back to Paris and other visitors have left, so the usual schedule resumes at Itesa. Tea, a snooze for Paul, while I look at books or write sitting on Paul's cushion in the salon. Wait for Abdelouahid to return for dinner. End the night with the Spanish news. But today after dinner there's a break in the normal order of things. Abdelouahid is annoyed with Paul because he hasn't walked in a long time.

"If you don't get out of that bed you'll never get up again," he barks. So slowly Paul rises. Wrapped in his white Yves St. Laurent robe he struggles to stand, grabs his cane, and begins the laps, which take him from the bedroom door to the fireplace in the salon, to the bookshelves and to the woolen curtain and back again.

He still hasn't eaten the big scoop of vanilla ice cream that was his dessert. He places it on a shelf, takes a mouthful, which he then holds there until it melts as he completes his laps. After three, he sits and rests.

"See, Pablo, you don't walk—you've become weaker," says Abdelouahid. Paul just sits there quietly and I hear him gasp for breath.

While Abdelouahid snoozes in Paul's old cushioned seat I watch Paul from the divan as he shuffles back and forth, white hair, white robe, white shoes. I decide to leave them to themselves and get ready to go. As I hug Paul I think of dancing with him as we've done in the past but I could see he was suffering so I held him for an instant in a dance pose and I remembered the dream and began to feel awkward. He stood there stiffly feeling distant and far away from me so I kissed his cheek, and before I even thought about kissing his lips he said, "I've got my mouth full of ice cream."

So I kissed him on the "Frida Kahlo" spot on his forehead and let him go. Before slipping through the curtain I turned: *"Hasta mañana."*

And he stood there all wrapped in white leaning on his cane. His eyes were serious and slit like the Cheshire Cat's: "I *hope* I'll be here tomorrow," he said.

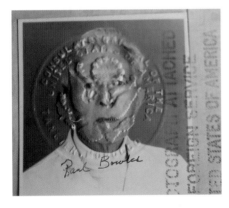

Encounter

JEREZ: "What countries have you been to, Paul?"

    (exasperated pause . . . TAP tap tap tap . . .)

PAUL: "Oh my God!—What?"

JEREZ: "Well, have you been to so many that you can't even count them?"

PAUL: "Of course!!!" (as if speaking to a small child)

Well-travelled Valise

Abdelouahid

Abdelouahid came a little late so Souad answered the door. His nephew, who had lived in Belgium, arrived in a box today. He died in a bus crash in Thailand and his family wanted the body returned so it could be interred in holy Moslem ground. Abdelouahid says when you're dead, you're dead, and finds the expense a waste of money.

Though he doesn't smoke either cigarettes or kif and doesn't drink alcohol, Abdelouahid claims that he is not a Moslem. "There are no Moslems," he is fond of repeating.

"But I see you praying by the drain pipe on the terrace every day, and you do Ramadan," I say.

But he tells me this does not mean he is Moslem. He maintains a Moslem must follow every detail of the religious law. While the concept is pure and the man who can follow it in its entirety perfect, very few can lay claim to this.

Unlike many of the followers of Allah, Abdelouahid does not consider himself superior in the eyes of God to anyone else. He makes no judgments of others as he feels this to be God's concern and not his, though he still believes the Moslem way to be correct. I see him practice his religion seriously, quietly, and with determination but without self-pride.

Paul's nephew's last will was in English so I read it to him and then he left for the airport. Souad and I ate dinner while Paul snoozed. I have a headache today and red splotches have suddenly appeared on my face. Paul says it is a symptom of indigestion. Paul's friend, Philip Krone, arrives with his wife tonight, so I leave early feeling ill. I fall asleep as soon as I get home but I awake in shock—a bolt of lightning passes through me and I see the moon between the curtain and the rim of the window looking down on me in the bed and suddenly it hits me—I am leaving.

"The apartment will be empty without you," Paul said when I told him I would have to leave in two days' time.

"Oh, I'll miss you," I moaned, burying my head in his chest.

Stroking my hair lightly with his fingertips he abruptly changed the subject and began to talk about photography.

"It's a documentary process, freezing the instant of time for eternity," he said.

"Well, what about . . ."

I squinted at a small crack in the wall by his bed.

"What about that crack? What if I manipulated the exposure and printing process so that what is printed bears no resemblance to the image in the here and now so it, through my conscious intervention, becomes something totally different?"

"It's still a crack in time," he replied. "But now it's also a study in technique. A portrait can be a study in technique too—what happens to it in the process. . . ."

I got up to leave but his hand gripped mine.

"Your hands are so cold."

I gently disengaged them.

I turned round at the door.

"I will see you tomorrow."

"Tomorrow—there will be no tomorrows," he said.

A Dream Before Departure

I am in Morocco living my daily life in the Charf.

Abdelouahid stands in the background.

I come upon a large room with a high curved ceiling, and there are many rows of wooden fold-up chairs. It is a palace or an assembly room where people meet for a special purpose. The room is empty. Half of the chairs are open, the remainder folded, some set in rows but others just scattered across the floor.

I take one and sit. I am here for a reason but I don't know what it is. I turn and see Mrabet nearby sitting in a corner. I hadn't noticed him before. Our eyes meet briefly. Mine hold no anger though I am distant, but Mrabet's eyes dance and flirt and he tries to give me a kiss. I laugh and push him away and we talk. He asks why I don't have children and I explain it is a weakness in my family genes. He is sad for me and takes my hand. I am not sad about this inability to conceive but I know that a Moroccan can't understand how a woman could not want children so I just smile and say, "Si." His empathy is a sign of peace and we are again friends. He places his hand on my knee—looks into my face with his dark deep eyes and tries to console me by saying,

"Well, then, you would make a good housewife." I know this is supposed to be a compliment and I laugh to myself knowing this is the last thing I'd like to be, but I say, *"Gracias."*

I notice that during our conversation the room has filled with people. I see a former friend and I am on my way to tell her that Mrabet and I have made peace when suddenly I find myself sitting on Paul's shoulders up above the crowd. I am high and happy and the star of the room as we weave through the throng. I notice the back of a man in a baseball jacket and I think I know him, so from Paul's shoulders I reach down and tap this man's shoulders and he turns around. It is not who I imagined it would be; it's my first husband, Meko, who had overheard my conversation with Mrabet and had watched me sail around the room on Paul's

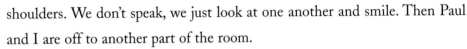

shoulders. We don't speak, we just look at one another and smile. Then Paul and I are off to another part of the room.

A young girl comes into the doorway. The light is behind her and she glows. She wears a leotard and elf boots and her hair is cut short like a pixie. Is it me in my youth? She certainly looks just like me, youthful and at my best, but she is European, not American, and so with a sense of melancholy I realize she can't be me. She is young and I am old, jumping and leaping, doing a Scout-like dance, and then suddenly she disappears. I comment on her prettiness wistfully though I am not upset that I am no longer young. Up here on Paul's shoulders I am at peace with my friends and respected by my enemies. I salute them.

"You will be missed—the house will be empty without you flitting around," Paul said again tonight. "But you have work to do in New York."

Then he switched off and began to look at a New Zealand literary magazine that contained a piece about him. It seemed like any other night and I felt momentarily safe in my normal routine of reading in the salon. But I knew it was all a facade. I went to the window that opened onto the Cherífa plant and stood blowing cigarette smoke through the branches trying to keep calm. I went and sat and watched the fire. Soon I heard the tap of his fingers, which was his daily signal to say it was okay to come in. He was distant tonight, and I was exhausted and aloof. I lay beside him on the narrow bed and though his fingers tapped he continued to read as I lay there in silence. He looked up.

"I'm pretending that it isn't the last night."

"I know."

Abdelouahid brought tagine. *"La ultima cena."*

So I took a photo of "the last supper."

"That's what they call rat poison in Spain," Paul said and we burst out laughing.

"Perfect," I said.

After the food we smoked kif.

Looking up I thought of his old Mexican parrot and I said: "Lop Lop."

"Rop," he replied, playing the game he often played with Jane where he was "Bupple," a parrot with the shape of a man who was capable of the most monstrous behavior. Jane would be "Teresa Braun," his mother/governess, and he'd alight on her hand and she'd pull him toward his cage scolding him.

So I lifted him up, placing my arms completely around him. I began to shake him up and down and back and forth.

"Do that if it makes you feel any better," he said, tense and unresponsive in my arms. I shook him once more and I was afraid—afraid I'd never see him again.

"I'm losing you," I moaned.

"But you never *had* me."

Yet he took my cold hands in his to warm them and kissed me, his lips met mine, and I got up to go— this goodbye is too long, I thought. I moved away but he took my hand again and started another story. This happened three or four times until I snapped a photo—stepped back—snapped another, and then the film ran out. I stoically said goodbye just as Abdelouahid came in the room and told Paul, "get into your cage"—*ponte en tú jaula*—and get ready for his *gotas*—eyedrops. I changed my mind—an excuse for a last shot—I changed film, jumped back into the room, and snapped. Paul looked up surprised.

"Like a firefly," I heard him say as I left.

I got back home so shattered and drained I immediately fell into a deep sleep.

And I dreamed of the time Paul and I went to look for dream flowers.

And when we found them in front of a stork's nest he picked one and handed it to me saying:

"The illicit bouquet that smelled of yesterday's perfume."

I woke at dawn.

Abdelouahid came to drive me to the airport.

As I closed the door behind me I could smell jasmine on the early morning air.

The illicet bouquet that smelled of yesterday's perfume.

Fax to: Cherie Nutting
           29th March 1998.

Dear Jerez,

So here I am, smoking the contents of my 'pistillera,' all by myself. Abdelouahid has gone home and I assume the night watchman is in the other room asleep. In any case, it's quiet and we hope for rain. Now there's no food for the sheep and cows, and there will be no good crops of food for the people. Not a drop of rain for more than two months. Today there was a shower, which is a good sign.

I wonder how you are? I hope the air trips weren't too much for you. Probably you are resting, recuperating from the stress. You should be. Phillip just telephoned, and was surprised to hear you were in New York. He said he'd call you right away, as perhaps he has by now.

The Krones have gone, so now I can dedicate myself to getting the car I was talking about. The salesman in Casablanca offered to drive the new car to Tangier if I wanted to complete the purchase but perhaps Abdelouahid will want to go himself to Casablanca.

Anyway, you didn't see the 'cotorro' Krone presented to me in a huge cage. It seems to me he wants to fill the flat so full of large objects that there will be no room for me. That way I'd end up in Chicago, or so he may imagine.

It's empty without you at Itesa.

Your roses are still beautiful

Paul

About Film

Black and white
Preserves the light.
Color is somehow duller.

Paul B.

Postscript: Msk ḍḷ Liḷ
(Perfume of the Night)

With financial help from Paul and Philip Krone I was able to spend the summer of 1999 in Tangier. And so on July 4, I took off for Morocco.

It was, I see in retrospect, a strange time, prefigured perhaps by the fact that the shell I found all those years ago had vanished from Paul's apartment. He himself was frail and could now see only shadows and shades of gray. But things seemed to go on much as before, largely due to Abdelouahid's care and Phillip Ramey's irrepressible sense of humor. We joked a good deal with Paul and listened to his stories, and he continued to relate some of his dreams to me. There were days, however, when Paul seemed silent and far away, as if he were listening to a distant tune.

We spoke often of the changes he had seen in the half century he had lived in Tangier and it was shortly after one of these conversations that we heard, with great regret, of the death of King Hassan II. After a thirty-eight-year reign, he was succeeded by his son Mohammed VI, who vowed to modernize Morocco. The end of the old regime, the coming eclipse, and Paul's frailty made me realize that a new era was dawning.

Paul talked about the eclipses, solar and lunar, he had seen during his lifetime, and I thought of how the one that was about to occur might mark for him a final transit. On August 12, the day of the eclipse, even at Tangier's distance from the line of totality, the light seeped away, the birds fell silent, shadows dissolved into dreams, and nothing seemed the same. And as the apparition moved across the sky and was gone in seconds, I remembered a conversation with the photographer David Seidner, who had died earlier this year in Florida. In Tangier in 1986, we had walked along the beach and that night at the San Remo I had told David how I always hated to leave Tangier because Paul was so old he could die. David just said, "All things that are jewels are wonderful because of their precarious state. That they can be either lost, stolen, or broken is why they are so special. So you shouldn't feel bad if you lose someone. Be glad that you had them at all."

I am.

People in the Book

Karim Jihad Achouatte—Moroccan singer, dancer, and soccer player.

Bachir Attar—virtuoso performer on the lira, guimbri, and ghaita. Leader of the famed Master Musicians of Jajouka.

Abdeslam al Bakkali—Moroccan acrobat.

Abdelouahid Boulaich—longtime chauffeur and companion of Paul Bowles.

Jane Bowles, née Auer—American author of, among others, *Two Serious Ladies* and *In the Summer House.* Paul and Jane were married in 1938, and she moved with him to Morocco in 1948. Subsequently, her health declined and in 1968 she entered the Clinica de los Angeles, in Málaga, where she died in 1973.

Claudio Bravo—Chilean painter who lives on The Old Mountain in Tangier. He is represented by the Marlborough Gallery in New York.

Cherífa—Moroccan woman born in Mraiehr, near Tangier. She was working in the grain market when she was introduced to Jane Bowles and remained involved with Jane until her illness.

Karim ("Snake") Debbagh—young and upcoming Moroccan filmmaker.

Brion Gysin—Canadian-born painter, writer, and recording artist. Author of *The Process* and a friend and traveling companion of Paul's.

Pociao de Hollanda—She is the translator into German of many of Paul's books and is married to Roberto de Hollanda, a literary agent for several Moroccan authors.

Libby Holman—American torch singer who met Paul and Jane in 1945. She commissioned Paul to compose an opera based on Lorca's play *Yerma.*

Philip Krone—Chicago political consultant who often visited Tangier.

Kenneth Lisenbee—an American friend and neighbor of Paul's.

Joseph A. McPhillips III—longtime headmaster of The American School of Tangier, friend and executor of Paul's estate.

Jeffrey Miller—bibliographer and editor of *In Touch*, the letters of Paul Bowles. Owner of Cadmus Edition.

Mohammed Mrabet—Moroccan storyteller, author of numerous books transcribed and translated into English by Paul Bowles.

Phillip Ramey—American composer. Neighbor and friend of Paul Bowles. From 1977 to 1993 the program editor and annotator for the New York Philharmonic.

Ned Rorem—Pulitzer Prize–winning composer and author of a dozen books of essays and diaries.

Rodrigo Rey Rosa—Guatemalan writer translated by Paul Bowles; Paul's literary executor and protegé.

Jonathan Sheffer—young American conductor of the Eos Orchestra in New York.

Virginia Spencer-Carr—authorized biographer of Paul Bowles.

Claude-Nathalie Thomas—Paul's preferred translator into French of, among other titles, *The Spider's House* and *Too Far from Home;* friend of many years.

Ahmed Yacoubi—Moroccan painter born in Fès; met Paul during the writing of *The Sheltering Sky* and traveled extensively with him over the years.

Some Places in the Book

Cap Spartel—It was the view of this promontory that inspired Paul Bowles to write *Let It Come Down.*

El Charf—the hill across the bay from Tangier where, thanks to Pociao and Roberto de Hollanda, I lived during my visits from 1997 to 1999.

Immeuble Itesa—the apartment house where Paul lived in Tangier.

Ksar el Seghir—a fishing village east of Tangier. Bordered by the river Ksar, it is near Farsioua, where Abdelouahid was born.

Mraierh—about 5 kilometers outside Tangier, near Cap Spartel, this is the village where Cherífa came from and the site of Cherie Nutting's house Charchumbo.

The Old Mountain—a favorite excursion for Paul, and once the base of the Moroccan forces who besieged Tangier during its occupation by the Portuguese and British. The old established cork woodland of the Old Mountain has now mostly given way to expensive villa properties.

Slâ—the former name of Salé, a town on the Atlantic coast just north of Rabat.

Socco Chico—at the turn of the century, the "small" market was roughly twice the size it is now. The cafés and hotels that surround the square were once the haunts of the Beat Generation.

Selected Glossary

Aid-el-Kebir—the annual sacrifice of the sheep.

Baraka—a mysterious, supernatural, beneficial force given to saints, certain people, animals, trees, and places as well as mountain passes.

Cherqi—an easterly wind.

Djellaba—a hooded garment with sleeves. Formerly a man's garment, now worn by both sexes.

Jilala—"to Europeans the music of Jilala is Moroccan folk music being played on long, low-pitched transversal flutes (qsbah) and large flat drums (bendir). To a member of the cult, however, it is a sequence of explicit choreographic instructions, all of which are designed to bring about a state of trance, or possession." –Paul Bowles.

Kif—the fine leaves at the base of the flowers of the common female hemp plant, chopped and mixed (ideally in a ratio of 7 to 4) with tobacco grown in the same earth.

Medina—the Arabic word for city. In North Africa it indicates in particular that part of the city that was built by the Moslems and that existed before the arrival of Europeans.

Msk dl lil ("Perfume of the Night")—a small star-shaped flower that exudes a sweet honey scent in the North African summer.

Sebsi—a long thin pipe for smoking kif.

Souk—properly souq, the word is used throughout North Africa to mean market.

Tagine—a stew.

Taifor—a low round table.

Tchar—a village; hence "Charchumbo—the place or village of the cactus."